Applied Anthropology

Applied Anthropology
A PRACTICAL GUIDE

ERVE CHAMBERS

University of Maryland, College Park

PRENTICE-HALL, INC., Englewood Cliffs, N.J. 07632

Library of Congress Cataloging in Publication Data

Chambers, Erve.
  Applied anthropology.

  Bibliography.
  Includes index.
  1. Applied anthropology. I. Title.
GN27.C45 1985   306   84-15010
ISBN 0-13-039371-1

Editorial/production supervision: Colleen Brosnan
Cover design: 20/20 Services, Inc.
Cover photo: Bernard Pierre Wolff
Manufacturing buyer: Barbara Kelly Kittle

Printed in the United States of America

10 9 8 7 6 5 4 3 2 1

ISBN 0-13-039371-1 01

Prentice-Hall International, Inc., *London*
Prentice-Hall of Australia Pty. Limited, *Sydney*
Editora Prentice-Hall do Brasil, Ltda., *Rio de Janeiro*
Prentice-Hall Canada Inc., *Toronto*
Prentice-Hall of India Private Limited, *New Delhi*
Prentice-Hall of Japan, Inc., *Tokyo*
Prentice-Hall of Southeast Asia Pte. Ltd., *Singapore*
Whitehall Books Limited, *Wellington, New Zealand*

Contents

Preface

This book is meant to provide a coherent view of the field of applied anthropology. The task has not been as simple as it might seem. Applied anthropology has only recently begun to emerge as a distinct mode of conduct within the profession, and there is not general agreement on what applied anthropologists do or what they should be doing. The notion of using anthropology in direct application to human problem solving has in recent years released a tremendous amount of thought and energy and has helped anthropologists realize a variety of career goals which were virtually unheard of even a decade ago. This might be thought of as a period of experimentation and exploration, out of which an idea that has been with us for some time has finally begun to prosper. But new prosperity often brings confusion with it, challenging more traditional views and favoring diversity over unity.

Writing a text in such a climate of new experiences and diverse opinions requires something more than a straightforward account of the state of our craft. What I have aimed to accomplish here is to provide a scheme (or, actually, several interdependent schemes) for evaluating the field of applied anthropology within a common framework—a construction to which our efforts might cohere despite striking differences in the types of work applied anthropologists do, and even despite differences in the values and ideologies they bring to their work. This book is a report on the state of our craft, and it is also an attempt to advance our endeavors a few stages by seeking a unity from our diverse experiences, ideas, and opinions.

The first chapter of this book offers an overview of applied anthropology. Chapter 2 describes several aspects of policy decision making. A major portion of this chapter is devoted to a summary of United States policy priorities and of several major strategies for decision making which have developed in this country over the past hundred years. Information of this kind has become indispensable for both understanding and realizing our efforts to apply the skills and knowledge of our profession.

The next two chapters provide a survey of major areas of specialization within applied anthropology. Each of these areas is described in terms of the several kinds of contributions anthropologists have made—to both basic and applied research, to knowledge transfer and utilization, and to decision making. In Chapter 5 I have described some fundamentals of applied social research and related these to examples of anthropological practice. The sixth chapter is devoted to a discussion of what I term the "cultures of policy." Here, I argue the importance of not only understanding the contexts of decision making, but of also furthering that understanding through basic research. One type of research which I especially recommend lies in the area of knowledge utilization. We understand too little of the ways in which decision makers use knowledge and are too often ignorant of the conditions attending both the use and misuse of the research we conduct.

The final chapter of this book is a review of some of the ways in which the larger profession of anthropology is adjusting to the growing visibility of applied work. It includes discussions of professional ethics and of recent approaches to training a new generation of applied anthropologists.

My presentation is, of course, shaded by my perception of what is critical in the field. I have tried to be as comprehensive as possible, both in the body of the text and in special sections I have added to each chapter. Every chapter begins, for example, with an informal story, usually in the form of a conversation between myself and others. The specifics of these stories are made up, although they represent types of conversations that I have had many times during the past several years. Obviously, I have great control over the way each story goes and have used them to highlight points I want to make in the chapters. A partial corrective to my biases is offered in the sections called "Perspective," which appears at the end of each chapter. I have used this vehicle both to summarize the chapters and to point out some of their limitations, often by citing views which are different from my own.

The "Recommended Readings" sections added to each chapter are meant to provide a more complete and useful bibliography of the field and its several subjects than could be offered in direct citations appearing in the text. In the interest of readability, I have tried to reduce the number of textual citations to a minimum. In "Recommended Readings" I have described other material which should be of interest to persons wishing to pursue a particular discussion in greater detail.

Of the many decisions I had to make in planning this book, two deserve special mention because they are likely to be controversial. The first of these has to do with the history of applied anthropology. I have taken what some readers will regard as an unusual step by incorporating earlier contributions to the field in the main body of the text rather than setting aside a special section for their discussion. My reasoning is twofold. First, many of these early achievements have never been duplicated in either their scope or in the quality of work done. In this sense, they are as current as they are dated. Second, I feel that the "story" of particular applications in anthropology cannot be reasonably separated from either the topical areas of interest they represent or from the larger social and political contexts out of which they emerge. Accordingly, I decided to subordinate the history of a profession to the story of its ongoing relationship with the rest of the world.

The second decision has to do with the sharp distinction I make between basic and applied research in applied anthropology, especially in the beginning of Chapter 6. This distinction is made primarily to give due attention to modes (and means and ends) of doing research which have received little attention in the past. Some readers will find this part of my presentation to be controversial.

A number of people have been of considerable help and support. I want to thank my students for their tolerance, enthusiasm, and many insights. Of these, Mike Pardee and Pat Sorrells merit particular thanks. Gil Kushner deserves special mention for his encouragement and good advice, as do Mike Agar, Helen Wadsworth, Al Wolfe, and Bob Wulff for the long and often late hours they have devoted to helping me think through many parts of this book. Several others have provided invaluable assistance in commenting on parts or all of the manuscript. These include Leslie Barger, Linda Bennett, Nancie Gonzalez, Setha Low, Harland Padfield, and Debra Schuman. There are many others, including the publisher's "invisible" reviewers, and Stan Wakefield, Editor at Prentice-Hall, who has shown more patience than I had a right to expect. Responsibility for the content of this book is, of course, my own.

Applied Anthropology

1

The

Beginning

"What have you been up to these days?" an old friend asked.

"Well," I answered, "among other things I'm writing a book about applied anthropology."

"What kind of applied anthropology?" my friend asked. I did not have difficulty understanding the question. After several years of involvement in both doing and teaching applied anthropology, I was fully aware that there were a great many different ways to conceptualize the field. The variety of work which has been described as applied anthropology is tremendous, and the connection between one type of activity and another has in many cases been far from obvious.

"I'm hoping," I told my friend, "to write something that's fairly comprehensive."

"That must be quite an undertaking," my friend observed.

She went on to say that she would not know where to begin the sort of book I was describing. I agreed that it was a problem, and that seemed like an understatement. In actuality, I had already begun the book several times. Part of the problem was that I wanted to write a textbook, a guide that would be useful to students and professionals alike. But there is something special about textbooks.

They often reduce a subject to its most common and easily agreed upon concerns. There tends to be little ambiguity in textbooks. The prevailing attitude seems to be that readers should be introduced to a field gently. The field of applied anthropology, on the other hand, is full of ambiguities. Although there are solid precedents of application throughout the history of anthropology, it is only during the past decade or so that the profession as a whole has begun to grapple seriously with the idea that anthropology not only has a potential to be useful, but that we should be committed to ensuring that it be useful. Ten years is not much time in the life of a profession. There are bound to be huge gaps, occasional inconsistencies, and plenty of disagreement as to what we are all about. These can be glossed over in a textbook, but only at the expense of failing to provide an accurate view of the subject.

My friend agreed with my assessment and asked me how I was going to resolve the problem.

"I'm going to try to be as considerate as possible," I said, "without compromising the difficulties."

"And how will you begin?" my friend asked.

"At the beginning," I answered.

Ten years ago, at a professional meeting of anthropologists, I attended a gathering of anthropologists who were distinguished by the fact that they were all employed outside academic settings. Within the space of an hour, I met anthropologists who were working for a fascinating and slightly bewildering variety of government and private institutions. These included an anthropologist employed by a major utilities company whose job was to help the company work with American Indian tribal organizations in the development of (some would say exploitation of) reservation energy resources. I met another anthropologist who had been employed by an American Indian organization in order to help them achieve tribal status. One anthropologist was working for the United States Air Force, and another was an information specialist for an antinuclear organization. Among the anthropologists I met were individuals working for city or county planning agencies, hospitals, mental health centers, professional associations, major corporations, international development agencies, public and private research institutions, newspapers, education planning agencies, and a variety of advocacy and public interest groups. One anthropologist was a training specialist for a city police department, another trained social workers, and yet another was teaching in a hospital. What impressed me about the group was that no matter how different their individual interests and careers were, each felt enough of a common bond to his or her profession to attend a professional meeting of anthropologists.

WHAT IS ANTHROPOLOGY?

The perspectives anthropologists bring to their work are the products of a relatively young, hybrid discipline which has attempted to explore aspects of the human condition that other sciences often seem determined to pull apart. Anthropologists tend to be *generalists*, seeking parallels between the physical, social, personal, cultural, and historical bases of human existence. They are also *comparativists*, having a longstanding interest in the diversity of human culture, custom, and form. Anthropologists are committed to achieving an in-depth and *holistic* understanding of the contexts from which observations about human activities, behaviors, and values are derived; they have often excelled as critics of grand theories and explanations of the human condition which discount both the diversity and depth of our being. The concept of *holism* is central to anthropological understanding. It holds that human events must be viewed in the larger contexts in which they naturally occur, and that much of the meaning which people attribute to their lives is specific to their cultural surroundings.

The idea of *cultural relativism* is a part of the anthropological perspective which is closely allied to the concept of holism. Anthropologists believe that distinct cultures and lifestyles can only be understood in relation to their unique integrity, and they admonish against trying to judge the behaviors of one group on the basis of the values of another group. Early in their careers, anthropologists are advised to avoid their own ethnocentrism in attempting to understand the ways in which other people manage their lives. A relativistic perspective is important to anthropologists because it encourages them to make sense of a social or cultural situation from a position of value impartiality. This *does not* mean that the anthropologist must necessarily withhold judgment on the conduct of human affairs, but only that his or her judgment is best informed by an impartial view of the cultural antecedents to specific human behavior and values.

Another aspect of the anthropological perspective is the *cross-cultural* mandate, which broadens the concept of holism to a rule of thumb extending to human societies in their entirety. Here, it is maintained that we can understand neither the limits nor the potentials of the human condition until we can account for the distinctiveness of human behavior occurring in different geographic and social settings. A sense of cultural diversity is of considerable value in extending our range of experience and knowledge beyond the moral and phenomenological blinders of our own cultural milieu. In the past, anthropologists participated in the cross-cultural perspective by conducting the major part of their research work in societies other than their own. More recently, as increasing numbers of anthropologists choose to work in their own society and in settings more similar to their own life experiences, their appreciation for diversity both among and within societies remains intact, although their sense of the parameters of culture and the range of cultural processes is not nearly as fixed as it once was.

These major perspectives of anthropology offer a guideline for social inquiry and are closely related to the way anthropologists go about their work. They not only stand as analytic and interpretive tools, but also help inform the values of anthropologists. Respect for the integrity (or wholeness) and diversity of peoples is a paramount concern of most anthropologists.

The Importance of Culture

One of the major organizing concepts for anthropology is that of *culture*. The term has not been used consistently by anthropologists, but even in its most diverse applications we can find enough agreement to enable us to fashion a sense of common intent. Culture is shared and therefore is attributed to groups rather than to individuals. It can be transmitted or communicated from one generation to the next. When anthropologists use the term *culture,* they are generally referring to a people's total way or style of being. While they may for the purposes of analysis pay special attention to only one or a few elements of culture, such abstractions usually are seen by anthropologists as being arbitrary and of limited explanatory power. One of the central concerns of anthropology has been to demonstrate relationships between the different elements of culture. Another has been to reveal how social and behavioral differences between discrete groups of people can be explained as variations in cultural understanding.

In this book, the term *culture* will be used to refer to the ideational and symbolic aspects of a group's way of being. Culture is not what people do, but the ideas and standards which guide their behavior. Our subject matter is the interpretation of the phenomenal world; it is the meaning that people ascribe to things and events and, in a more profound sense, the way they learn to make meaning. A culture is, therefore, a group of people who share standards of behavior and have common ways of interpreting the circumstances of their lives. It is important to keep in mind that a sharing of major cultural elements does not necessarily imply a similarity in behavior. Members of a culture may, for example, share a common idea of marriage, but the ways in which individuals respond to that idea are likely to vary considerably. In this sense, a cultural idea serves as a kind of reference point for people. As much as an individual's behavior might seem to divert from a cultural standard, the interpretation of that behavior invariably refers back to a common cultural idea. In our society, for example, events such as divorce and homosexual marriage are made meaningful only when they are considered in light of the significance we attach to the term *marriage.*

How different do people have to be in order to be considered members of different cultures? Anthropologists have not always been clear as to how they define a cultural unit. In the past, when they worked almost exclusively among relatively isolated groups of people who had distinct and seemingly exotic traditions, this did not seem to be much of a problem. Cultural units could be roughly identified on the basis of a people's geographic, linguistic, or technological distinctiveness. More recently, as increasing numbers of anthropologists choose to work in their own society, or in other social settings which are similar to theirs, the delineation of cultural units has become more complicated. Some anthropologists have used criteria such as ethnicity, occupation, status, and wealth to highlight subcultural differences between people who share a common culture. These distinctions have been useful to the extent that they have helped anthropologists broaden our understanding of the diversity of modern, complex societies. There is the danger, however, that overzealous attention to subcultural differences tends to obscure important cultural similarities among the various groupings of modern societies.

There is another aspect of culture which is important to keep in mind. Many of the cultural ideas and standards for interpretation which guide the ways in which people ascribe meaning are not well understood by the people who use them. Explicit standards of behavior, well known to the members of a culture, may actually serve to obscure more tacit cultural ideas. People may *know* these implicit modes for interpretation, but they may not understand or fully appreciate their relationship to behavior. One of the great contributions of the cultural perspective has been to uncover the more tacit dimensions of human thought and to demonstrate how these hidden grammars of meaning help shape our lives.

Anthropological Research

Traditionally, anthropological inquiry has encouraged long-term, empirically based field research. Anthropologists often describe themselves as "being where the action is" and emphasize the importance of observing human behavior in naturally occurring contexts. The *fieldwork* approach associated with anthropology is often contrasted to two other modes of social and behavioral research. First, it is different from most *experimental research*, in which behavioral responses are observed in a laboratory or similarly contrived setting. Anthropologists argue that the laboratory setting routinely employed, for example, in psychological research lacks the information-rich, value-laden flavor of the "field" in which humans normally behave. The stimuli and information introduced into a laboratory setting in order to elicit specific behaviors or responses may differ significantly from the total complex of environmental stimuli occurring in natural settings. Laboratory research is "cleaner" than field research, because it reduces the complexity of any setting in which behavior might occur. But, by the same token, an appreciation of the complexity that frames and intrudes upon naturally occurring behavior is an important feature of our understanding of the human condition.

Fieldwork is also often contrasted to *survey research*, a second major mode of social inquiry. Surveys rely on brief information exchanges between an interviewer and a respondent. Their success depends on the rigorous control of these exchanges. Do respondents understand and properly interpret the questions? Do they tell the truth? How do variations in interview style affect the range of responses given to a particular query? These are but a few of the difficulties survey researchers encounter, and they are not substantially different from those encountered by other social researchers. The major problem with survey research lies in the brevity of the exchange, which allows little opportunity for testing the validity of informant responses. Survey research can also be biased by the extent to which the researcher, in preparing a survey instrument, might unintentionally distort or limit the scope of an inquiry. On the other hand, surveys are an efficient approach, because a great deal of information can be collected quickly from a large sample of respondents. For some types of inquiry, surveys seem entirely adequate to the task. In other cases, the limitations of surveys can lead to spurious and misleading conclusions.

As their preferred mode of inquiry, fieldwork offers anthropologists an opportunity to sift meanings and discover relevant conditions of human behavior from the settings in which persons normally interact. The intensity of inquiry associated with fieldwork permits the anthropologist to probe the social and cultural background from which particular human activities emerge. A sense of surprise is endemic to fieldwork, and anthropological research has proven particularly adept at discovering the unintended consequences (both positive and negative) that attend human attempts to understand, respond to, and alter the conditions of their existence.

One of the great advantages of the fieldwork approach is that it encourges anthropologists to try to see the world in much the same way as the people they are studying. Cultural differences between the investigator and the subject of an inquiry are reduced when anthropologists strive not only to discover what a people think, but also to share in their thinking. This perspective is often called taking an *emic* or "native" point of view. Of course, anthropologists can never fully shed their own culture and learn to think in precisely the same manner as their subjects. If they could, they might well lose another valued part of their approach, which is attention to the more tacit dimensions of culture. The kind of understanding anthropologists acquire as a result of their close familiarity with other people blends the view of the outsider with that of the insider. From this vantage point, anthropologists are often able to account for important differences between peoples which would otherwise be ignored or minimized.

The fieldwork approach is often associated with qualitative methods of data collection, such as participant observation and intensive interviewing. These methods require that the anthropologist act as an instrument of inquiry, carefully recording human events as they are derived from his or her direct experience of a distinct cultural setting. This is an important aspect of the anthropological approach, but it does not preclude the use of additional research strategies which are based on quantitative or statistical procedures. Most anthropologists routinely employ both qualitative and quantitative research techniques, often using the one as a check upon the reliability of the other.

THE APPLICATION OF ANTHROPOLOGY

At the beginning of this chapter, we noted that there have been some changes occurring in the field of anthropology. One of these changes is that anthropologists have begun to apply their expertise to a wide variety of employment settings. Another is that many of the individuals who are doing this continue to identify themselves as anthropologists through participation in the activities of their profession.

Professional meetings are one of the ritual occasions of anthropology. They represent a renewal of professional ties and provide the opportunity to increase one's knowledge of the discipline. Anthropologists tend to work closely with people whose backgrounds are different from their own. One way for them to maintain a perspective on their work is to discuss it with other anthropologists, many of whom have had similar experiences. Professional meetings are a good place to do this. The anecdotes anthropologists exchange on these occasions are more than mere gossip, although they may sound that way to an outsider. The sorts of things anthropologists talk about when they gather, and their manner of talking about these things, provide useful information for understanding the ways in which the profession is changing. Implicit in nearly every discussion are a host of ideas about what it is that anthropologists do, how their work affects other people, and the sorts of behaviors they value.

Anthropologists have always had special ways of communicating among themselves. "*Where* did you do your fieldwork?" has been a common form of greeting, and until recently the response to a question like this usually evoked the image of a faraway, exotic refuge from modern industrial life. Some anthropologists spend a lot of time talking about "their" people, an odd and revealing form of possessiveness toward research subjects which has become increasingly difficult to justify. Many of the stories anthropologists tell are humorous and some of them are hair-raising, reflecting both the strangeness and dangers of fieldwork in isolated places.

Anthropologists continue to work in many different places, often under trying circumstances, and their conversations reflect this diversity. But in recent years there has been an added dimension to the stories they tell. At a professional meeting we might, for example, hear one anthropologist ask another, "*Who* do you work for?" Even a decade ago, it was generally assumed that nearly all anthropologists worked for universities. Today probably fewer than half the anthropologists in the United States are employed in academic settings. The tales told by these relative newcomers are often as exotic as the more traditional stories. What is it like to work for a major business corporation? How will a new government regulation affect people who are living in poverty? What are the ethical problems associated with working for the military? How does one explain what anthropology is to a personnel officer in a government agency? What is it like to do fieldwork in Peoria, Illinois? How does an anthropologist end up as the director of a health planning agency in Atlanta, Georgia?

A tendency for increasing numbers of anthropologists to work outside academic settings is not the only indication of change within the profession, or even within applied anthropology, but it is certainly an important development. In a larger sense, and after a generation of relative neglect, the profession as a whole has begun to embrace the promise of applied work and to accept the idea that a concern for utility should be an integral part of the anthropologist's identity. The idea of applied anthropology is not simply an addition to the more traditional goals and ambitions of anthropologists; it has become a powerful stimulus to a rethinking and modification of some of the basic tenets of the profession.

A Separate Identity

Applied anthropologists use the knowledge, skills, and perspective of their discipline to help solve human problems and facilitate change. Does this mean that applied anthropology is simply anthropology made more immediately practical, or is it something significantly different from the usual pursuits of the profession? It is not an easy question, and there are good examples that go both ways, but my inclination has been to argue that applied anthropology is different enough from other kinds of anthropology to merit a distinct position in the profession. It is not, as some have suggested, simply a matter of taking what we learn of anthropology and trying to use these insights in practical problem solving. Along the several lines which make any profession unique—including its subject matter, sponsorship, theory, roles, methodology, and intentions—applied anthropology has come to differ significantly from other ways of doing anthropology.

To appreciate these differences, we need to understand how radically the profession of anthropology has changed during the past decade. While all these changes have precedents in the more distant past, it is only over the last 10 years that they have come to be generally recognized as having the potential to force a rethinking of the profession as a whole.

Most of the changes find their roots in an earlier tendency to view anthropology as being predominantly an academic profession, with the great part of its disciplinary intent slanted toward the study of non-Western, preliterate peoples. At least four major events have conspired to erode this once-favored image of anthropology.

One of these events has been the maturation of the discipline. Anthropologists have found it increasingly difficult to defend the idea that they should confine their interests to the cultural experiences of relatively isolated peoples. As they have gradually extended the range of their inquiries, they have also expanded and improved upon their techniques of inquiry. Anthropologists today are as likely to find their work in urban settings as they are to situate themselves among the more isolated peoples of the world. They are less likely to limit themselves to work in a single village or community, and they have become considerably more interested in the regional, national, and even international implications of their work. The rapidity of this change is intriguing. Even less than 10 years ago, anthropologists who chose to forsake the imagery of the jungle for modern suburbs and cities ran the risk of being considered as somewhat less than "real" anthropologists by their colleagues.

Another event which has helped reshape the profession has been the increasing difficulties anthropologists have faced in working with peoples of the Third World. Many of the traditional subjects of fieldwork have matured in their relationship to anthropologists. In some ways, they have forced the profession to view them less as unique and "primitive" peoples and more as partners in a rapidly modernizing world. Access to tribal and peasant peoples in many parts of the world has become more difficult to achieve. These people are now more likely to complain that, while anthropologists have taken a lot from them, they have left very little in return. They have sometimes insisted that anthropologists demonstrate how their work will directly benefit their communities. Many anthropologists have become sensitive to the one-sided nature of much of their past work and are now more likely to consider how their endeavors might be of practical use to their subjects. This sense that the presence of an anthropologist should entail more than the acquisition of knowledge and ought also to be of practical benefit to the community in which research is being conducted has contributed substantially to the overall development of the field of applied anthropology.

Anthropologists have also become much more likely to undertake work in their own society. This third major event results from a number of factors. In practical terms, it has become difficult for many anthropologists to receive grants to work outside the United States. Some anthropologists seem to have turned to an interest in their own society out of a sense of fair play if not guilt, as if to compensate for the profession's earlier tendency to focus critical attention upon the institutions of other societies. But many anthropologists have become genuinely interested in the problems of their society. At least in the United States, much of this interest parallels the introspection and demands for relevance in higher education that accompanied this country's journey into the 1970s. Whether for good reason or not, or for some combination of reasons, many anthropology students of this era began to question the desirability of a career in the "ivory towers" of academia. Some of these students were simply lost to the profession, but others began to face their futures and the potential of anthropology with fresh insight and determination. Their efforts have contributed to a major change in the profession's attitudes toward career development.

A fourth event contributing to the recent development of applied anthropology is that anthropologists have found it increasingly difficult to secure academic employment. Over the past decade, an increase in the number of anthropologists being trained has been accompanied by a decline in opportunities for university employment. Students and their professors alike have had to face the obvious fact that the profession must either shrink or prepare its students for a greater variety of employment possibilities. Over the past decade, an increasing number of anthropology departments have begun to offer programs designed to prepare students for employment outside academic settings. These efforts have helped change both the content and style of instruction in anthropology.

It is not one or another of these events but their occurrence together which has encouraged rapid change in the way anthropolgists have come to view their profession. They have led to an increased concern for the uses of anthropology, and thereby to the exploration of different ways of connecting the profession to the rest of the world. These changes have not only increased anthropology's field of vision; they have altered the lens through which many anthropologists accord significance to their work. The new images captured in this lens are not altogether clear or consistent. There are profound differences of opinion as to the appropriate styles of work and proper roles to be played by applied anthropologists. Still, while keeping these differences in mind, it is now possible to discern the principal features of what amounts to a distinct approach to doing anthropology.

The Public Setting of Applied Anthropology

Like most scientific professions which find their roots in an academic setting, anthropology is heir to an intellectual tradition which places a premium on the independent development of inquiry and the accumulation of knowledge more or less for its own sake. Anthropologists are accustomed to deciding for themselves what is worth understanding, to determining how such understanding is best reached, and to being the sole judges of the worth of their colleagues' contributions. This sense of professional evaluation is not absent in applied anthropology, but it is significantly altered by the public setting in which nearly all applied anthropologists work. Specialization in applied anthropology represents a conscious decision to enter a setting where interests that are strictly disciplinary play alongside concerns of a more diffuse and public nature. While all knowledge can be useful, the knowledge sought by applied anthropologists is much more deliberately so— it is typically derived from a need to make a decision concerning some aspect of human behavior.

The applied anthropologist is accountable to other professionals and to the public in ways other anthropologists seldom are. Whether an applied anthropologist works as a researcher or as a program administrator, or in some other role, the results of his or her work are normally subject to public scrutiny. Other persons besides anthropologists are often responsible for judging the worth of the anthropologist's contribution. Outside critics are often greater skeptics than one's colleagues, who after all have already accepted most of the assumptions of the profession.

The public setting of applied anthropology provides several important evaluative criteria that are minimized or absent in other expressions of anthropology. Foremost among these is the *criterion of judgment*. The goal of application is to facilitate a wide range of judgmental processes. Normally, the only kinds of judgments in which anthropologists have been consistently interested concern the nature and quality of scientific inquiry— how do we know what we know, and what are the criteria by which we can judge the validity and reliability of our knowledge? However, applied anthropologists need to be equally attentive to considerations of what is desired and valued. The criteria for evaluating desires and values are not nearly as clear cut as are those by which we evaluate the acquisition of empirical knowledge. Since people often desire and value different things according to strikingly different criteria, the work of applied anthropologists regularly involves efforts to mediate claims upon a society's resources, or to reconcile the different cultural processes which influence the ways in which people express and attempt to realize what they value.

This is not to say that anthropologists have in the past been disinterested in values. To the contrary, the *study* of human values has been a major concern of anthropology, and in another sense many anthropologists have been outspoken in letting their own values be known. The difference is that in applied anthropology knowledge and value assume their significance in relation to acts of decision making. These acts are often exceedingly complex and tend to blur the distinction between what is empirically known and what is valued. What is more, the contexts of decision making typically require sifting through a great variety of kinds of knowledge and respecting a much greater range of public and private values than anthropologists are accustomed to dealing with.

The differences between problems of empirical knowledge and those of value, and the interaction between the two, can be better appreciated with an example. For this purpose, let us take a brief look at the public welfare system in the United States. Public welfare is a system represented by a complex set of attitudes, information, and expectations concerning how a society perceives its responsibility to the economically least fortunate of its members. This particular system is in turn linked to others, such as the overall administrative and bureaucratic procedures by which a society collects and allocates resources. Within such a maze of intentions, the processes of valuing, knowing, and judging play important but not necessarily identical roles. The idea that a society has a responsibility to economically marginal people is based primarily on value. This value might be reinforced or contraindicated by empirical knowledge. Historical knowledge, for example, suggests that some classes of people in the United States have been consistently deprived of access to educational opportunities which would qualify them for a more substantial position in society. Other knowledge might suggest that current approaches or attitudes toward public welfare in the United States do not in actuality serve to maximize or improve the position of poor people, and might in some cases function to guarantee the presence of a permanent underclass in our society. In these cases, and many others, knowledge may inform our values, but it does not take the place of value-based judgment. Does a history of neglect indicate that some people *deserve* public assistance? No amount of empirical knowledge will make this decision for us. Is the purpose of public welfare simply to aid people who are without resources, or is it to help people make their way out of poverty? Knowledge may help us to understand how particular responses to welfare problems lead to specific goals, but it alone will not provide us with the goals.

The interactions between empirical knowledge and value discussed above relate primarily to problems of *policy formulation*. How does a society decide what is of sufficient importance to merit the expenditure of scarce resources? There are other kinds of decisions which relate to problems of *program planning* and *implementation*. Once it has been decided that something is worth doing, what is the best way to do it? How can we insure that our goals are being met and that our values are being reinforced through purposive action? In the case of public welfare, how do we decide to direct and redirect the resources we have committed to this activity?

In the United States, public assistance to the poor is a matter of considerable complexity. There have been many different programs dedicated in one way or another to the relief of poverty—such as the food stamp program, aid for dependent children, basic medical and educational assistance, housing programs, job training, legal assistance, and the like. Each program has its own constituency, extending well beyond the client population to which assistance is directed and involving, among others, professional care administrators, medical and legal institutions, housing developers and agents, social researchers, and a myriad of public and quasi-public agencies. Our society legitimizes the claim these people and institutions have on administering to public welfare goals, valuing not only the goals but the manner in which they are implemented. What is more, public welfare programs are necessarily enacted at the local level and are subject to tremendous regional variation. A job training program in a major East Coast city is not, for example, likely to be the same kind of job training program as might be found in a rural community in the Southwest, even though both programs share the same legislative and policy intent. Differences in the clientele served by a program, in local values and public needs, as well as in the ways in which programs are administered and implemented, all add to the complex and sometimes awkward fashion by which public intentions become actions.

Empirically derived knowledge related to these processes of planning and implementation, informing us of the results of our actions and predicting further outcomes, is an important contribution to efforts to judge the worth of what we are doing. Much of this book is devoted to this kind of knowledge—how it is acquired, communicated, and used by decision makers. But this book is not only about knowledge. In every case, what we know must be considered in light of what we value, and in a sense what we value actually dictates what we come to believe is important to know. Knowledge itself often must be adjudicated, for it can be incomplete, contradictory, and misleading. The criterion of judgment, fused in the public setting in which applied anthropologists work, helps mediate the claims of scientific-empirical knowledge and those of value. The philosopher Soren Kierkegaard wrote, "We can only understand backwards, but we must do our living forwards." This recognition that the world will not wait for us to know it as well as we might wish is central to the idea of applied anthropology.

STYLES OF WORK IN APPLIED ANTHROPOLOGY

A number of factors help account for the variety of ways in which applied anthropologists respond to the public setting of their work. Like any field of endeavor, applied anthropology is partly a product of the history and perspective of its parent discipline. At any point in its history, applied anthropology is also broadly influenced by its relationship to current policy commitments and concerns, including attitudes and conventions as to what constitutes effective public decision making. Applied anthropology is further subject to the ideological currents of the society in which it develops and is partly a product of the individual value commitments and special interests of its practitioners. It stands to reason that there will always be different views of what applied anthropology is and what it should be.

Applied anthropology shares this amorphous style of response to its mission with most other professions. Among health practitioners, for example, there is considerable difference of opinion as to what constitutes effective health care. This difference can in part be understood from a historical perspective. Witness, for example, the rise in prestige of surgeons from a practitioner status roughly equivalent to that of a barber during much of the nineteenth century, to an exceptionally high-status profession during much of the twentieth century, and now perhaps to a slightly declining status as a result of recent trends in the health profession to consider much surgery as unnecessary and perhaps detrimental to a patient's well-being. Pronounced differences of opinion in health care can also be seen within the limited perspective of our time, as in recent ethical conflicts between medical doctors, nurses, health service administrators, patients, paraprofessionals, and lay practitioners (Yezzi 1980).

As with most other professions, applied anthropology is a product of the interaction of varied practitioner orientations in response to a wide array of human needs. Looking at it this way, we avoid the temptation of trying to rationalize a single "right" approach to the profession, and rather adopt the attitude that complex societies with diverse populations and uncertain needs are best served by professions which have the inherent capability of responding to human needs on the basis of a great variety of skills and orientations.

Research and Practice

There is a useful distinction to be made between the acquisition of knowledge and its practical application. In applied anthropology, this distinction provides insight into two different ways of conceptualizing the profession. Historically, the literature of applied anthropology has focused most of its attention on the role of basic research in policy and decision-making contexts. This preference is not at all surprising when we recall that, until recently, the favored career choice, even of applied anthropologists, has been to work in a university setting, where professional success is built largely upon a person's ability to conduct inquiries which are meant to further the state of our knowledge in traditional fields of scholarship.

Although generally in the minority, there have always been other anthropologists who elected to devote their careers to activities other than basic research. Their conviction that knowledge is not inherently useful, but must deliberately be *made* useful, provides a valuable precedent for the future of the profession. We can draw one example from the early days of professional anthropology in the United States.

W. G. McGee's career as an anthropologist (he was also a geographer) began in the 1890s when he served as Ethnologist in Charge of the United States Bureau of Ethnology. He worked in this capacity under John Wesley Powell, another anthropologist-geographer, and the Bureau's first director. The contrast between Powell and McGee is an instructive page in the history of applied anthropology. In his position as director of the Bureau, Powell followed the model of the dedicated and patient basic researcher. His conviction that policy decisions must await a solid foundation of scientific evidence led him to avoid entanglement in major policy issues involving the federal government and North American Indians. Instead, he guided the Bureau through a major attempt to document Indian life—a work which he felt would eventually lead to sound decision making (Hinsley 1979).

Certainly, the work of the Bureau was to become a rich and enduring source of information about Indian life at the turn of the century. Some of it would in fact come to have direct policy relevance. But, at least in retrospect, it seems unfortunate that the Bureau's labors did not have more immediate returns. This is an especially poignant consideration when we realize that the early years of the Bureau of American Ethnology correspond to a period of serious misunderstanding and massive exploitation of the Indian people of the United States.

There is no evidence that McGee disagreed with Powell during his tenure with the Bureau of Ethnology. But his career after Powell's death appears as a radical departure from the Bureau's carefully neutral stance. When he went to St. Louis to head the Anthropology Department of the Louisiana Purchase Exposition, McGee became actively involved in promoting a major waterways development which would encourage commerce between the midwestern United States and Latin America. Later, he returned to Washington to make perhaps his greatest contribution to applied anthropology. McGee became, in the words of the historian Hays (1975: 102), "the chief theorist of the Progressive conservation movement" and "one of its most crucial promoters." McGee worked closely with Theodore Roosevelt's conservation-minded administration, and his involvement during this period was intensely political and thoroughly practical. His design for multipurpose waterways development, which was never fully accepted in his lifetime, found application some 20 years after his death in the depression era's plans for the Tennessee Valley Authority and similar waterways developments. Although an ardent supporter of anthropology, McGee operated outside many of the most accepted strategies of the still young profession. He published little and, unlike Powell, did not use his considerable influence in Theodore Roosevelt's administration to promote basic research devoted to his concerns for conservation and economic development. McGee perceived the issues related to natural resource management to be urgent and chose a role closer to that of a planner and advocate. Still, his position was clearly anthropological; his model for multipurpose waterway development was based on a strategic and holistic notion of the interdependence of human resource use.

Although McGee served as a principal founder of the American Anthropological Association, his example was lost on subsequent generations of anthropologists. He was chided by both Robert Lowie and Alfred Kroeber as being careless in the sporadic bits of basic research he attempted. Other anthropologists, such as John R. Swanton, accused McGee of being great at talking but not much in the way of originality. Such evaluations speak more clearly to the rapidity with which basic research became the nearly xenophobic focus of United States anthropology than to the significant organizational and planning contributions made by people like McGee.

Opportunity has found other anthropologists working outside the favored research role. During the 1930s and 1940s, anthropologists Philleo Nash, John H. Province, and James Officer played prominent decision-making roles in the Bureau of Indian Affairs. Several of those who worked after World War II as government anthropologists in the Trust Territory of Micronesia found their jobs required more administrative acumen than research skill (Fischer 1979). These and similar involvements remained, however, isolated from the mainsteam of anthropological endeavor. Only after the events discussed earlier in this chapter, events barely more than a decade in the making, did the profession as a whole have an opportunity to reconsider some of its most fundamental commitments to the way its members pursued their work.

The idea of a *practicing anthropology* emerged during the 1970s as a way of identifying anthropologists who were employed outside academic settings. This crude distinction came about primarily because the profession could no longer afford to be so thoroughly dominated by the concerns of individuals who were employed in universities. There have been two major difficulties in the subsequent use of the concept of practice. First, the designation remains vague, and there have been few attempts to account for the wide range of activities and styles of work in which practicing anthropologists are engaged. Second, while the distinction between practice and academia has encouraged anthropologists to rethink their commitment to different career models, it has also obscured important continuities between education and profession. As the idea of practice begins to infiltrate colleges and universities, the original need for a distinction of this kind becomes less persuasive.

However awkward and uninformative the designation might be, the term *practicing anthropologist* has been widely accepted as a meaningful expression of change within the profession.

Applied Anthropology and Practice

Rather than continuing to serve as a fragile distinction between academically situated anthropologists and some vague category of others, the term *practicing anthropology* can be better used to identify those styles of work which are heavily invested in making anthropological knowledge useful. This work is in contrast to, but certainly not in conflict with, efforts to acquire knowledge which have a potential to be useful but which originate without any clear framework of utility. An applied anthropologist might be engaged in either type of work, and at various stages of his or her career is likely to take an interest in both.

It is helpful to view applied anthropology in terms of four complementary but distinct styles or models of work. The first of these is *basic research*, or independent inquiry. In a context of application, basic research is directed to general problems of social and cultural change, and increasingly to problems in the utilization of knowledge. Applied anthropologists conduct basic research in order to gain a greater understanding of human behavior, especially as it relates to issues of policy concern. Basic research is "independent" by virtue of its primary allegiance to canons of scientific discovery.

The other three models of work relevant to application relate to the idea of *practice,* or to the notion that knowledge must deliberately be made useful. Common to each of these styles is the idea that the major role of applied anthropology is to mediate knowledge and its uses, and that a profession which presumes to be useful requires practitioners who are specialized in such acts as mediation. Each of these models is tied closely to processes of decision making.

The first model of practice is that of *applied research,* or collaborative inquiry. The most fundamental distinction between applied and basic research lies in the manner in which its problems are identified and the criteria by which it is evaluated. Applied research is subject, for example, not only to scientific criteria of validity and reliability, but also to various criteria of utility—such as relevance, significance, and credibility. In like manner, the identification of applied research problems results from collaboration between the producers and users of knowledge and is heavily invested in concerns of value as well as in those of strictly scientific-empirical knowledge. (The distinctions between basic and applied research, and criteria of utility, are discussed in greater detail in Chapters 5 and 6.)

Another model of work based on practice is that of *knowledge transfer.* Many applied anthropologists do not produce new knowledge but rather act as purveyors of knowledge—organizing, evaluating, and interpreting our vast store of knowledge. This is an often-neglected but critical role played by many anthropologists. There are two major ways in which anthropologists have contributed to the transfer of knowledge: *teaching* and *planning*.

Teaching has rarely been regarded as an applied activity, although it clearly is. Consider, for example, that most of the students enrolled in college-level anthropology courses do not become anthropologists. Teaching is one of the major ways in which the profession reaches beyond itself, effectively influencing many people with a wide variety of professional and social interests. Anthropologists have also been hired to teach in other professional programs—in schools of education, business, medicine and nursing, agriculture, social work, law, and architecture and design—where their contribution to issues of human problem solving is even more direct.

Planning is an activity of knowledge transfer in that it typically involves the collection, evaluation, and presentation of information. Anthropologists have worked in a variety of planning settings—including health planning, education, city and regional development, transportation planning, and natural and historical resource development. These anthropologists typically report that their anthropological training in judging the quality of research, in holistic perspective and systems analysis, and in familiarity with cultural process, is of considerable benefit to their work.

The fourth model of work for applied anthropologists derives from their participation in the actual processes of *decision making*. Anthropologists and persons trained in anthropology have worked as decision makers, both in the administration and management of programs of planned change, and in the implementation of programs or direct-service activities. A counselor or nurse trained in anthropology functions primarily as a decision maker in determining the type and quality of care given to individual clients. A sensitivity to cultural differences has proven invaluable in these settings. Similar backgrounds have been useful in employment involving the administration and management of people, particularly in situations involving considerable cultural diversity.

The models of work discussed above are not exclusive. Many of the positions occupied by applied anthropologists require the ability to work in several different capacities in a single setting. Margaret Boone (1981) described her employment in a public hospital setting in such a light. Assigned to a large urban hospital, Boone worked variously as a researcher, teacher, intermediary (or cultural broker), and administrator. In effect, her involvement was determined by the multiple ways in which her training and expertise could be used in a particular work situation. This mode of performance is far from unique.

These models represent ways in which applied anthropologists connect with the rest of the world. For the most part, the three models of practice have only recently been admitted to the profession, and even then partially by default. It is possible to encounter anthropologists who would exclude one or more of these activities as being inappropriate. The argument underlying this book is that all four models are not only appropriate but essential to the continuing development of applied anthropology.

CLIENTS AND SUBJECTS

In addition to their responsibilities to their profession, applied anthropologists are generally accountable to two parties—their "clients" or employers and the "subjects" of their activities. The actual situations of applied work can be more complex than this. There is often a hierarchy of clients as well as considerable diversity among subjects. In any event, the distinction between clients and subjects is important. Styles of applied work vary according to the way individual anthropologists recognize their obligation toward and their dependency upon others. Although applied anthropologists rarely consider their work as decidedly favoring the interests of either their clients or subjects, a recognition that the concerns of clients and subjects may be different has led to two additional models for applied work. These are based on orientations toward the needs of clients and subjects and can be identified as the *administration* and *advocacy-action* models.

The Administration Model

This approach includes all those efforts which are directed toward assisting in the administration of programs of planned change which have developed out of government or private initiative. In this style of work, there is generally a clear distinction between the client or sponsor of the effort and the subject population to which policy issues are directed. In many respects, this is the classic model for applied anthropology. Much of the early impetus for applied anthropology was at the bequest of government agencies which had encountered difficulty in translating their policy goals into effective action in culturally diverse settings.

One example from the work of George Foster (1969: 23-27; 1978: 205-216) illustrates this. In the early 1940s, Foster and several other anthropologists became active participants in the Institute of Inter-American Affairs, which among other tasks assisted in establishing regional health care centers in a number of Latin American countries. One of the anthropologists' jobs was to help evaluate the success of these health care centers after 10 years of operation. It was already known that the centers were not being fully utilized by the people they were intended to serve. The next question was "why"?

The anthropologists came up with two explanations. The first was that the new facilities were found to be in competition with local practitioners of folk medicine, who enjoyed a long and popular tradition in the areas where the "Westernized" health centers had been established. The second reason related more to a cultural difference in health perceptions. As Foster explains:

> With respect to bureaucracy and planning, the anthropologists discovered a principle that had become axiomatic in the best technical aid programs: you cannot transplant an institution unchanged from one culture to another and expect it to function as effectively as in the place where it developed. In the case of public health centers, the organizational and philosophical relationship between preventive and curative medicine was the issue. In the United States good curative medical services developed under private auspices relatively early in the country's history. Public health in its contemporary form came later, and since it is largely a government enterprise, it has had to avoid offending the vested interests of private medical practice. It has therefore concentrated on preventive medicine, in the form of environmental sanitation, immunization, maternal and child health servics, and the like. The pattern of curative medicine as largely private and preventive medicine as largely public therefore grew up in response to the conditions of American society. American health advisors in Latin America naturally followed the American pattern, emphasizing preventive to the relative neglect of curative medicine. (1969:25-26).

This "American pattern" was found to be inconsistent with the needs of the low-income Latin American population which the health centers were meant to serve. The center clients expected curative attention. Because private medical practice was less well established in many of the areas being served, this was a realistic need which the centers were not fulfilling. Many potential beneficiaries lost interest in the centers after discovering they would not receive primary health care.

This evaluation project is fairly typical of the uses of applied anthropology following the administration model. It places the anthropologist primarily in the role of a researcher working for a government or private agency which is attempting to provide services or effect change within a target population. Most often, the relationship between the research client and the target population is one in which the client has some basis of authority to effect the desired changes. In these cases, anthropologists have usually been asked to provide information and insights concerning the target population which will help determine the most effective programmatic approaches to implementing and administering such changes. In some instances, anthropologists have been engaged in the actual administration of the programs.

Although it is often the case, the subjects (or presumed *beneficiaries*) of such change efforts are not always the least powerful or most economically marginal members of a society. For example, much of the applied work in education focuses on the *providers* (teachers and administrators) of educational services rather than on the *recipients* (students). Several recent government-sponsored social experiments directed toward evaluating innovative programs for income assistance have focused as much on the agencies that provide such assistance as on the people who receive the services. Anthropologists working with some of these projects have found themselves carrying their notebooks into the offices of middle-level managers much more often than into the homes of the poor.

The Advocacy-Action Model

This approach derives from the realization that a government or corporate view of policy issues often favors the value orientations of middle-class planners and managers. As a result, the views of the people whose lives might be most dramatically changed by a new policy are sometimes seriously "misread" or underestimated. This has been especially true for those persons considered to be "problems" in a modern society. Drug abusers, the unemployed, pregnant teenagers, slum dwellers, subsistence farmers, and minority children all have one thing in common. They are the focus of a considerable amount of public policy interest, and they have had little or no opportunity to say anything about it.

Advocacy anthropology seeks to redress this imbalance in the different approaches to problem solving by representing and furthering the perspectives of the less powerful. As Stephen Schensul and Jean Schensul (1978) point out, advocacy work finds its roots in the earliest history of professional anthropology, with the founding in 1838 of the Aboriginal Protection Society in London. In the United States, the Women's Anthropological Society, founded in 1885, played an active role in advocating housing improvements for low-income families in Washington, D.C.

The distinction between administration and advocacy approaches to applied work is partly a result of historic circumstances. Anthropology, perhaps more than any other social science, has maintained an advocacy perspective throughout its development, and most anthropologists who have worked in an administration setting have assumed that their work would benefit both clients and subjects.

Distinct models for advocacy work did not emerge until the 1950s, as anthropologists (and the public in general) became more sensitive to situations in which the interests of those who governed did not seem to coincide with the interests of those who were being governed. One such model is epitomized in the Vicos Project, conducted by Alan Holmberg and other anthropologists from Cornell University (Holmberg 1958, 1962).

Vicos was a large-scale demonstration project in Latin American rural develoment. Holmberg and his colleagues rented a Peruvian *hacienda* (a large landed estate) with the express purpose of breaking down the reign of exploitation that traditionally existed between a landowning elite and the Indian tenant farmers who occupied *haciendas* throughout Latin America. In the initial phases of the project, the anthropologists assumed the role of *patron* to the Indians, but with the aim of guiding them to self-sufficiency rather than of perpetuating the chain of dependency normally associated with Latin American agrarianism.

Over a period of years, the Vicos administrators were able to guide the Vicos Indians to a form of elected representation and to reverse the traditional authority structure of the *hacienda*. At the same time, they managed to carefully introduce a number of agricultural and social innovations. In slightly more than 10 years the Indians were in a position to purchase their *hacienda* from its previous owners and thus ensure themselves a measure of self-sufficiency which, until that time, had been thought impossible.

The Vicos Project is atypical in the degree to which anthropologists took a firm hand in directing the course of social and economic change. The more usual approach has been similar to the *action anthropology* described by Sol Tax in reference to his work with the Fox Indians of the midwestern United States (cf. Tax 1958; Gearing 1970). Action anthropology begins with the premise that the anthropologist should operate within the framework of goals and activities initiated by groups seeking to direct the course of their own development. The action anthropologist may use his or her technical skills to help a group clarify its goals, but generally avoids the temptation to direct the project. Recent examples of action anthropology include work with urban community action groups (Peattie 1968); a program of assistance rendered to a Chicano community, which included helping justify funding for a community-operated drug counseling program (Schensul 1974); and work with a free neighborhood health center (Jacobs 1979).

A number of recent advocacy projects have also centered on international issues. *Cultural Survival Inc.*, an organization of action-minded anthropologists, has worked with the Sam hunters-gatherers of Botswana in documenting their legal claim to land they occupy (Bevis 1979). A similar group, the *Anthropology Resource Center*, has taken a special interest in the plight of Indian peoples in the Amazon basin, lending their active support to the establishment in Brazil of an "Indian Park" intended to ensure the survival of the Yanomamo Indians.

In its most basic expression, advocacy-oriented anthropology seeks to reduce any possible disparities between the interests of the clients and subjects of applied work. For action anthropologists, this aim is accomplished by regarding the client and the subject of their activities as one in the same. The justification for an advocacy model can be both practical and moral. People who are at the forefront of change (that is, who are actually undergoing a radical change in their lives) sometimes have a better feeling for what is needed and possible than do decision makers who are several steps removed from the problem. Most advocacy researchers also feel that people who are subject to programs of planned change should have the *right* to be actively involved in the management of their destinies, and consequently to avoid becoming the victims of others' good intentions.

The administration and advocacy settings for applied work represent different points of departure based on the anthropologist's relationship to clients and subjects. There are no hard fast boundaries, and much of the activity originating from one setting can be expected to overlap into the other. While the distinction is meaningful and represents significant differences in the attitudes of some anthropologists, the actual practice of applied anthropology is seldom so easily categorized. Applied anthropologists in administration settings are more inclined today to incorporate the views of people who will bear the weight of policy decisions than they were several decades ago—if for no other reason than that public involvement of some sort is now often required by law. On the other hand, much of the advocacy anthropology undertaken in this country has been accomplished with the sponsorship and policy overview of the federal government. And even action anthropologists have sometimes found that taking the subject's goals as their own does not always save them from becoming embroiled in differences of view and value conflicts that exist within the subject population.

Recent Trends

The variety of clients and subjects with whom applied anthropologists work cannot be fully explained by making a distinction between administration and advocacy-action models. The distinction has begun to fade as increasing numbers of applied anthropologists find themselves engaged in activities in which the status and economic positions of clients and subjects are no longer as clearly disparate as they were in most traditional anthropological endeavors.

For the past several years, the American Anthropological Association's *Anthropology Newsletter* has been publishing brief profiles of anthropologists employed in different applied settings. A sampling of these profiles will help demonstrate the variety of client and subject relationships to which some anthropologists have adapted.

1. Steve Barnett is employed by the Planning Economics Group of Boston. The firm conducts marketing and consumer education research, and Barnett was the first anthropologist in their employ. His clients are the firm's clients, and the work he has done involves integrating cultural analysis with the types of research his firm normally conducts. Barnett explains how this is done.

> Imagine a union offering its own health plan in competition with other standard health plans. Suppose further the union doesn't understand why so few

workers switch to the union plan even though it ostensibly provides more benefits. Three kinds of research are needed to understand why. First, there is consumer economics and demography. Are the benefits "really" better, or are they better for some and not for others? How do the benefits affect different population segments broken down in terms of family size and houshold budget? Second, there is behavioral or marketing research. What do the workers say are the reasons for choosing one plan over the other? How do they make trade-offs? Third, there is cultural research. What are the underlying, non-verbalized reasons for worker choice? Do workers think negatively about the union in general and does this affect their confidence in a union-run health plan? Is there a tension between cultural oppositions like public/private, family/self?

Once we know which kinds of worker segments tend to think and act in which ways based on quantitative evaluations of these three kinds of research questions, we can map the segments onto each other and devise an effective strategy for the union to both change certain aspects of its health plan and to communicate more effectively the strong features of the plan to the membership. In this case it turned out that young householders most strongly resisted the union plan because, as they married and started households, they feared losing their autonomy and were reluctant to grant dependence to anything else, especially their union. (*Anthropology Newsletter*, Vol. 21, No. 4, 1980)

2. As a management analyst with the Naval Weapons Center in California, Karen L. Buehler is "responsible for conducting problem-definition and problem-solving studies" and "providing information and/or decision alternatives to top- and middle-level managers." She admits she could fill her position without anthropological training, but not as well:

> I view anthropology in a very general sense as a method for making order out of chaos. That is, we explore culture(s) from a variety of different frameworks in an attempt to understand the whole, its parts and their interrelationships. Many management studies, in a very focused way, do (or should do) much the same thing.
>
> An anthropological education provided me with several methodological principles which are of continuing value to me as an analyst. These include: (1) never assume anything—question your own assumptions and all apparent "facts" or observations; (2) recognize your own preconceptions and ethnocentrism (including academic centrism); (3) there are a lot of ways to observe and evaluate the same situation; (4) "garbage in, garbage out"—if you ask the wrong questions, or the right questions the wrong way, you probably won't learn much; therefore (5) you must go to the people you want to learn about in order to find out what the right questions are—your questions are not necessarily their questions. (*Anthropology Newsletter*, Vol. 23, No. 3, 1982)

3. In her position as Vice Chancellor for Academic Affairs at the University of Maryland, College Park, Nancie L. Gonzalez found that her clients were not substantially different from those of a university faculty member. As an administrator, however, her relationships to the university's constituencies were both more diffuse and intense. She reports that her background in anthropology played an important part in her work.

> The most important transfer from my anthropological training is the broad and holistic view it has given me of the world. Anthropologists have an appreciation of how technology, economics, social organization, art forms and ideologies are all intimately interrelated in any sociocultural system. A university resembles a whole culture or society in two different ways. First, its various departments or disciplines present in microcosm the "parts" of culture, and any anthropologist who has studied a whole culture has perforce learned something of the content of each of them. Secondly, a university is itself a social system; and an ability to sort out the various components of that system, together with an ability to understand the various "political" forces which determine the behavior of the various groups vis-a-vis each other and elements outside the university gives an administrator a great advantage. (*Anthropology Newsletter*, Vo. 21, No. 2, 1980)

4. Gwen Stern has worked with a variety of community-based health programs in Chicago. Much of her work has taken an advocacy or action perspective:

> My role as coordinator involves administration of the program, staff supervision, development of a documentation system, continued gathering of basic research data as follow-up to the Latina Mother Infant Research Project, liason with health care institutions, advocacy for changes in hospital policies related to perinatal health, curriculum development, public relations for the program, and the securing of additional funding. (*Anthropoligy Newsletter*, Vol. 19, No. 9, 1978)

In reporting on her work, Stern alludes to several of the adjustments she has made from the orientation of basic research to that of applied research:

> Applied work has led me to reexamine the role of the anthropologist vis-a-vis various constituencies: informants, employers, funding agencies, etc. Once you've left the role of the detached, "objective" observer, you must struggle with such issues as commitment to your constituencies, power, and your identity as a professional versus your ability to work with community groups as an advocate or applied researcher. (*Anthropology Newsletter*, Vol. 19, No. 9, 1978)

5. H. Clyde Wilson has served on the city council and as mayor of Columbus, Missouri. His work involved serving a diverse set of clients and placed him clearly in the role of decision maker. Like the other anthropologists mentioned here, he notes close parallels between his employment and his anthropological training:

> I feel there was a close relationship between my public service and my career as an anthropologist. My council experiences had many parallels with my two years of fieldwork with the Jicarilla Apache. The diverse interest groups with which I had to work required that same facility with interpreting new value

systems, learning new systems of signaling information, and so on. There were, or course, significant differences as well. With the Jicarilla I was a neutral observer; on the city council I interjected my values and had the power to determine outcomes . . . anthropologists have an important contribution to make to the public sector. I suspect most of us are not aware of the considerable skills we have to bring intellectual order out of seemingly chaotic and complex situations. This is what we are trained to do well, whether the situation is another culture, a strange language, an improbable distribution of gene frequencies or pot sherds scattered across the floor. This type of analytical ability is transferable outside the areas traditionally considered by anthropologists, and it is in very short supply in the public sector. (*Anthropology Newsletter*, Vol. 23, No. 1, 1982)

Applied anthropologists have demonstrated that the skills and perspective associated with their profession can be useful to a considerable array of clients and subjects. These relationships can be further described in terms of the particular roles anthropologists assume as they undertake applied work. As the following discussion suggests, how anthropologists determine their relationship to both clients and subjects rests in large part with how they perceive their contribution to the processes of decision making.

THE ANTHROPOLOGIST AS CULTURAL BROKER

Applied anthropologists have often described themselves as cultural brokers, maintaining that their activities involve some kind of transfer of knowledge, skill, or service between distinct cultures. The idea of cultural brokerage is often tinged with a sense of advocacy for the economically marginal and least powerful members of society.

As laudable as the anthropologist's willingness to leap to the defense of the downtrodden has been, this unidimensional sense of advocacy limits and strains the role of the cultural broker. As action anthropologists have pointed out, there is a measure of paternalism in assuming that one can represent the special interests of another group of people better than can the members of that group. There may have been some merit in this perspective during the early days of applied anthropology, when practitioners found themselves in close contact with peoples who had little understanding of the social and political processes bearing down on them as a result of the forceful encroachment of Western industrialized nations. Unfortunately, some anthropologists have been reluctant to lay down the reins of their original authority or to recognize that their continued utility rests with their ability to adapt to changes in the alignment of a society's bases for public decision making.

Consider anthropology's involvement in the affairs of American Indians. Anthropologists have always had a kind regard for the lifeways of

American Indians, but their interest and concern has also generally followed the major social and political currents of their time. The earliest period of professional interest in the native peoples of North America is marked by a commitment to scholarly intent. As George Hicks and Mark Handler (1978) have noted, anthropologists originally showed little interest in the contemporary problems faced by the Indians they studied. Their first concern was salvaging ethnological materials (for example, the direction defined by John Wesley Powell for the work of the Bureau of American Ethnology). These matters began to give way during the 1930s to an interest in processes of acculturation. This work closely followed the popularity of the "melting pot theory," which assumed that United States ethnic minorities would eventually be absorbed by dominant Anglo-cultural values. Much of the work of anthropology initiated during this period was clearly paternalistic, devoted to helping edge the American Indian into the "American" mainstream with a minimum of stress and discomfort.

But during the late 1950s and early 1960s it became increasingly apparent that the idea of a mainstream of American culture was yielding to another imagery of powerful and distinct ethnic tributaries, and that ethnic and cultural minorities were beginning to insist on the distinctiveness of their place in society. This insistence was articulated by spokespersons who came from the ranks of the minorities, and who early on demonstrated that their disadvantage in relation to the dominant society was not so much a matter of their inability to understand their relationship to the rest of society as it was a problem in countering prevalent public images of their cultural status. Outspoken Indians such as Vine DeLoria (1970) went so far as to partly blame anthropologists for the public's mistaken ideas about contemporary Indian life. While DeLoria's remarks are misleading in some respects, discounting the extent to which anthropologists had contributed positively to our understanding and appreciation of Indian life, they are painfully accurate in other respects. Anthropologists had shown a greater interest in studying the most traditional elements of Indian culture than they had in more recent phenomena, such as the increasing sophistication of the American Indian rights movement. When anthropologists dealt with the contemporary situation of the Indian, it was often to look at pathological behaviors (such as alcoholism) rather than at these people's efforts for self-improvement and self-determination.

In the perspective of contemporary society, the role which finds the anthropologist serving as a spokesperson for people who cannot speak for themselves is becoming increasingly inappropriate and, at its worst, has become ludicrous. An uncritical approach to advocacy also hinders the anthropologist's ability to locate a human problem in its larger context. In the past, applied anthropologists have spent most of their time explaining why socially and economically marginal people often resist outside efforts to alter their behavior. They have spent much less time trying to understand people who originate and attempt to implement programs of planned change. The view "from the ground up" which anthropologists have offered is an important and critical contribution to our understanding of the effects of public decisions. But it is not an adequate view on which to base a profession of applied anthropology.

Neither the impulse of the advocate nor the role of the cultural broker are discounted by these observations. As we begin to realize that there are many ways of approaching applied anthropology, we need to consider that styles of brokerage will also be subject to considerable variation, depending on the way in which an anthropologist approaches a particular policy issue. Within these variations of practice, at least five roles of cultural brokerage are easily defined.

The Representative Role

In this role, the anthropologist serves as a spokesperson or representative for a particular group of people, usually in reference to their relationship with the larger society. An example of this style of brokerage is when anthropologists are called on to report or testify on behalf of a people they have studied. In the 1940s, for example, anthropologists were asked to respond to the Bureau of Indian Affairs' new Indian Reorganization Act. On the basis of his extensive study of the Navajo and other Indian peoples, Clyde Kluckhohn played a significant part is seeing that many of the provisions of the Act were changed. In this role, Kluckhohn was clearly speaking on behalf of the American Indian, with his efforts devoted to representing the Indian "point of view" before federal policy makers.

As we have seen, the viability of this role is reduced as the minority groups with which anthropologists have traditionally worked become more outspoken and as representatives of the dominant group better listen to what is being said. We should all be pleased with the assurance that this form of brokerage is rapidly becoming a thing of the past, because it thrives only in the face of gross societal neglect of the rights, authority, and power of representation of peoples who are culturally distinct.

The Facilitator Role

The style of brokerage suggested by a facilitator role involves those activities which are directed toward making something happen in a relationship between two or more groups of people. Facilitation may be from the top down, as when an anthropologist assists a development agency in introducing a programmatic activity in an alien cultural setting. This is the role predominant in Ward Goodenough's (1963) discussion of the role of the field-situated change agent. Facilitation may also occur from the bottom up, as represented by the assumptions underlying action anthropology.

In some cases, the two directions of facilitation might be combined, as they were in a project described by Philip Young (1980). In 1978, Young was hired as a project director for Plan Guaymi, a program sponsored by the United States Agency for International Development with the cooperation of the Panamanian Ministry of Education. The project called for training Guaymi Indians as change agents who would eventually return to work in their rural communities. Young's role was to direct and facilitate the training of the young Guaymi men selected for the project. While many of the change goals associated with the project were related to policy assumptions developed outside the Guaymi communities, the long-term benefits of the project focused on developing the skills and confidence of the Guaymi participants. As a result of their training, the Guaymi were better equipped to assume initiative in future relations with representatives of the Panamanian national government.

In most respects, we can expect (and hope) that the role of the facilitator will also begin to decrease in importance for the applied anthropologist. Like the representative role, the facilitator's activities are based on an assumption that certain peoples are not fully able to negotiate with a dominant society. In many cases, this is no longer true. Some of the most promising attempts at facilitation are those which, like Plan Guaymi, emphasize the training of indigenous leaders.

On the other hand, some anthropologists might remain indefinitely as facilitators and representatives for minority or special-interest groups. This is particularly true as members of these groups choose to become anthropologists in their own right. Bea Medicine (1978), an anthropologist and a Sioux, has declared a unique responsibility for her work with American Indians. "I am part of the people of my concern and research interests," she reports. From this perspective, Medicine has both studied and advocated for the interests of Indian people.

The Informant Role

While anthropologists have shown little reluctance to identify the subjects of their research as "informants," they have seldom been eager to acknowledge that their own participation in public affairs is often limited to a similar role. In this style of cultural brokerage, the anthropologist serves primarily as a conduit in transferring knowledge about one sector of humanity to another, usually dominant, sector. The important characteristic of this role is that the anthropologists involved usually have little control over how the information they supply will be used.

Anthropologists are generally sought as informants on the basis of their special knowledge of a group of people, or because of their skill in obtaining such knowledge in culturally diverse settings. At the close of World War II, for example, United States anthropologists were employed by the Department of the Navy to collect basic information concerning the peoples living in the newly acquired Trust Territories of Melanesia. British anthropologists have similarly been hired by their government to conduct basic research among the peoples of the British colonial empire. The possible use of such information is seldom as clearly specified as it is when anthropologists are serving as representatives or facilitators. In the above cases, reports provided by anthropologists were certainly of general use in familiarizing government administrators with the people of a region under their jurisdiction, and no doubt were also useful in formulating subsequent administrative policy.

The use of anthropologists as informants has continued as a model for recent applied work. Many of the large evaluation research projects sponsored by the United States federal government during the 1970s and 1980s have employed anthropologists as "on-site researchers," with their major responsibilities being to provide information as to how local-level service clients and delivery agencies respond to federal policy initiatives (Clinton 1975: Chambers 1977). Anthropologists also continue to serve, wittingly or not, as informants to international development agencies (Almy 1977).

The possibility that information supplied by anthropologists might be misinterpreted or inappropriately used by others has sometimes been offered as an argument against becoming involved in applied research. We should keep in mind that *all* the knowledge of anthropology, and not simply applied work, has the potential of being misappropriated. If anything, applied work has the greater potential for offering an antidote to this problem as applied anthropologists become more sophisticated in their approach to the problems inherent to knowledge transfer and decision making.

The Analyst Role

The roles of the representative, facilitator, and informant are all typified by a tendency for anthropologists to permit others to define and delimit their participation in applied work. They are also a result of the fact that, until recently, most anthropologists who were engaged in applied work have been content to accept part-time and sporadic involvement in policy issues, while their major professional interests remained directed toward basic research and academic careers. The word that describes many of these assignments is *consultation*. As consultants, anthropologists are called upon to respond to specific needs for information or insight. Their contribution is rarely an integral part of the project on which they are working.

The analyst role reflects a change from short-term to long-term involvement in applied activities. Here, we recognize the importance of an anthropologist becoming an active participant in the formulation and analysis of applied research activities, rather than simply a provider of information. Although the analyst role is much more common today than it has been in the past, there are important precedents. During the 1930s, for example, a number of anthropologists were engaged in a long-term interdisciplinary study of labor and management practices in association with Elton Mayo's Western Electric research project. This work not only served as a milestone in applied anthropology, but more significantly contributed to major changes in human relations and organizational theory and, consequently, to changes in the management practices of United States' industries (Arensberg 1978).

Despite the example of the Western Electric studies, it was still possible as late as the mid-1970s for most research in applied anthropology to be described as being predominantly in the informant role. M. G. Trend does so in his description of the anthropologist as a "go-fer":

> When I was in the building trades, and Malinowski was Stan Malinowski, a guy I once worked with on a raising gang, a familiar figure at the construction sites and in the shops was the "go-fer." He was usually the most junior person who happened to be around when it was coffee time, an apprentice whose informal duty it was to "go-fer" the coffee and "go-fer" the doughnuts, or whatever. In the words of a fellow tradesman, "Somebody has to be the coffee boy," (Mike Cherry, *On High Steel: The Education of an Ironworker*, 1974). When it wasn't time to make a run down to a nearby restaurant or liquor store, the go-fer gave a hand wherever it was needed. He'd fetch tools or stock, and he did a lot of the "bull work"—tasks that required some muscle but not too much finesse . . . unless applied anthropologists can offer . . . some other skills besides observational ones, the likelihood is great that they will become the go-fers of the policy research world. (1980:13)

Trend goes on to argue that, at least in applied work, the data-gathering phase of a research project is low in prestige and effectiveness when compared to the subsequent analysis of that data. He suggests that anthropologists are often hired for work on large-scale, interdisciplinary research projects because of their observational data-gathering skills, and that they often leave the projects before the analysis begins.

Trend's personal experience with the informant role, and his subsequent employment as a policy analyst with a large research firm, has led him to comment more explicitly (Trend 1978a) on the importance of the anthropologist playing an active role in policy analysis. He notes that the anthropologist who manages to make the transition from the role of fieldworker to that of policy research analyst has begun to carve out a new professional status. It "probably means that the individual has learned to separate *anthropology* from a single research *method* (participant observation)." At the same time, Trend does not discount the anthropologist's prior experience in the field. The informant-turned-analyst is a valuable addition to an "in-house" research staff because of his or her in-depth knowledge of the human contexts surrounding a research effort.

The analyst role has distinct advantages over the informant role. In the first place, by encouraging anthropologists to become involved at all stages of policy research, the profession as a whole gains through a fuller and less distorted view of what policy research is. Individual anthropologists engaged in policy research also gain by having the opportunity for greater input into the design, interpretation, and implementation of their work.

The Mediator Role

Just as the analyst role is an outgrowth of dissatisfaction with the informant role, so is in many respects the mediator role an improvement over those of the representative and facilitator. The analyst and mediator roles are complementary in many respects, with mediation becoming an active manifestation of the analyst's research perspective. A difference between the representative and facilitator roles and the mediator role is that in mediation the distinction between "subject" and "client" often becomes usefully blurred. The mediator recognizes that there are many parties to any given policy issue and attempts to treat each party as an equal partner and participant in deriving solutions from complex human problems.

There is a slight but important difference in the ideologies of representation and facilitation and those of mediation. The mediator tends to be less concerned with single, correct answers or ultimate solutions to most policy problems. Rather than seeking the best of all possible worlds, the mediator is more likely to look for possibilities of detente in which various special-interest groups can agree on a course of action. Like the role of analyst, the mediator role generally requires a long-term commitment to the resolution of a particular problem. In the careers of individual anthropologists, it has sometimes developed out of frustrations similar to those expressed by Trend. This is the way Mim Dixon (1982) has described her involvement in responding to the social impacts of the trans-Alaska oil pipeline, a major and controversial construction project started during the early 1970s. Dixon was originally hired to do a study of the probable social impacts of the construction project while it was still in the planning stages. She was later discouraged by the extent to which her findings were not used to help mitigate the social costs of future energy development in Alaska. Rather than giving up, Dixon found herself taking advantage of opportunities to become more involved in planning and in the development of legislation and state policy related to energy development. She came to see effective participation in the policy process as requiring a long-term professional commitment to helping mediate the claims of a variety of groups with a special interest in the energy and quality-of-life resources of the state.

Mediation has become an increasingly popular approach to resolving conflicts in modern societies. In some areas, such as in resolving labor disputes, mediation has been an accepted practice for some time. It has more recently been applied to issues of environmental concern and community development. The major alternative to mediation is the always lengthy and often arbitrary course of legal process. The role of the mediator is compatible with the perspective of the anthropologist; it encourages a holistic view developed around issues and events, supports public participation in decision making, and acknowledges cultural diversity as a major concern in public decision making.

As cultural brokers, applied anthropologists assume a variety of roles in relation to the people with whom they work. Anthropology is not unique in this respect. The broker role is central to the activities of most professions. The nurse, for example, is often called upon to be a broker among patients, physicians, hospital administrators, and patients' families and friends. The attorney is a broker among a client, a contestant, and the courts. A teacher is a broker among pupils, school administrators, and parents. The anthropologist's professional role calls for a brokerage between cultures, or at least between the divergent values and distinct life opportunities of recognizable groups or constituencies of people. The complementary roles of analyst and mediator represent a maturation of the ways in which anthropologists have responded to opportunities to participate in decision-making activities.

PERSPECTIVE

Understanding a profession is not easy, and this book is as much about the profession of anthropology as it is about some of the phenomena on which anthropologists reflect. Our task is complicated because the ideas and demands associated with criteria of values, judgment and utility (as compared to those of basic science) impose a different way of thinking about the sorts of things applied anthropologists do. It is not enough to accept a notion that the knowledge and insights of anthropologists *should* be useful; we need to follow the laborious if intriguing routes by which utility can be assured.

The viability of applied anthropology as a profession rests on our ability to imagine that anthropologists can do a lot more than conduct basic research. This is not to denigrate the important role of basic inquiry; it is a foundation for all our endeavors. At the same time, we cannot rely upon others to do the work of applying our insights. The most important single event in applied anthropology during the past decade has been the rapid expansion of anthropologists into roles of applied research or collaborative inquiry, knowledge transfer, and decision making.

Some anthropologists will have trouble with one or another of the models of work or client orientation described in this chapter. Solon Kimball (1978) has, for example, argued against an advocacy orientation in the professional activities of anthropologists. Other anthropologists have argued that the profession should not make its services available to particular clients, ranging from the military to business and industry to any institution representative of the "status quo." For the most part, I trust in an open market for anthropology and with very rare exceptions I do not believe it should be the business of any profession to tell its members where or where not to practice. There *are* important ethical considerations connected with the practice of anthropology, but I do not believe these problems are adequately resolved simply by insisting that anthropologists should avoid working for one or another client. Such an approach virtually guarantees that the skills of anthropologists will not be widely acknowledged. Most professions have held that their services should be available to practically any group or individual requiring them. The thinking behind this latter approach is that a profession should not generally exercise moral control over the granting of its services. A doctor should not, for example, have the right to deny life-saving services to any clients. Similarly, our legal system mandates that, at least in principle, all citizens should have an equal right to legal representation.

I acknowledge that this is a difficult issue. What a society offers its citizens in principle is often represented in practice by tremendous gaps in the quality of professional services to some segments of that society. Anthropologists should be sensitive to this problem in the practice of their profession. On the other hand, the best guarantee of equitable practice does not lie in denying services to some while making them available to others, but rather rests with a professional commitment to make those services as widely available as possible.

These observations do not exhaust the range of ethical dilemmas faced by applied anthropologists. We will have occasion to return to the problem in the last chapter of this book.

RECOMMENDED READINGS

A somewhat different view of the relationship between applied anthropology and the rest of the discipline is offered in Edward Spicer and Theodore Downing's "Training for Non-Academic Employment: Major Issues," appearing in *Training Programs for New Opportunities in Applied Anthropology* (American Anthropological Association, 1974), as well as in *Some Uses of Applied Anthropology* (Anthropological Society of Washington, 1956) and Bela C. Maday's *Anthropology and Society* (Anthropological Society of Washington, 1975).

The relationships between applied work and the profession have been explored in a number of books. In his *Applied Anthropology* (Harper & Row, 1971), Roger Bastide offers a theoretical discussion of the scope of applied anthropology and an interesting argument for viewing applied work as distinct from other branches of the profession. Cyril Belshaw's *The Sorcerer's Apprentice* (Pergamon, 1976) probes some of the ambiguities that reside in efforts to make anthropological knowledge useful. In *Anthropology and Contemporary Human Problems* (Cummings, 1976), John H. Bodley relates anthropological insight to major environmental issues.

Until quite recently, most published accounts of applied work in anthropology focused on planned change in the context of overseas development. These include George M. Foster's *Applied Anthropology* (Little Brown, 1976), Ward H, Goodenough's *Cooperation in Change* (Russell Sage, 1963), Charles J. Erasmus' *Man takes Control* (Minnesota, 1961), Conrad M. Arensberg and Arthur Neihoff's *Introducing Social Change* (Aldine, 1964), Homer G. Barnett's *Anthropology and Administration* (McGraw-Hill, 1956), and Laura Thompson's *Toward a Science of Mankind* (McGraw-Hill, 1961). Glynn Cochrane's *Development Anthropology* (Oxford, 1971) offers a critical perspective on most of these contributions and a brief but compelling description of the public context for overseas development work.

Cases studies in applied anthropology, again mostly devoted to overseas development projects, are provided in Edward H. Spicer's *Human Problems in Technological Change* (Russell Sage, 1952), Arthur H Neihoff's *A Casebook of Social Change* (Aldine, 1966), and James A. Clifton's *Applied Anthropology* (Houghton Mifflin, 1970).

More current case studies devoted largely to applied anthropology projects conducted in the United States can be found in Elizabeth M. Eddy and William Partridge's *Applied Anthropology in America* (Columbia, 1978), Michael V. Angrosino's *Do Applied Anthropologists Apply Anthropology?* (Southern Anthropological Society, 1976), Patricia Tway's *Anthropology and the Public Interest* (a special edition of the *Anthropological Quarterly*, 1976), Elizabeth Hegemen and Leonard Kooperman's *Anthropology and Community Action* (Doubleday, 1974), Donald D. Stull and Felix Moos'*Symposium on Anthropology and Public Policy* (a special edition of the *Policy Studies Review*, 1981), Peggy Reeves Sanday's *Anthropology and the Public Interest* (Academic, 1976), Ruth H. Landman's *Anthropological Careers* (Anthropological Society of Washington, 1981), and Donald H. Messerschmidt's *Anthropologists at Home in North America* (Cambridge, 1981).

Two edited contributions to applied sociology should be of interest to anthropologists. These are Phillip Hammond's *Sociologists at Work* (Basic Books, 1964) and Howard E. Freeman, Russell R. Dynes, Peter H. Rossi, and William Foote Whyte's *Applied Sociology* (Jossey-Bass, 1983). Lisl Klein's *A Social Scientist in Industry* (Wiley, 1976) offers a detailed accounting of a British sociologist's role as an applied researcher in industry.

2

The Policy Idea

I once asked another applied anthropologist what he thought was the most important thing for applied anthropologists to learn.

"How to overcome their innocence," he told me.

"What do you mean?" I asked.

"I know it's been difficult for me," he said, "and I see the problem reflected in the attitudes of many other applied anthropologists. We're always in danger of forgetting that our work has a context and a history that is virtually independent of our profession."

"Why is that?" I asked.

"It has something to do with the way we normally teach applied anthropology," my colleague said. "When we talk about the history of our profession, for example, we often describe it as though our predecessors had simply invented their particular interests and the way they went about their work. The truth is that they were generally following the public concerns of their time. We can't really understand why they got interested in particular problems unless we pay attention to the larger social context out of which those problems evolved."

"Like Franz Boas," I suggested. "We know he was interested in United States immigration policy. But sometimes we forget that his interest was part of a much greater national concern with immigration issues."

"Exactly," my friend said. "But there's a lot more to it than that. What we need is a good sense of the structures which underlie policy concerns. What are the rules for making and facilitating policy decisions? It isn't just a matter of what people get interested in. The greater problem is how they translate their concern into action. There are institutional structures and behaviors which greatly influence the way things get done in our society, or in any society for that matter. These structures and the standards of behavior which support them change over time . . ."
. . .

"That sounds like something anthropologists should be aware of," I suggested. "It actually sounds very cultural."

" 'Should be' and 'are' can be two different things," my colleague said, "and anthropologists know that, too. The best of applied anthropology is informed by a clear understanding of the contexts of policy decision making. But we have done a lot of work which leaves much to be desired in this sense."

It is clear that applied anthropology is a profession of many possibilities. There is no single line of work, type of training, philosophical orientation, or political perspective which adequately describes the kinds of activities applied anthropologists engage in or are capable of claiming for the future. One of the few relationships of enduring significance to the profession is its intimate association with the idea of policy. Applied anthropologists work closely with public and private decision makers and special-interest groups in attempting to understand, measure, manage, and sometimes actually direct social and cultural change. Whatever they do, their work can never afford to progress apart from the concerns of the rest of the world. The anthropologist's sensitivity to cultural processes helps guide his or her interaction with others. At the same time, successful applied anthropologists must develop a keen understanding of the contexts, strengths, and limitations associated with programs of deliberate change.

In this chapter, the idea of policy is introduced as a vehicle by which we might better grasp the essential connections between applied anthropology and public decision making. Our task will be to gain at least an elementary understanding of the larger political, economic, scientific, and administrative contexts of social action (and inaction) which have helped shape and influence the practice of applied social science in this country. We will see that the idea of policy is as central to the development of applied anthropology as the concept of culture has been to the anthropological profession as a whole.

A good part of this chapter is devoted to a historical overview of the past century of public policy activity in the United States. For the most part I have emphasized the development of structural, legal, and administrative precedents for policy activities rather than describing the emergence of particular policy ideas in any detail. It will be worthwhile to understand how these former mechanisms arose and to appreciate the extent to which they came to influence the way people arrive at public decisions.

WHAT IS POLICY?

The word *policy* is a lot like the word *culture*. It can mean almost anything, practically nothing, or it can be operationalized to mean something very particular. In the most general sense, the policy idea represents those intentions which can be associated with deliberate action in any sphere of human activity. Any action, whether it affects a single life or millions of lives, is preceded by some notion of the outcome of that action. It is these notions which represent policy: they may be vague or clear, accurate or inaccurate, appropriate or bizarre, but in every case they form the intentionality of human activity.

With this definition in mind, we must realize that applied anthropologists are most concerned with certain kinds of policy; that is, with those policies which are institutionally sanctioned and have the potential for affecting a large number of people. Anthropologists are interested in both *public* (or government) policy and in the *private* policies of business and industry, although they have paid considerably more attention to the former.

The value of forming an idea of policy is that it enables us to start thinking about human issues and problems in terms of their intentionality. Programs and activities of change do not just happen. They are thought about, planned for, and put into action by human beings for particular reasons. Neither do attempts to change something always turn out the way they were intended. We can seldom approach the policy idea with a unidimensional idea of intentions. In nearly all cases, it is much more accurate to envision the world of policy as an arena where people with varied and frequently conflicting intentions meet. The outcomes of these confrontations, imperfect as they often are, represent much of the social world we know.

The range of policy is immense. Some policies are subject to rigorous debate; others are either so much or so little a part of our lives that we tend to take them for granted. People and societies differ in the attention they pay to public policy. In many traditional societies, important policies are well understood, and a long-term consensus has been reached in many areas of social concern. But in less traditional societies, noted for their diversity of public interests and a tendency for rapid social change, we can expect lively debates centered on policy issues. This is obviously the case in our own society, where public consensus on particular issues tends, if it is reached at all, to be fragile and short-lived.

People are generally most interested in policies which are controversial and which they perceive to directly affect their lives. Similarly, societies tend to focus on those policy issues which relate most closely to current crises. However, in a rapidly changing society, it is often the neglected, ignored, and only vaguely felt policies of the past which contribute to the crises of the present.

The usual interests of applied anthropology can be further narrowed to those policy ideas which have been translated into a "language" of social and cultural change. These ideas have developed into a manner of speaking in which a wide range of assumptions are made implicitly, including the various *stages* and *levels* of policy decision making as well as the institutional base of control or authority for implementing programs of planned change. This language underlying policy also guides the ideology and circumstances of change—key terms like *federalism, private sector, revenue sharing, cost-benefit ratio, deregulation,* and *quality of life* represent segments of discourse which help define the character of specific public policies. Understanding the language of decision makers is a prerequisite of effective applied work.

PUBLIC POLICY AND AMERICAN VALUES

Trying to make sense out of existence appears to be an inexorable part of human nature. Still, anthropologists are well aware that people have different ways of arriving at an acceptable view of the cosmos. These views and the value systems which support them help us understand why a particular society responds to policy issues in the way it does. In our society, for example, public policy issues reflect two distinct sets of ideas about *control*. Our approaches to policy are based on the belief that we can control and shape some major portion of our destiny. The policy idea is also based on our belief that some people and institutions should be allocated considerable responsibility and authority for controlling significant parts of other people's lives.

Like any other people, Americans are heirs to a set of rational expectations, not the least of which in our case is a clear idea of progress. We tend to believe that individual and collective destinies can be willfully altered, adjusted to match the times, and improved upon. We often disagree on how our social lives might best be changed, and many promised improvements have never come about. Many of our attempts to manipulate our future have created more problems than they have solved. But these realities only seem to spur us on. Most Americans believe that the world can be made better.

If recent times have tempered this belief, it is mostly to our advantage. The pioneer heartily chopping a meaningful life out of a piece of wilderness is no longer an appropriate image for most Americans. Our circumstances have changed very rapidly and simply keeping up with those circumstances has become increasingly difficult. Americans have begun to discover that a belief in orderly progress is not enough. Far-reaching changes in nearly every area of human endeavor have, paradoxically, brought us nearer to each other in some respects and drawn us further apart in others. Rapid transformations in communication, transportation, and even in human opportunity have broken down old community boundaries. The interrelationships between people and events have never seemed so complicated or so immediate. Access to places, people, and information has never been so easily obtained. And yet, the more aware we are of our surroundings, the more the myth of a single-minded American public seems to give way.

Modern Americans are incapable of acting in total concert or complete harmony. For one thing, it is simply not in each of our best interests to do so. The widespread recognition of this fact has served to challenge many of our earlier and more naive ideas about progress and beneficial social change. But it has not led us away from the fascination we hold for tampering with the parameters of our present social condition. If many Americans are now more keenly aware of the limitations of past efforts to transform society, most of us remain convinced that we must keep trying.

Americans accept, although sometimes uneasily, the trappings associated with their desire to control their destiny. We are a bureaucratic people, relying heavily on institutional arrangements of centralized authority and coordination, processes which Richard N. Adams (1975) describes as an inevitable consequence of societal complexity. Most Americans accept that major decisions concerning their lives will be made by others and readily yield large measures of personal autonomy to people and groups who are (or should be) in a position to know both the short- and long-range benefits of particular courses of action. Only in rare cases do we even question the degrees of autonomy we have surrendered for the sake of a relatively secure and orderly existence.

Like their belief in progress, the way Americans respond to bureaucracies has been tempered over time. Unpopular wars, periodic economic and social crises, and the demonstrated irresponsibility of many representatives of our governing bodies have served both to challenge the present bases of authority in our society and to give rise to new avenues for expression of the "public will." At the same time, traditional forms of bureaucratic control, such as those described half a century ago by the sociologist Max Weber, are yielding to the very complexity they helped create. The idealized manager of good intent and consummate wisdom, whether a politician or a corporate executive, has come to rely increasingly upon the opinions of specialists. On some fronts the "authority of office" has yielded almost completely to an "authority of expertness," with many critical public issues being decided outside traditional channels (Blau and Meyer 1971). Equally important, as more public issues are shaped and decided within the authority of expertness, we begin to witness a significant breach between bureaucratic *authority* and *responsibility*, the latter of which remains with the office rather than with the specialist.

Expertness, of course, has its own limitations. The more a society comes to rely on specialists, the more closely we witness that many important policy issues do not entirely yield to an expert's point of view. A specialist's interests and opinions are shaped much like everyone else's—by his or her specialization, by political and philosophical orientations, and by perceived loyalties to employers, friends, and associates. Just as many Americans now realize that there is no single conception of the public good, so have many of us begun to question the link between bureaucratic authority and expert opinion. At the same time, our basic beliefs in the legitimacy of some body of authority and in the value of expertise remain strong.

The idea of policy emerges most clearly (and is most subject to public expression, debate, and negotiation) under the conditions described in this chapter—where it is clearly recognized that no single authority or expert can respond to the totality of needs and interests of a diverse public. Our growing interest in public policy over the past decades is in fair proportion to the doubt and uncertainty that we face whenever we must make decisions that affect the lives of others. The development of viable means for assessing public interests, for responding to human problems, and for measuring the effects of particular kinds of responses has become one of the most pressing needs of our society.

STAGES OF POLICY DECISION MAKING

Involvement in public policy is involvement in the intentions of human actors. It is also engagement in a continuous process of organized efforts to clarify, actualize, and refine what is intended. The language of policy generally recognizes several stages of decision making, including those of *policy formulation*, *planning*, *implementation*, and *review*. Ideally, each of these stages receives due consideration in any attempt to investigate, determine, or influence public policy. At the same time, we must realize that major policy decisions generally involve a great many people. Seldom will the applied anthropologist, or any other professional, be fully involved in all four stages through the development of any particular policy issue. It is also important to recognize that these several stages of policy decision making often overlap and are seldom as closely followed in practice as they are described in ideal terms.

The stage of *policy formulation* pertains to those activities which result in an initial idea or set of ideas concerning social action. A rational approach to policy formulation prescribes that such ideas be as explicit, clear, and internally consistent as possible. While there is an unavoidable and often useful idealistic slant to most policy formulation, it is also desirable that policy ideas developed at this stage should be realistic, based on an understanding of the social facts of the issue, and on availability of the strategic resources and time needed to accomplish a given social action.

Needless to say, many public policy formulations do not meet these criteria. Policy goals may be vague and little understood even by those who are responsible for formulating them. A community organization, for example, might be sincerely dedicated to neighborhood improvement without its members ever sitting down to try to determine what they mean by "improvement." A federal agency charged with formulating policies for the support of bilingual education in public schools may act with the *a priori* assumption that bilingual education is desirable, never bothering to seek evidence which might indicate otherwise. It is not at all uncommon for agencies and organizations to formulate policies which are clearly unrealistic in terms of available resources and appropriate time frames. For example, an association representing an ethnic minority's interests might establish the immediate end of all forms of employment discrimination as its only policy goal. While that is a laudable aim, it appears naive and impractical in the absence of more specific and realistic supporting goals.

Vagueness and impracticality obscure many policy formulations. In other cases, important policy goals can be made deliberately unclear or kept purposely concealed from the public view. Groups organized locally to oppose enforced school busing programs seldom publicly acknowledge all the feelings that lie behind their policies. University departments sometimes develop and advertise impressive graduate programs with the avowed policy of better serving students and their profession, whereas much of their implicit and unstated policy lies in serving the department faculty's personal interests and career goals.

One of the most difficult tasks of policy formulation is to ensure some kind of consistency among policies. This is particularly true in organizations and agencies which assume responsibility for a wide range of public activities and try to be responsive to a large variety of special interests. The United States Department of Agriculture, for example, strives to consider the interests of the farmer, the farm employee, the consumer of agricultural products, and the merchant, as well as the special interests of low-income consumers and producers. Where these interests conflict, inconsistent ideas about policy issues are likely to develop within the single agency.

The second stage of policy is *planning*. Planning differs from policy formulation in that it is directed to specific program activities, becoming the bridge between a policy idea and its implementation. Of course, if policies have not been clearly formulated to begin with, it is unlikely that program goals arrived at through planning will be any clearer. There is also the possibility that initial policy formulations and programs will be strikingly different from each other. This is especially possible in situations where policy formulation and program planning are clearly separate functions, conceived and acted upon by different agencies or organizations or at different levels of public decision making.

Again, federal policy in this country provides a good example. In our time, many major policy ideas are initially formulated within the federal government. Policy planning, however, usually requires the cooperation of state and local governments. While agencies at these levels have little opportunity to participate directly in the initial formulation of a policy idea, they do have a crucial role to play in translating policy at the local level, particularly as they plan for specific types of program activities. Consider, for example, the fate of a federally sponsored rape information program in two different cities. Significant actors in one city agree that one of the reasons these crimes are so seldom reported is because police do not understand and are unsympathetic to the victims' experience. This city develops an energetic program to educate police officers. In the other city, significant decision makers are convinced they have the finest police force possible. While they are concerned with the problem of rape, the program they plan emphasizes public meetings which are designed to tell women they have nothing to fear in reporting attacks.

There is nothing wrong with varied planning responses to general policy concerns. It is from a variety of approaches that we learn which sorts of responses work best under what conditions. Still, it is important to realize that planning *is* policy and that plans for specific activities always reflect the special beliefs, perceived strengths, and limitations of the planners. Like policy formulations, plans can be vague, inconsistent, and impractical.

The test of both policy formulation and planning lies in *program implementation*. The best of policies are simply paperwork exercises if they cannot be brought to fruition. But implementation is not simply a testing ground for previously established public policies; it is also a framework for new policy responses. Program planners are often not responsible for the broad-scale policy formulations on which they model programs, and people who put policy ideas into practice are often one or several steps removed from the planners. Consider, for example, the case of a local school district. Reacting to some segment of public opinion, the school board decrees that there should be more emphasis upon the "three R's" and traditional teaching methods. Administrators of the local elementary schools are charged with planning revised curricula which will reflect the board's policy. However, the classroom teachers who are expected to implement the new plans may feel differently about the goals of education. If so, the teachers may not give the new policy the test the school board expects.

Even when policy planners and implementors generally agree, there are possibilities for striking discrepancies between program planning and practice. For example, planners may not have been realistic in assessing their resources or may not have understood the environment for which they are planning. In these instances, new policy ideas may have to be formulated to carry out a vague plan.

Consider a case where two local housing agencies in different parts of the country implement a new rental housing program for low-income clients. The program purposefully promotes racial desegregation. One of the agencies realistically assesses the local situation and comes to the conclusion that the program might not be well received by local landlords, many of whom openly oppose housing integration in their community. This agency decides to approach the problem directly and hires an attorney to represent low-income clients in possible discrimination complaints against landlords.

Although facing a similar housing environment, the other agency chooses to ignore the problem, hoping that enough landlords will cooperate to make the program a success. In neither case, however, do landlords cooperate. The first agency follows through with legal action, and many landlords drop their opposition to the program. The second agency, unable to find rental housing for its clients and unwilling to take legal action, begins to blame their low-income clients for the program's failure. Eventually they abandon the policy of housing desegregation and adapt their program standards to meet the wishes of local landlords.

The fourth stage of policy is *review*. At this stage it is recognized that policy making is a continual process and that past experiences in implementation contribute to future policies. Thus, the goal of review is to assess the effectiveness and impact of these prior implementations. Policy review is subject to many of the same pitfalls of the other policy stages. If goals and expectations are not clearly stated for programs, it is almost impossible to assess program effectiveness. If discrepancies between plans and their implementation are deliberately ignored, it becomes difficult to measure program impacts.

Still, policy review has become an important part of the policy process, and in many cases has helped indicate weaknesses in the prior policy stages. As more agencies and organizations call for systematic review of their public programs, they begin to realize the need for greater care in approaching public policy as a process of closely related activities which merits close attention at each stage of development.

Discrepancies among the stages of policy decision making do not always yield negative results. There is room for creative activity at each stage of development, as broadly based policy ideas are molded to local circumstances and continually adapted to changing social needs and priorities. One important justification for policy review is that it provides a record of both successful and unsuccessful adaptation.

There is no precise formula or set of procedures that will guide us through the four basic stages of policy decision making described above. The actual process of deciding upon a public policy will vary according to the particular contexts or circumstances. The one thing that all these efforts seem to have in common is that they lack finality—at its best, policy decision making is a continual cycle of action and introspection.

POLICY DOMAINS

Policy issues can be categorized into specific *domains* of public concern and activity: health care, education, economic development, energy use and conservation, community development, historical preservation, product testing, and marketing. The list can be continued to the full extent of our interest. At first glance, the boundaries between policy issues seem clear. However, when we consider each issue as a domain of activity, we are implying a sense of control and responsibility which has an institutional base, and here the common-sense distinctions between public activities are often easily disassembled. For example, the institutional base for health care in this country is divided among several government agencies, public and private institutions (such as hospitals), and professional associations. The assignment of control and responsibility in this domain frequently overlaps, and conflict between one or another institutional base is common.

Policy domains are often dispersed even within the limits of government control. For example, different agencies of the federal government have responsibility for a variety of public activities in the areas of education, cultural resource management, the enforcement of equal opportunity legislation, and the protection of human research subjects. As new or more complex policy issues arise, the assignment of an institutional base is often a matter of considerable controversy. One policy issue might be effectively "buried" by assigning policy responsibility to an already overburdened government agency. Another issue might be highlighted by creating a new institutional base, as occurred when the federal government created the cabinet-level Departments of Education and Energy during the 1970's.

The dispersion of policy domains among several different institutional bases, both private and public, suggests that any given policy issue might be subject to a variety of interpretations. The ability to recognize and mediate the several possible interpretations of an issue is an important component of applied work.

PUBLIC INTERESTS AND POLICY LEVELS

Why is there so much uncertainty about public policy issues? Whenever a major policy problem finds its way to public awareness, it is almost immediately clouded in debate. People begin choosing up sides and, before we know it, what might have once seemed like a relatively simple concern has become transformed into a decision maker's nightmare. Recent discussions concerning this country's energy policies provide a case in point. Even though energy policy has become a serious issue for most Americans only during the last decade, many of us are now convinced of the need to conserve our dwindling energy supplies and develop new sources of energy. But how? Every major effort in a particular direction seems blocked. Every good suggestion for a solution, such as increasing gasoline taxes or building new nuclear power plants, is countered with an equally good argument against it. And both are supported with a wealth of "reliable" documentation. After reviewing much of the literature on the safety of nuclear power plants, a Seattle attorney concluded that there was no conclusive evidence to say that nuclear power was safe within reasonable limits, or to say that it was not. "The problem," the attorney remarked, "is what to do when you don't know the answer."

We can rephrase the attorney's comment by saying that much of the problem is what to do when there are *too many* answers. Few responses to public policy issues are in the best interests of everyone. Almost invariably, some kind of public confrontation occurs. For example, the United States Army Corps of Engineers was recently involved in a project to improve a transportation waterway through a predominantly rural area of three Southern states. Most business executives and politicians within the area supported the project wholeheartedly on the expectation that local communities would profit from the development. But the same project threatened to displace dozens of small family farms and to destroy much of the original waterway's natural environment. These farmers and local environmentalists opposed the project with all the enthusiasm and sense of virtue of modern-day Quixotes. The railroad interests, faced with a potential loss of transportation revenue if the waterway was improved, supported the farmers and environmentalists. The issue became even more complex when the President of the United States called this project and dozens of others into question, noting that the "cost-benefit ratio" (the relationship of the cost of the project to the benefits to be realized from it) for the waterway was very low. Less concerned with what the project would cost the

entire nation, and considerably more interested in anticipated local benefits, governors and representatives for the three states turned out to support the project. On the surface, the Corps of Engineers tried to maintain
an image of neutrality. The image was somewhat tarnished, however, by
this semi-independent federal agency's long history of opposition to
executive control over its policies.

What this case illustrates is that one of the factors which often
obscures public policy is the existence and active participation of so many
different *public interests*. This is a fact of life in the contemporary United
States, as well as in most of the world. Confrontations between levels of
government, public and private bureaucracies, and numerous special-
interest groups have become commonplace. There is, of course, nothing
new about confrontations between various segments of a society. But the
ways in which societies institutionalize conflict, the degrees to which they
encourage confrontation, and the means they utilize to resolve differences
have varied considerably both across cultures and through time.

Many factors contribute to variations in dealing with conflict and
confrontation concerning public policies. In our time, major advances in
communication have provided the means for rapidly transmitting information to nearly all sectors of our society. The emergence of a computer
technology has permitted us to store and easily retrieve vast amounts of
information that was previously inaccessible. At the same time, and partly
as a result of these factors, the form of our government has been changing.

Government, in its most elementary sense, is simply a product of
explicit and tacit public policy. At the base of every system of government
we find important assumptions about societal authority and responsibility.
Who will make public policy? Who will be charged with implementing
policy decisions? And, importantly, who will be held accountable for poor
decisions? In some societies, the lines of authority and responsibility are
quite clear. This seems true, as we noted above, for most traditional
societies. We assume that it is also reasonably true of modern totalitarian
societies. But this sort of clarity is less apparent in modern democracies.
Here, the balance between effective social action and the equitable representation of public interests seems always to be in question. In recent
decades, special-interest groups have come to play major roles in both
determining and responding to policy issues.

Public policy is not only influenced by confrontations between special-
interest groups; it is also affected by the various levels on which policy can
be made and implemented. In American society, there are many such *policy
levels*, and by being sensitive to their presence and their particular vul-
nerabilities, we can better understand why arriving at effective public policies is seldom a simple matter.

Like special-interest groups, policy levels represent ideas about how
social authority and responsibility are to be allocated. One such idea in

American society is the belief that democratic principles are best served by a clear separation of governmental powers. The *federal level* of policy making is itself composed of several parts. For example, the executive, congressional, and judicial branches of federal government all play major roles in determining public policy at the federal level. Ideally, they represent a system of separation of powers which many Americans feel is essential to ensuring the continued existence of a democratic state.

Another idea that clearly influences policy in the United States is the notion of a *state level* for public policy. Americans believe that state governments should retain significant political controls and decision-making capabilities within their territories. Much of our policy-making history involves state versus federal rights.

The idea of territorial jurisdictions and the possibilities they provide for policy confrontations multiply when we include *local levels* of policy making, such as those found in city and county governments. Again, these governments have traditionally maintained a degree of control over their own affairs. The amount of authority and responsibility invested at these levels varies greatly from state to state, as well as in proportion to the size and style of government practiced by local jurisdictions. Even smaller policy levels, such as those representing neighborhood interests, have emerged and proven to have an effect on the policy process.

On each of these governmental levels (federal, state, and local), elected officials and their administrative support systems play a major role in determining and implementing public policy. But our view is hardly complete there. Americans have always maintained a precarious balance between the rights of government and the rights of the governed. The American blend of democracy, capitalism, and commitment to industrialization has encouraged the development of many other *private levels* of policy. The principle of *laissez faire*, for example, indicates a long-standing commitment to the right of private businesses and industries to determine "company" policy in their own best interests, even though these policies often have a profound effect on the general public. Business and industry are also generally recognized as having the right to use their resources to attempt (at least within the limits of ever-changing laws) to influence government policies in their favor. Some industries, such as those connected with the media, have come to play a major role in influencing public opinion and, consequently, in shaping public policy.

Similarly, our ideas about the rights of the individual have played a major role in determining American public policy. We generally maintain that there are certain areas of individual authority and responsibility in which neither government nor any other institution should interfere. Where these rights have been threatened, either by government or private interests, we have seen the emergence of labor unions, professional associations, and countless other special-interest groups.

Other policy levels have developed, not so much as a reflection of American ideals, but as a result of our attempts to deal with the increasing complexities of administering a modern nation. This is particularly apparent in the federal government, which has seen over the past century the unprecedented growth of a semi-independent administrative bureaucracy. Cabinet-level federal agencies (such as the Departments of Agriculture, Housing and Urban Development, and Health and Human Services) have assumed major responsibility and authority for public policy directed toward special areas of national concern. Administrative agencies within particular cabinet offices (such as the Bureau of Land Management, the Federal Housing Authority, and the Bureau of Indian Affairs) have also played important roles in designing and implementing public policies. Semi-independent regulatory agencies (such as the Food and Drug Administration, the Federal Communications Commission, and the Interstate Commerce Commission) also constitute specific levels of public policy concern. What is more, federal research agencies (such as the National Science Foundation, the National Institute of Mental Health, and the National Institute of Education) have come to play an important role in influencing policy decisions by virtue of their power to encourage research priorities through selective federal funding.

The fact that these segments of the federal bureaucracy came into being at the will of the federal government is not nearly as significant as the fact that their growth has fostered subtle (and sometimes not so subtle) independence from government control. It is also important to recognize that similar administrative structures exist at state and local levels. All in all, the number and variety of possible policy levels which might play a role in any critical exercise in public decision making is truly staggering.

The interplay of policy issues with various special-interest groups and at numerous policy levels is an everyday process. Through this process, policy issues are decided and the particulars of authority and responsibility are determined. But no policy is ever determined once and for all, and the balance of power between particular special interests and policy levels is never entirely settled.

HISTORICAL DIMENSIONS OF U.S. PUBLIC POLICY

A society's approach to the policy process does not just happen, but is the result of specific social and historical experiences. During the past century in the United States, profound shifts have occurred in our orientations to public policy, with one of the most significant changes being the emergence of the federal government as a potent force for social control and change. Prior to the Civil War, many of the governmental policy-making functions we now take for granted did not exist. Neither did most Americans foresee many of the social problems we now accept as the inevitable consequences of rapid technological development and uneven social change.

Industrialization

The last half of the nineteenth century was a period of considerable unrest as the nation experienced a civil war and its aftermath, as well as the transition from an agrarian society to a major force in the world's rush to industrialization. The abrupt and far-reaching changes of this period helped bring about a new consolidation of power and influence. In his biography of Abraham Lincoln, Carl Sandburg suggested that the Civil War marked the time when Americans stopped saying "the United States are" and started saying "the United States is." Certainly the war was a decisive step in settling part of the issue of states' rights versus the rights of the nation as a whole.

As the confederate states lost their bid for sovereignty, the federal government was significantly strengthened. However, the federal government was ill-equipped both politically and administratively to handle the problems of a rapidly industrializing nation. In addition, most people did not want to grant the federal government additional powers. On the rural front, the Populist party, emerging in the midwestern United States, stressed the virtues of rural life, individualism, and self-determination that party adherents felt to be at the core of the American dream. In the nation's growing urban areas, business leaders, industrialists, and local politicians merged their self-interests in demanding that the federal government remain true to the principles of *laissez faire* and stay clear of their "private" affairs. For awhile, it looked as if the federal government would lose the significant measure of authority it had managed to build during the war.

However, the forces opposing a strong federal government contained many of the seeds of their own destruction. By the turn of the century, it had already become clear that the United States was no longer a land of unlimited resources. If there were virtues to be associated with the fierce independence of American farmers and ranchers, so were there mounting costs to the nation. A few visionaries could already see that Americans were despoiling their natural resources far more rapidly than they could be replaced. Yet no regulatory mechanism existed, either in the federal government or anywhere else, to develop effective land use policies and conservation measures, let alone to enforce them.

On the second front, in the nation's urban and industrial zones, the public's faith in unbridled progress had also revealed an ignoble side. The press, in one of its early all-out attempts to influence public policy, revealed that America's leading cities were rife with corruption and greed. New waves of immigrants were finding that most of the opportunities open to their predecessors were closing fast, and many were forced to accept miserably low wages and uncertain futures for themselves and their children. At the same time, many of the earlier and now-well-established immigrants were beginning to question the country's liberal immigration policy in the face of a large influx of Italian, Jewish, and Asian newcomers. The foundations of a new wave of ethnic prejudice and racism were being laid in a not very subtle fashion. It had also become clear that *laissez faire* for American businesses and industries cut both ways. The railroads, for example, once credited with building the American West, were by the beginning of the twentieth century so hopelessly enmeshed in inefficient and outright cutthroat competitive practices that the nation's entire transportation system seemed threatened.

The Progressive Era

The desperation of the decades surrounding the beginning of the twentieth century lent support to important new ideas about public policy and American government. In the absence or relaxation of other controls, the federal government rapidly came to assume unprecedented authority over national affairs. "The Search for Order" is how the historian Robert H. Wiebe (1967) chose to typify this period of our history, and the rise of the Progressive party under Theodore Roosevelt is generally seen as a cornerstone to these important new beginnings.

If any word can summarize the Progressive movement and its many ramifications, the word is *efficiency*. Many of the ideas behind the movement were not new; the genius of the Progressives was their ability to apply these ideas to a burgeoning sense of national policy. To do this, Roosevelt relied heavily on the business and scientific communities, setting a pattern that continues, albeit with important modifications, to the present. Business leaders were brought into the national government to help model a new administration based on the principles of sound business practice. They brought with them a keen sense of planning and a strong appreciation for the merits of a statistical basis for public decision-making, a practice already proven particularly effective in the insurance business (Boorstin 1974). Scientists and business leaders alike stressed the need for research and *scientific management*. The entire effort seems to have been undertaken with an extreme air of confidence and a sense of having come up with the perfect system of governmental administration. To the chaos of rapid social and economic transformations, the Progressives offered a new discipline which they fully expected would return the nation to an already idealized vision of American life before the Civil War.

One of the first tests of the new "gospel of efficiency" (Hays 1975) came in the area of natural resource management. Concentrating primarily on the western United States, the Progressives sought to develop sound national policies in areas of land use, range and forest conservation, and water resources management. The policies were not nearly as widely accepted or vigorously enforced as Roosevelt and his cohorts would have liked. But even where they failed, as in the development of a national policy for multiple-purpose river basin development, they provided much of the basis for more successful subsequent efforts.

Urban reform also became a major interest of the Progressives. The city as a system of patronage and political bossism began to yield to interesting new ideas of city planning which stressed, among other things, broad-based citizen participation in civic affairs. Similarly, urban poverty was attacked seriously for the first time in American history. Puritanical ideals associating poverty with sinfulness began to give way to a more scientific approach to understanding the social and economic conditions which lead to poverty. As a consequence, the idea of aid to the poor as a form of charity began to be replaced by an entirely new, professional approach to social welfare (Lubove 1975).

The Progressive movement took hold wherever it could get a grip. Even the seemingly sacred ideology of *laissez faire* in American business and industry began to erode in the face of major reform efforts. In 1877, with the establishment of the Interstate Commerce Commission, the federal government touched down on the nation's powerful railroad magnates by creating the federal government's first regulatory agency. Other "watch-dog" agencies, such as the Federal Trade Commission and the Food and Drug Administration, soon followed.

These are but some of the Progressive movement's contributions. In the large view, the movement was both the beneficiary and stimulus to a new approach toward public policy. In its wake, the ideas of scientific management and long-range social planning became commonplace. The movement also profited from and helped create a new spirit of professionalism in American society—particularly in areas of social service, such as medicine, law, education, social work, and the planning professions. Many of the policy-makers of the future would come from the ranks of these fledgling professional associations.

The actual achievements of the Progressive Era, many of which fell far short of expectations, are perhaps not as important as the ideas about policy which were developed at that time. Although significant, the change in the way government was administered was less noteworthy than the change in the kinds of social problems and policy issues with which the federal government, and consequently state and local governments, were concerned. Policy-makers began to use a partially scientific approach to decision making, placing great emphasis on discovering the causes of social problems. However, the essential optimism of the Progressives was to receive severe blows in future decades. Scientific management did not turn out to be as simple a process as had been expected. There were many policy issues which the Progressives did not anticipate, and which would later emerge as serious social problems. And it would soon be discovered that the gospel of efficiency, while admirable on some counts, was not in itself a sufficient or practical basis on which to formulate public policy.

In retrospect, we can see that all the policy responses of the Progressive Era were not laudatory. During the last decades of the nineteenth century, for example, American minorities began to pose serious policy concerns in this country. The response of those in power was primarily one of containment and control rather than any serious attempt to promote the interests of minority groups. The brief period of reconstruction after the Civil War, in which the federal government had maintained strict political and economic control over the southern states, was mostly over by 1875, and the cultural gaps between slavery and emancipation were quickly filled with wide-ranging discriminatory policies which most Americans would not even begin to question for another half century.

Racism in America was not confined to the southern states. The nation as a whole had a strong ideological commitment to widely held beliefs in white Anglo-Saxon superiority, and in the social, mental, and hereditary inferiority of other "races" (Hofstadter 1955). At the turn of the century, the doctrine of Social Darwinism and an increasingly popular eugenics movement helped justify blatant policies of discrimination throughout the country. American Indians, recently "emancipated" from "savagery," were to experience systematic attempts to destroy their heritage and to render them the helpless dependents of a supposedly superior national mentality. This was also a period in which ethnically discriminatory immigration policies came in vogue, with deliberate attempts on the part of the federal government to curb the growing numbers of immigrants of Asian, Jewish, and Mediterranean heritage.

The notion of Social Darwinism was not limited to domestic policy. Closely linked with the concept of a "Manifest Destiny" for the United States, the ideology developed even more dramatically into a pronounced shift in American foreign policy. If the Progressives were mostly reformers at home, they were imperialists abroad. Emerging from a century-old policy of isolationism, the "Open Door" policy of the Progressives informed the world that Americans now proposed to play an active and proprietary role in world affairs. The Spanish-American War of 1898 left the United States with its first colonies (Puerto Rico, Guam, and the Philippines). The annexation of the Hawaiian Islands and territorial claims in Samoa occurred durng the same year.

Thus, the United States joined the other world powers in an era of expansionism that would soon leave most of the globe divided and claimed like slices of a huge pie. And, as did nearly all the other powers, America would approach the task with the conviction and missionary zeal of a people who were certain that their way of life was vastly superior to that of the peoples who fell under their new-found dominion (Bodley 1975). Many of the policies for administering native peoples which ensued were well intended, but all of them maintained a sense of the superiority of the Western way of life.

World War I and the New Deal

Although the Progressive Era continued into the 1920s, many of the domestic and foreign policy aims of the federal government were temporarily set aside during World War I. At the same time, in mobilizing for war, the federal government's hand was again strengthened. During the presidency of Woodrow Wilson, successful business leaders were once more called into government service. Industrialists and farmers alike accepted wartime controls they would have opposed bitterly in peacetime. The war enabled the federal government to build an administrative structure capable of responding to critical national issues, something which had been lacking during the Progressive Era. Further, the ever-present problems created by wartime shortages encouraged the government to develop means for maintaining an accurate inventory of national resources and for projecting future national needs, both essential ingredients to developing an effective policy process.

Many of the controls and much of the federal government's administrative structure were abandoned after the war. But they left a legacy of experience that would soon prove useful. The wartime build-up of the federal government was still fresh in the minds of Americans when, in 1932, Franklin Delano Roosevelt assumed the presidency on a promise to put an end to the Great Depression. It is doubtful whether Roosevelt's interventionist strategies would have met with the acceptance they did had not much of the foundation for a strong federal government with substantial executive powers already been laid over the previous half century.

Major policy issues of the depression included natural resource depletion, unemployment, and poverty. Each of these problems was met with social and economic programs which anticipated and began to fulfill the policy goals of the "welfare state" that have become so apparent in our time. The earlier conservation movement of the Progressives provided a model for much of Roosevelt's "New Deal" response to resource depletion. The Tennessee Valley Authority project, for example, brought many of the Progressives' plans for multiple-purpose river development to fruition. Conservation principles and employment policies went hand in hand with depression era programs like the Civilian Conservation Corps and the Works Progress Administration. The problems of poverty were approached with a variety of new welfare programs, including the nation's first comprehensive public housing program and the founding of the Social Security Administration.

Interestingly, there was a considerable rural bias to the New Deal. For the first time, the federal government exhibited concern for national population policy, and efforts were made to control the flow of rural migrants to the country's crowded cities. Once again, the values and lifestyle of the American countryside were idealized: only this time, rather than as a Populist cry from the back country, the virtues of the small rural community were being touted by the most powerful and influential (and in many respects thoroughly urbanized) federal administration in the nation's history.

Progressive Era ideals for social planning and scientific management were at the core of the New Deal administration (Graham 1976). The successful, efficient, and cost-effective private business operation was applauded by public administrators as a model worthy of emulation. The concerned scientist was viewed as a crucial participant in the decision-making process. Equally important were significant changes in the country's economic policy. Never before had a federal government spent so much money in supporting its domestic policies. The growth of the welfare state went hand in hand with the development of accurate fiscal monitoring procedures and standardized mechanisms for determining how limited resources could be allocated most efficiently. Federal spending had begun to be viewed as a potentially creative tool for encouraging social and economic reform.

The Planning Society

From an administrative point of view, World War II was the capstone to the New Deal's efforts to transform the federal government, and particularly the executive branch, into a powerful and effective force in public decision making. Once again, added government controls were accepted in the face of a threat to the nation's well-being. But something else happened between the outbreak of war and its aftermath. Perhaps it was that, in the interim, many Americans came to realize that the United States was itself transformed. In any case, the two presidential administrations folllowing the New Deal did not pursue the welfare state with anything like the same intensity as Roosevelt had. They did not really have to. The welfare state was there, and the problem was not so much how to build or even dismantle it, but simply how to mangage and keep up with it. And that was not all. When Dwight Eisenhower surprised much of the American public by denouncing the rise of the "military-industrial complex" toward the end of his administration, he was giving words to another modern phenomenon. In America's rise to world influence, it was not only the federal government which had grown powerful, ambitious, and deeply involved in a wide range of public policy concerns. The entire scale of the nation had changed.

During the late 1940s and well into the 1950s, human rights became a clear issue in American domestic policy as the New Deal became Harry Truman's "Fair Deal." In retrospect, it appears to have been a time for setting noble and well-intended goals, sometimes with only a modicum of understanding of how difficult it might be to reach those goals. It was also a time when the federal bureaucracy played a major role in broadening the dimensions of what the public could expect from their government. Federal aid to education and scientific research increased substantially during these years, setting a pattern that would not be questioned for decades to come. In the area of human rights, Truman repeatedly pressed Congress to establish a commission that would investigate racial discrimination in employment. With the federal Housing Act of 1954, the government proclaimed that every American had a *basic right* to decent housing.

Still, many of the executive branch's efforts to establish new human rights during the 1950s were overshadowed, first by extremes of public resistance on some fronts, and finally by the monumental Supreme Court decision of 1954 *(Brown v. Board of Education of Topeka)*. In one grand sweep, racial discrimination in American public schools became a major battleground for establishing minority rights. Equally important, the decision brought the courts squarely into the policy-making arena. In the decades to come, federal courts would continue to play a major role in establishing the limits of human rights and providing the bases for new policy decisions.

The years following World War II were especially significant in areas of United States' foreign policy. In the Pacific, Americans acquired major new colonial commitments. Elsewhere, economic and political ties between the United States and other nations were altered and strengthened. American foreign aid became a vehicle for encouraging redevelopment in war-torn Europe and, somewhat later, for promoting economic and social change in the lesser developed countries of the world.

There is no reason to doubt that most of the resulting overseas development programs sponsored by the United States government were sincere. Still, much of the altruism and seeming magnanimity of post-war foreign policy commitments were being called into question by the early 1950s. Accused of engaging in a "neo-colonialism" which in effect forced the lesser developed countries into a relationship of economic dependency and perpetual poverty, Americans were confronted with overwhelming evidence that their foreign policies were directed more toward a kind of economic imperialism than to promoting the interests of other peoples. In fact, much of the foreign "aid" of the United States, which served primarily to protect United States investments abroad and to ensure access to natural resources, actually seemed detrimental to the economic growth and political independence of the lesser developed countries.

In both domestic and foreign policy, it was during the "New Frontier" administration of John F. Kennedy that many Americans first began to realize the far-reaching consequences of a new "fourth branch" of the federal government—the bureaucratic maze of departments, agencies, commissions, and offices which had grown up in response to the government's expanding public responsibilities. Of particular interest and concern was the vast army of career service employees who, firmly placed in their jobs, sometimes seemed less receptive to the public will than many people felt was desirable. This "permanent government," as Schlesinger (1968) described it, had in itself become a potent force in policy making by the 1960s.

But it was not simply that the federal government had grown larger or, as some people felt, less receptive to the public weal. State and local governments were similarly affected. The practices of private business and industry had also become more complex, and the public began to take a close look at the influence of business on public affairs both at home and abroad. It was clear that the various policy levels operating in America were having difficulty communicating with each other, were often working at cross-purposes, and were sometimes actually engaged in outright sabotage of each others' missions. What is more, new and unanticipated policy levels were becoming manifest, a clear example being the rise to influence of multinational corporations. None of this, of course, was entirely new. But what seemed apparent by the time Kennedy took office was that the problem was getting out of hand. The need for greater coordination among government agencies and between the government and other policy levels, as well as the need for more careful planning of public programs, was clear.

A Tightening Federal Spending Policy

It was a businessman, Robert McNamara, who introduced the Kennedy and Johnson administrations to advanced systems analysis and operations research, and more specifically to the Planning-Programming-Budgeting-System (PPBS), which was to dominate federal planning efforts throughout the 1960s. PPBS was developed primarily as a budgeting control device (Wildavsky 1974), but its implications stretch much further and its life span extends far past the time that Richard Nixon decided to abandon it. By then, PPBS had spread to state and local governments (it was already well established in business and industry), and its principle of operation, known as cost-benefit analysis, had gained wide acceptance in government and planning agencies throughout the country.

Associated with PPBS was the call for more accurate social reporting, which had its strongest expression in a social indicators movement originating in the United States Department of Health, Education and Welfare. The goal of the social indicators movement was to emulate the kinds of statistical documents produced by the President's Council of Economic Advisors and the Bureau of Labor Statistics, ultimately to measure such phenomena as public well-being and satisfaction as accurately as economists measure the country's Gross National Product. Again, the movement soon found expression not only at the federal level of government, but also within state and local planning agencies.

In many respects, PPBS and the social indicators movement represented a final big push in the efforts to quantify public decision making that had begun during the Progressive Era. To the consternation of some social scientists and a few professional planners, both movements seemed to represent the triumph of traditional economic analysis at the expense of other possible approaches to public decision making.

What is most clear is that, during the 1960s, the policy process in this country became an extremely sophisticated activity. PPBS and social indicators research are complex procedures, requiring the participation of skilled practitioners. Business executives like Robert McNamara and social scientists like Daniel Patrick Moynihan rose to important advisory positions in the administrations of both Kennedy and Johnson. Accurate social accounting was now a recognized national need. Evaluation research, which was designed to assess the effectiveness of government programs, became, like PPBS and social indicators research, a byword of the federal bureaucracy. At the same time, government agencies, hard pressed to respond to the information needs they had helped foster, came to rely heavily on the cooperation of private research firms. During the next decades, right up to our time, these firms would come to play a major role not only in studying public policy, but in determining it.

The Congresses of the 1960s also contributed substantially to changes in the American policy process, particularly as their members began to encourage the idea of "comprehensive planning" on state and local levels. Comprehensive planning is based on the realization that local governments often do not have the resources or inclination to view the planning process much beyond their jurisdictional boundaries. The results of their short-sightedness include the waste of natural resources and duplications of public services. When Congress began to call for the creation of area-wide planning agencies, it was with the intention of encouraging greater coordination among local governments. Congressional concern was backed with fiscal muscle by requiring that local applications for federal grants in areas of housing, transportation, water and sewer projects, and dozens of other policy areas be approved by comprehensive, area-wide planning agencies before being submitted to the federal government.

Lyndon Johnson's push for the "Great Society" was, in many respects, the culmination of Kennedy's short-lived New Frontier. Not only were substantial changes made in social reporting and in the ways public service programs were planned, but there was also a quantitative advance in the building of the welfare state. Not since the New Deal had there been so many new public programs as were promulgated during the early years of

Johnson's declared "War on Poverty." Few previous presidents had ever shown the keen interest in urban problems that Johnson did. Many of his policies, such as those apparent in the Model Cities Program, have in retrospect been criticized as being too ambitious. But one thing seems certain— the optimism of the Kennedy-Johnson years, backed on the local level by numerous federally sponsored aid programs for minorities and the poor, contributed substantially to these groups' discovery of a new identity vis-a-vis the rest of the nation. The programs of the Great Society openly encouraged and to some extent institutionalized citizen and community involvement in public affairs. In a major attempt to reform welfare policies, they brought the inadequacies of past policies to the public's attention. It was a point from which it has become difficult to retreat. The promises of the 1960s, culminating not only in the Great Society programs but also in the Civil Rights Act of 1964 and the Voting Rights Act of 1965, became in many respects the demands of the 1970s.

The practice of foreign policy in the United States during the 1960s is complicated and confused by such issues as the Vietnam War and a growing public awareness of clandestine involvement of the United States in the domestic affairs of other nations. Revelations of political intrigue and conspiracy which continued into the Watergate crisis of the 1970s demonstrated to many Americans how little they actually knew about the working of their government.

The New Federalism

In domestic policy, an interesting reversal to much of the philosophy of the Great Society occurred when, in 1969, Richard Nixon proposed a "New Federalism." Offered both as a curb on the awesome new powers of the federal bureaucracy and as a means of returning much of this "power to the people," the key policy vehicles of the New Federalism emerged early in the 1970s. Through a *revenue sharing plan*, the federal government now provided large-scale funding for programs developed and administered at the local level. Unlike previous administrations, which had dispersed federal monies to local governments primarily in the forms of grants for programs initiated at the federal level, revenue sharing permitted local policy makers to exercise greater discretion in determining how the new funds were to be spent. A program of *general* revenue sharing, passed by Congress in 1972, gave local governments considerable leeway in deciding how to spend the money. A second program, initiated two years later in the form of *special* revenue-sharing block grants in the areas of human resource training, education, community development, and law enforcement, imposed limitations on some of the spending, but still gave local governments a considerable amount of discretion in determining specifically how funds would be used.

Nixon's revenue sharing plan was felt at all levels of government. Like many of the programs of the Great Society, the plan encouraged community and citizen involvement in local planning. Revenue-sharing grants required that the public be informed in advance of local plans for projects funded under the program, and that the public have an opportunity to help develop local policies.

The 1969 passage of the National Environmental Protection Act (NEPA) has become a milestone in recent policy legislation. Not only does it provide planners and environmentalists with a powerful legal tool for safeguarding the environment, but it also gives firm footing to the idea of formulating specific public policies on the basis of attempts to *forecast* the probable results of any particular course of action (an approach to policy which, interestingly, also rose to popularity in defense planning during the Vietnam War). Environmental impact assessment, mandated under NEPA regulations, has become the basis for a wide variety of forecasting research. The idea of impact assessment was both broadened and strengthened with the passage of the Clean Air Act of 1972 and the Water Quality Act of 1974. Legislation requiring impact assessment in particular areas of policy development, such as transportation planning, community development, and land use regulation quickly followed.

This new emphasis on forecasting research corresponded to a continuing interest in improved social accounting and evaluation procedures. The trend toward comprehensive planning and applied research received added emphasis in the area of public health with the 1974 passage of the National Health Planning Act.

By the mid-1970s, the policy idea was firmly established as a planning and research activity in the minds of many Americans. While some would (and will) continue to ignore its implications, there probably has never been another time in our history when the expression of public policy has been so thorough or, in many respects, so public. In recent years, it has become increasingly apparent that fiscal control plays a major role in public decision making in the United States. Aaron Wildavsky (1974) has described this process clearly in his description of federal budgeting during the early 1960s. At that time, under the impact of PPBS, policy priorities were ideally established according to strict budgetary and fiscal accounting procedures which presumably determined the relative costs and benefits of competing programs. With this system, the Federal Office of Management and Budget assumed a large measure of responsibility for determining the level at which most public programs would be funded and, hence, played a major role in federal policy making.

During the Nixon administration, much of the policy role of the Office of Management and Budget was usurped by the President when PPBS was replaced with a new procedure called Management by Objectives (MBO). Under this practice, the President and his newly established

Domestic Council assumed primary responsibility for determining policy priorities, although their decisions were still to be based largely on measures of cost effectiveness. MBO was in its turn replaced during the 1970s by President Jimmy Carter's Zero-Based Budgeting (ZBB) system, which returned considerable policy influence to the Office of Management and Budget. ZBB is a controversial procedure which has yet to prove its utility for federal decision making. Unlike PPBS and MBO, which were designed to help establish program priorities, ZBB appears to be most useful in assessing the cost effectiveness of already established programs.

While all three of these recent budgeting and decision-making procedures have received considerable attention at the federal level of public policy, it is important to realize that they are also widely used at other policy levels. Both PPBS and MOB actually originated in business and industry. ZBB was well established as a policy tool for many state and local governments long before it was adopted by the federal government.

Another highly significant characteristic of all these procedures is their reliance on cost effectiveness as a primary consideration in determining public policy priorities. The advantage of making policy on the basis of cost is that it sensitizes decision makers to resource limitations, and encourages them to think in terms of the relative costs of particular activities as compared to their anticipated benefits. On the other hand, reliance on measures of cost effectiveness is problematic because some policy goals are more easily measured than others. Economic costs and benefits are, for example, easily quantified and compared. Many social or human costs and benefits are not as easily measured, and there is a tendency for decision makers to discount these factors in their calculations of cost effectiveness.

It should be clear by now that Americans have, over the past century, experienced profound changes in the ways they make and respond to public policy. These changes have affected each of the stages of the policy process. Policy formulation and planning have steadily become more systematic and, with the phenomenal growth of the social and behavioral sciences, have consistently sought to become more scientific. The links between planning, program implementation, and review have grown stronger over the decades as more policy makers and citizens have come to realize that we can no longer afford to treat any single part of the policy process in isolation.

We can see that, as the policy idea grows in importance, or at least in public recognition, the levels of policy making expand. The past century stands out as one in which the congressional and executive branches of the federal government have successfully assumed major authority and responsibility for much of public policy. Other major institutions, such as the courts and the press, have expanded their roles considerably. Social scientists and private businessmen have contributed substantially in promoting policy research as well as in helping determine the shape of public policies. A new but precarious balance between national, private, and state and local governmental interests has been forged, along with considerable rethinking concerning the measure of basic rights for individuals, for special-interest groups, and for the determination of the "public good."

In recent years, there has been a tendency to attempt at least to limit some of the broadly based decision-making powers that have accrued to the federal government. To an extent, the federal government has cooperated in these efforts, and in some cases actually initiated them. The administration of Ronald Reagan has given rise to deliberate attempts to curb government spending and to limit federal responsibility for the country's social well-being. So far, the results of both goals are inconclusive. The cutback in federal social programs experienced during the early 1980s has given rise to a new need for research and policy that is directed toward determining the effects of reduced social benefits (particularly for the poor and minority programs) and of similarly changed priorities in government authority and responsibility.

How the balance in spending and social benefit will be struck even a decade from now is difficult to predict; but a few things seem certain. The American commitment to the policy idea is not about to fade away. The involvement of the social sciences in policy-related research and in the implementation and evaluation of public policies seems secure. In many respects, the development of the policy idea in the last century is closely tied to the increased complexity of modern American life. The great optimism of the Progressives has been tempered with a realization that the policy process involves much more than simple equations of operational efficiency. While the goals of efficiency and cost-effectiveness continue to be significant factors in policy development, they are joined in our time with even more dramatic issues of *equity*. Increased sensitivity toward the pluralistic character of United States society, the civil rights movement, and the growing influence of special-interest groups have all led to new challenges in determining the allocation of limited and often scarce national resources. At the same time, the measure of equity and public fairness has proven elusive. The ability to determine the costs and benefits of social reform has become even more crucial during the past decade as the nation moves from an imagery of abundance to one of scarcity.

WHO REALLY MAKES PUBLIC POLICY?

In our society, the processes of public policy are complicated by several factors:

1. Americans live in a complex social environment that has given rise to conflicting social values. There are few public policies which can realistically satisfy the interests of all Americans and, with the rise of numerous special-interest groups, it

is becoming increasingly difficult to determine even where the "greatest good" lies.

2. Policy making is seldom a neutral process. Public policy must be enacted through numerous policy domains and levels which represent varying degrees of social and economic power. The relationships among these domains and levels, as well as the relative amount of authority and responsibility assumed by each, varies regionally and through time. The development of public policies has often provided a stage for skirmishes between participants in the process.

3. The *status* of the policy idea also varies regionally and historically. During the past century there have been far-reaching changes in the legal and legislative structures of policy making in the United States. Different parts of the country vary considerably in their receptivity and adaptation to these changes.

4. Although scientific research has come to play a major role in the policy process, the relationship between knowledge and public decision making is not always clear. Also, many of the techniques of applied research which are most useful to policy development, such as evaluation and forecasting research, are not well understood by the general public or by many social scientists.

These observations should convince us that the policy process is not a static exercise, nor can it be approached from a single perspective, such as that of politics, program administration, or scientific research. The policy idea is manifest in nearly everything Americans do, and the processes of public policy touch our lives in ways few of us understand.

Naive ideas about public policy and public decision making persist in our society. Most Americans seem content to accept public policy as something that just happens, much like the weather. Unless they are immediately threatened by a particular decision, these people are unlikely to show much concern. Others, though perhaps interested and concerned, often despair of playing an active role in public decision making: it is either too complicated or they are convinced the game is "rigged" and there is no chance of their views being heard.

Public policies are made by people, and although some people certainly have more influence than others, much of that influence is accrued by default rather than by virtue of any kind of absolute power to rule public affairs. Public policy decisions are frequently carried through in a climate of public disinterest and inaction. The question of who makes public policy can sometimes be answered by reference to one or more of the policy domains or levels we have discussed, but much of the answer also lies in what most people do *not* do.

A century ago, before the development of any organized land-use policies in this country, Americans nonetheless supported an implicit policy governing land use. In a sense, it was a policy not to have a restrictive policy, but rather to permit open exploitation of our land resources. Until recently, Americans maintained similar "nonpolicy" policies in regard to such now-popular issues as energy exploitation, equal employment opportunity, and child abuse. The existence of so many hidden and emergent policy issues is perhaps an unavoidable consequence of rapid social change.

The opportunities for Americans to participate in public policy decision making have seldom been greater. They are complicated, however, by the increasingly complex legal, political, and scientific structures of policy making. The contributions applied anthropologists make to the social well-being of our society and other societies rest on their ability to understand, interpret, and participate in these structures. In this sense, the policy idea is both the beginning and the end of applied work.

PERSPECTIVE

This chapter is obviously slanted—first to the idea of public policy in the United States, and second to the federal sector of government. Much more could have been said about any of the problems touched on here, and equally detailed accounts might have been written focusing on other policy levels or on the policy process in other countries, but I could hardly do them justice in so abbreviated a treatment. My choice has been one of economy.

There are two important lessons to be derived from this chapter which I believe apply to nearly all policy contexts. First, we can recognize that most policy issues have a long history of public involvement. Policy problems are not so much solved as they are responded to, with adaptations and cycles of interest more or less corresponding to changed social circumstances. Part of the frustration that sometimes accompanies applied work results from a failure to understand that there are no ultimate solutions to most human problems.

A second lesson to be derived from this chapter has to do with the decision-making structures underlying policy activities. The shifting of policy domains from one level of responsibility to another, mandates for comprehensive and regional planning, increased demands for social accounting, evaluation and cost effectiveness—each of these contributes to changes in the way policy activities are carried out. An understanding of these and similar structures of decision making is a vital component of successful applied work.

In a sense, there is a "culture of policy." Effective participation in policy activities requires an understanding of implicit cues and standards for behavior as well as of more formal and explicit rules of public administration. The culture of policy in the United States is all the more mysterious and exotic because we so often assume that we ought to be able to understand it with little or no effort. It is often more difficult to find a clear path through the forest in which one was raised than it is to blaze a trail through someone else's jungle.

RECOMMENDED READINGS

There have been numerous studies of American character and public values. The anthropological contribution to this area of inquiry began early, with such notable publications as Margaret Mead's *And Keep Your Powder Dry* (Morrow, 1943), Geoffery Gorer's *The American People* (W.W.Norton & Co., Inc. 1948), W. Lloyd Warner's *American Life: Dream and Reality* (Chicago, 1953), and Jules Henry's *Culture Against Man* (Random House, 1963). Other views on American values are offered by William F. Whyte, Jr., in *The Organization Man* (Simon & Schuster, 1956), C. Wright Mills' *The Power Elite* (Oxford, 1959), and David Reisman's *Abundance for What?* (Doubleday, 1964). The historian David M. Potter has summarized many of the earlier studies of American character in his *People of Plenty: Economic Abundance and the American Character* (Chicago, 1954), and Michael McGiffert has edited a highly recommendable selection of readings entitled *The Character of Americans* (Dorsey, 1964).

The reader interested in further introduction to the study of public policy in the United States will find the large part of the literature being produced by political scientists and economists. Good overall perspectives are provided in *Strategic Perspectives on Social Policy* (Pergamon Press, 1976), edited by John E. Tropman, et al., *Policy Studies and the Social Sciences* (Lexington, 1975), edited by Stuart Nagel, and *Social Science and Public Policy in the United States* (Praeger, 1975), by Irving Horowitz and James Katz. Policy formulation is concentrated on by Charles Lindblum in *The Policy-Making Process* (Prentice-Hall, 1968) and Thomas Dye in *Understanding Public Policy* (Prentice-Hall, 1972), while policy implementation is the focus of Erwin Hargrove's *The Missing Link: The Study of the Implementation of Social Policy* (Urban Institute, 1975) and Jeffrey Pressman and Aaron Wildavsky's *Implementations* (Campus, 1974). A good introduction to governmental levels of public policy making can be found in Thomas Dye's *Politics in States and Communities* (Prentice-Hall, 1973).

There is also a great deal of literature on the history of the policy idea in the United States. The Progressive Era is well covered in Robert H. Wiebe's *The Search for Order: 1877—1920* (Hill & Wang, 1967), and in Samuel P. Hays' *Conservation and the Gospel of Efficiency: The Progressive Conservation Movement, 1890–1920* (Atheneum, 1975). A study of the growth of professionalism during and after the Progressive Era which should be of particular interest to applied anthropologists is Roy Lubove's *The Professional Altruists: The Emergence of Social Work as a Career, 1880–1930* (Atheneum, 1975).

The ideology of the American instinct for reform is discussed, from different vantage points, by Richard Hofstadter in *Social Darwinism in American Thought* (Braziller, 1955), Eric F. Goldman in *Rendezvous with Des-*

tiny: A History of Modern American Reform (Vintage, 1955), and Arthur M. Schlesinger in *The American as Reformer* (Atheneum, 1968).

An outstanding summary of the development of the policy idea in recent times is offered in *Toward a Planned Society: From Roosevelt to Nixon* (Oxford, 1976) by Otis L. Graham, Jr. Policy advances during the years of the New Deal are discussed in Daniel R. Fusfeld's *The Economic Impact of Franklin D. Roosevelt and the Origins of the New Deal* (Columbia, 1956) and Charles E. Jacob's *Leadership In the New Deal* (Prentice-Hall, 1964). The politics and policy issues of the Great Society are discussed in several studies, including Eli Ginzberg and Robert M. Solow's edited volume *The Great Society: Lessons for the Future* (Basic Books, 1974).

Important developments in social accounting and policy research techniques during this era are examined in Daniel Bell's article "Toward a Social Report" (*Public Interest*, 1969(15):72–84) and Otis Dudley Duncan's "Social Forecasting—the State of the Art" (*Public Interest*, 1969 (17): 88–118). PPBS procedures are detailed in Aaron Wildavsky's *The Politics of the Budgetary Process* (Little Brown, 1974) and Edwin L. Harper's article "Implementation and Use of PPB in Sixteen Federal Agencies" (*Public Administration Review*, 29 (6):623–632). Walter A. Rosenbaum's *The Politics of Environmental Concern* (Praeger, 1973) describes many of the important changes in environmental policy making made during the 1960s. Laurence Tribe's *American Constitutional Law* (Foundation, 1978) discusses the emergence of the United States Supreme Court as an effective level of public policy making.

Richard Rose introduces the MBO decision-making practices of the 1970s in *Managing Presidential Objectives* (Free Press, 1976), and revenue sharing is discussed in Paul R. Dommel's *The Politics of Revenue-Sharing* (Indiana, 1974) and *Financing the New Federalism: Revenue Sharing, Conditional Grants, and Taxation* (Johns Hopkins, 1975) by Robert P. Inman, et al.

There are many journals which publish current articles related to the policy idea and social issues. The *Policy Studies Journal*, *Policy Analysis*, and *Policy Sciences* are particularly instructive for grasping the policy idea. Articles published in *The Journal of Interdisciplinary History* provide invaluable background to many of the significant policy issues of our time. Journals such as *Social Problems* and other periodicals such as *Social Policy* and *Society* (formerly *Transaction*) offer a variety of perspectives on contemporary social concerns.

3

Specialization in Applied Anthropology I

I don't think I was meant to overhear their remarks. Two men were standing in the hallway after class.

"This is pure nonsense," one of the men said.

"I can't believe they hired this jerk," the other added.

They were talking about my lecture.

Several years ago I was invited to speak to a group of soil conservation officers employed by the United States government. I was to participate in an ambitious project in which the conservation officers would be pulled in from various parts of the country to hear a group of professors tell them how social science could be useful to them. My task was to give two of the lectures.

When I walked in for the first lecture, I was pleased with myself. I had spent two days studing United States soil conservation policy and knew something about current issues and problems facing the conservation officers. I had what I felt would be a coherent and useful lecture drawing on several examples of effective applied social research. But the lecture was a complete flop. Fortunately, I ran out of material and acquired a dry throat before my time was up. When this happens, a lecturer usually asks for feedback from the audience.

As the conservation officers began to respond to my invitation for feedback, it became obvious to me that I had made two serious errors. First of all, my feeble attempts to impress the audience with my understanding of soil conservation were, however well-intended, lacking in humility. My listeners were seasoned professionals, most had been in their jobs for 10 years or more, and they knew more than I could ever hope to know about soil conservation policy. Secondly, most of the officers had worked with social scientists before, and from some of their comments it was obvious that the relationship had not always been fruitful. They seemed to regard many of the social scientists they had worked with as impractical know-it-alls, and my lecture had done nothing but reinforce their feelings.

I left the classroom hurt and embarrassed. Obviously, I had not done my homework and everyone had suffered as a result. I had done nothing to encourage these people to be more receptive to social science. If anything, I had done more harm than good. The prospect of going back into that classroom the next day was about as welcome as contracting a dread disease. As a matter of fact, I seriously considered calling in sick. I spent half the night being contrite and the other half trying to put myself in the soil officers' place.

"I want to start where we left off yesterday," I announced the next morning. I invited the audience to continue discussing how they had worked with social scientists in the past. What kinds of problems had they encountered? How had their efforts ended up? Several stereotypical characteristics began to emerge: Social scientists don't listen. They're not practical. They don't appreciate the constraints under which agencies operate. Their research is sometimes one-sided. Other times they use a lot of money, words, and fancy methods to tell you nothing more than you already know. They treat you as though you don't know anything.

The last observation caused me to twinge.

Stereotypes are generally based on half-truths. Several examples of useful cooperation between the soil officers and social scientists also emerged during our discussion. After about an hour, it seemed time to change direction. I told the soil officers that I felt the best thing we might do for the rest of the lecture would be to try to figure out two problems. First, if you're a soil conservation officer, how do you determine when social research will help you make a decision? And second, having worked that out, how do you find a social scientist you can count on? The two problems, I suggested, are closely related.

The lecture turned out to be a modest success, and I had learned a valuable lesson in humility. By the time it was over, the soil conservation officers had at least begun to acknowledge that their suspicion of social scientists was based as much on their ignorance of the potential uses of social inquiry as it was on the efforts of particular social scientists. Perhaps the lesson to be derived from this experience has to do with how hard it is for people with different backgrounds, and hence with different views of a problem, to communicate. Bridging the mental gaps between ourselves and those we work with is perhaps one of most formidable tasks facing applied anthropologists. This task is made all the more difficult by the fact that anthropologists work with so many different kinds of people.

Applied anthropologists generally claim special skill and expertise in one or several areas of topical interest. Their specialization often corresponds to particular policy domains—anthropologists have, for example, exhibited a keen interest in problems of international development, medicine and health, agriculture, education, and urban affairs. For the most part, these specializations demonstrate a convergence of disciplinary and policy-relevant concerns. Anthropological work in education, for example, has evolved from an early basic research interest in the importance of childhood socialization to include more directly applied research in bilingual education, the evaluation of educational programs, and similar activities.

In this chapter and the next, we will consider the major areas of topical specialization for applied anthropologists, and we will see how each area combines the interests of basic and applied research, as well as providing opportunities for practice other than research.

In Chapter 5, we will consider the major strategies associated with applied research. It should be noted here that some applied anthropologists have tended to specialize in one of these techniques rather than in a topical area of interest. An anthropologist with special expertise in evaluation research might, for example, apply those skills to a wide variety of policy domains.

MEDICAL ANTHROPOLOGY

Because health is a major concern for all human societies, anthropologists have long taken an interest in the health-related activities of the people with whom they have worked. The popularity of medical anthropology as a subfield can be attributed in part to the fact that the topic appeals both to biological and cultural anthropologists. While the focus of this book is on social and cultural examples of application, the close parallels between the interests of biological and cultural anthropology must be emphasized as we consider medical anthropology. Some of the earliest applied research conducted by United States anthropologists exhibited a combined concern with the physical and cultural. Franz Boas' *Changes in Bodily Form of Descendants of Immigrants* (1910), published under the auspices of the United

States Immigration Service, sought to demonstrate the influence of environment on human growth and changes in body form. The study corresponds to Boas' early interest in race and culture, and to his open criticism of the eugenics movement in the United States.

Early ethnographers, with their catholic interests in describing the minute detail of non-Western societies, captured considerable information about indigenous health practices around the world. These investigators showed a special interest in what people ate, in folk beliefs related to the health properties of foods and food preparation, and in culturally diverse curing practices. For the most part, they were not concerned with the practical uses of such knowledge. Their contribution was to begin to catalog the varied ways in which the world's peoples attended to their physical and mental well-being.

Another reason for the popularity of medical anthropology as an area of specialization is the importance of health-related and medical problems to Western industrialized societies. In some nations, health care is considered a basic human right, and governments strive to ensure that all their citizens have equal access to modern medical technology and health services. Other societies, including the United States, have a strongly established tradition of private medical practice which, while officially opposed to "socialized" medicine, is augmented with government and private programs designed to ensure everyone some access to medical care.

In any case, the health-care profession in Western nations is strongly committed to medical research, and research-oriented applied anthropologists have found it relatively easy to establish their worth in this domain. This has become even more apparent as other health-care practitioners and researchers have come to appreciate the important role played by social and cultural factors in both preventive and curative medicine.

Nutrition and Culture

The relationship between biological and cultural factors in applied medical anthropology is well demonstrated by nutritional studies, which generally subsume both physical and cultural relationships to nutritional studies under the rubric of ecological research. Thus, as explained in Jerome, Kandel, and Pelto:

> The strength of the ecological approach is that it makes it possible to relate biological and cultural factors on the same level of analysis. Thus, an ecological explanation of early childhood malnutrition in a Third World agricultural population might include patterns of family size and composition, infant weaning practices, cultural elaboration of high carbohydrate "superfoods," methods of crop production, high levels of chronic parasitic infection, and low levels of education and income as explanatory factors of the same magnitude. Similarly, epidemic rates of midlife overnutrition in the developed countries might be visualized as embedded in a matrix which

includes high cholesterol diets and cocktail parties, high stress white collar jobs and sedentary lifestyles, and the advertising and distribution tactics of food-processing corporations.(1980:4)

United States anthropologists began studying food habits in their own country relatively early (compared to their virtually ignoring most other aspects of United States life until very recently). Nutritional studies in rural American began during the 1930s and reached a temporary zenith during World War II. Much of this work was done under the auspices of a National Research Council Committee on Food Habits. Like most major applied and policy-oriented research, the work was broadly interdisciplinary, although anthropologist Margaret Mead served as the committee's executive secretary and much of the research involved ethnographic and case study contributions.

These early nutrition studies were clearly focused on policy problems, some of which were immediately relevant to life in a country at war. The researchers sought to identify regionally based dietary deficiencies in the United States, to explore ways to effectively encourage changes in the public's eating habits in the event of wartime shortages, and to assess public attitudes toward food relief to European countries (Montgomery and Bennett 1979).

Many of the more contemporary nutritional studies in applied anthropology deal with the causes and effects of malnutrition, both in the United States and in other countries. T.J. Marchione (1977) has found the existence of malnutrition in relatively developed countries especially puzzling. His research into the malnutrition of children in Jamaica indicates that the country's recent policies favoring an agricultural development plan that is capital intensive and oriented to an export market contributes to malnutrition, particularly among the children of landless agricultural wage earners. In this case, it would seem that one development goal (to realize profit from the export of agricultural resources) is being sought at the expense of the country's human resources.

In some instances, applied anthropologists have responded to nutritional problems from an advocacy base. The Human Lactation Center, founded by anthropologist Dana Raphael, has published a newsletter devoted to an understanding of breastfeeding practices and the public controversies which often surround them. Much of the Center's early work, funded by the United States Agency for International Development, was founded on extensive cross-cultural ethnographic study of breastfeeding. The Center has been embroiled in serious debate regarding the practices of major food corporations which are accused of marketing infant food formulas around the world without regard for differing nutritional practices and of using deceptive marketing techniques which actually contribute to the poor nutrition of infants in many lesser-developed countries.

The methods of anthropological fieldwork have repeatedly proven useful in nutritional studies, whether employed by anthropologists or others. Even the specific nutritive values of foods vary according to the local conditions in which they are prepared for consumption, thus necessitating a first-hand familiarity with varying social norms on the part of a nutritional researcher. Ann McElroy and Patricia Townsend cite a simple but telling example:

> . . . foods may vary considerably in nutritional value depending on the conditions under which they were grown, marketed, stored, and cooked. Unexpected factors may turn out to be important. Among the !Kung, for example, iron from cooking pots obtained in trade with the Bantu raises !Kung hemoglobin levels much higher than would be predicted from the foods alone. (1979:251)

Observation research methods are particularly helpful in many nutritional studies where the self-reports of research subjects may be found to be misleading due to forgetfulness or deliberate deception.

The Impact of Western Society

Many health-related practices are strained and threatened when an indigenous people are brought into contact with Western society, or even as the benefits (and costs) of medical services are differentially distributed among members of industrial societies. Some of the earliest contributions to medical anthropology were those which attempted to explain why relatively isolated peoples often rejected or misapplied opportunities to utilize "modern" medical services.

Anthropologists have correctly suggested that plans to introduce Western health services to societies which are unfamiliar with the corresponding Western concepts of health and illness will often be delayed or will fail. Similarly, status and cultural differences between Western medical practitioners and their clients may lead to serious misunderstandings and ineffective health care. Anthropologists have also pointed out that non-Western medical practices do not always make a sharp distinction between "mind" and "body" as the loci of particular ills—a recognition which modern Western practitioners have also begun to acknowledge, at least in relation to certain "stress-related" diseases such as asthma.

In truth, of course, modernization brings much more to the isolated peoples of the world than the "cures" of scientific medicine. It also brings many new and exacerbated ills. The rapid urbanization of the world's rural population often results in crowded living conditions, poor sanitation, exposure to industrial pollution, and radical changes in nutrition. A classic example of the unexpected harms resulting from contact between Western and non-Western peoples was the introduction of smallpox to the indigenous peoples of the Americas, who had not developed any immunity to the disease. The result was a drastic decline in the Indian population.

But the relationships between culture contact, modernization, and health practices can be much more complex than this. One example is the alarming spread of schistosomiasis, a parasitic disease of the blood that is known to have existed in relative isolation in Egypt for thousands of years, but which has spread to 72 countries and infected about 200 million individuals during the past few decades. McElroy and Townsend (1979) help unravel the mystery:

> Schistosomiasis is transmitted by snails that are commonly found in the quiet waters of irrigation projects, hence the disease's early association with Egypt.
>
> During the last several decades, developing countries such as Egypt have introduced new large-scale irrigation projects. Egypt's Aswan Dam, for example, "increased by one-third the amount of land available for cultivation" (1979:390). Of course, it also increased the habitat of the schistosomiasis-bearing snails.
>
> The parasite is transmitted to humans during bathing and other activities performed near irrigation canals. After several years, its eggs are reintroduced into the stream through human excrement.
>
> Population density and poverty contribute to the cycle since contact with the parasite is most likely to occur where communities do not have plumbing and are dependent on open water.
>
> Islamic religious practices also contribute to the spread of the parasite. Muslim males, for example, are expected to cleanse themselves several times a day before prayers. Religious practice also dictates washing with flowing water after urination and defecation.
>
> Finally, the large-scale migration of persons carrying the parasites into previously uninfected areas accounts for much of the rapid spread of the disease, which McElroy and Townsend report was recently brought to California by Arab farm workers.

Understanding and responding to the complex relationships between modernization and disease is not solely the responsibility of the applied anthropologist. Effective responses can result only from an interdisciplinary perspective combining the efforts of such a diverse group of practitioners as, for example, biologists, economists, agricultural and industrial engineers, medical researchers, and social scientists.

The Delivery of Health-Care Services

Whether it is to a village in rural Africa or to a large metropolitan area of the United States, the delivery of health-care services has drawn the attention of a number of applied anthropologists. Many of the problems related to providing health care to culturally diverse peoples have already been alluded to. In the following examples we can see how the methods and cultural orientation of anthropology are brought to bear on specific cases of health-care delivery.

Arthur Kleinman, a psychiatrist who has also trained as an anthropologist, studied the "languages of medicine," which he described as:

> . . . the divergent. . . conflicting, lexical and semantic systems operating in the different health care sectors and subsectors. These medical languages constitute and express separate clinical realities, and conflicts between them. . . create substantial difficulties for clinical practice. (1980:144)

Kleinman points out that differences in lay and medicial perspectives often result in tacit misunderstandings which are never fully understood by either patient or practitioner. The result can be poor care on the part of the practitioner, or failure to comply with prescribed procedures on the part of the patient. Cultural differences in describing illnesses can also result in misunderstandings. Kleinman's study of medical practices in Taiwan yields several interesting examples. Western patients, he notes, usually refer to problems related to their brains in psychological terms, while Taiwanese patients tend to refer to such problems as resulting from "brain damage."

A number of anthropologists have devoted attention to the delivery of health-care services to ethnic minorities and low-income communities in the United States. Often their work is based on an ethnographic study of a single group. Margaret Clark (1959), for example, based her research into health and health care among Californian Mexican-Americans on a detailed study of a single community. She was then able to relate problems in the delivery of health services to a wide range of characteristics of the people with whom she worked. "It is important to remember," Clark noted, "that in the eyes of medical specialists the world revolves around health, but to the patient it is only one of many aspects of everyday life" (1959:223).

The everyday life of the Mexican-Americans of Clark's study included economic, cultural, and language constraints to receiving adequate health care. She pointed out that there were not only important differences between the Mexican-Americans and the Anglo-American health practitioners of her study, but that members of the community differed significantly among themselves—local belief systems, for example, ran the gamut from faith in the curative powers of folk medicines, to the influence of Catholic religious practice, to participation in Protestant sects (some of which opposed the practice of scientific medicine).

Other anthropological studies in the delivery of health services to United States ethnic groups have focused on specific delivery systems and their response to a variety of patient populations. The Miami Health Ecology Project (Weidman 1978) was based on a study of the health beliefs of five ethnic populations in this Florida city. The five groups were Bahamian, Haitian, Puerto Rican, Cuban, and southern black. This major study not only reported on the distinct health-related beliefs of these diverse populations, but also traced how members of existing groups utilized the health-care facilities and treatments available to them, including folk as well as orthodox scientific medical systems. Among the study's conclusions, the following recommendations were directed to health-care personnel:

> Gain knowledge of the health beliefs and practices of local ethnic groups.
> Respect the fact that these beliefs and therapies, although perhaps running counter to the scientific medical systems, have survived in these populations for generations and may indeed be measurably effective. To try to change a deeply rooted health belief either by ridicule or by treating it as unscientific may not only fail but may also alienate the patient.
> Use a treatment plan which shows understanding and respect for the patient's beliefs and which builds on these in a positive way. (Scott 1978:69)

The role of the applied anthropologist defined for the Miami Health Ecology Project not only included providing basic social science information about ethnic health practices, but also serving as health professionals and "culture brokers." Anthropologically trained workers in this setting were called upon to represent the interests of ethnic clients and to mediate those interests and the concerns of orthodox health-care practitioners (Weidman 1978:870–893).

Examples of mediation cited for the project ranged from dealing with the complex discrepancies between folk and scientific concepts of mental and physical illness to more simple, practical suggestions. For example, Scott (1978:69–70) notes that many Puerto Ricans and Haitians adhere to a belief system based on a classification of food, illness, and medicine into categories of "hot" and "cold." In this system, the opposite treatment (say, a "cold" food or medicine) is prescribed to deal with a "hot" illness. The principle of treatment is to restore a proper balance of "hot" and "cold" in the body. Unfortunately, scientific medicine does not alway correspond to these categories. Pregnancy, Scott notes, is believed to be a "hot" condition. Vitamins and iron supplements which might be prescribed to pregnant women are also classified as "hot." One solution to this dilemma might be to prescribe taking the vitamins with fruit juice, a "cold" food, in order to maintain the sought-after physical balance.

The participation of applied anthropologists in work related to health care delivery and other aspects of health services has been encouraged in the United States through federal legislation which calls for health planning on the *local level* (cf. Cohen 1979), where the anthropological approach proves especially useful in identifying the clientele of health services, in clarifying their culture-specific health needs, and in evaluating the effectiveness of health-care programs. In recent years, applied anthropologists have not only come to do research related to health care, but have begun to assume administrative and implementative roles within the systems. Weidman (1978) has noted that the Miami Health Ecology Project provided regular staff positions for anthropologically trained, advocacy-oriented "culture brokers." Boone (1981) has described her role in a large metropolitan hospital, which included research, teaching, and administrative responsibilities. Wolfe (1980a) has outlined the ways in which anthropologists trained at the M.A. level at the University of South Florida have assumed significant administrative roles within the local health-planning system.

Anthropologists have not only counseled that folk medical beliefs should be respected, but in many cases have indicated that they can be *effective* responses to illness. In recent years, international health organizations have begun to accept this premise and, rather than attempting to wipe out traditional healing practices, have often attempted to cooperate with folk practitioners. In many lesser-developed countries, for example, public health personnel are working closely with midwives in order to share medical beliefs as well as to develop more effective means of distributing family planning information and devices. Similarly, in some countries, the World Health Organization has been working closely with national governments and folk healers in efforts to extend health services beyond the capacity of the region's existing scientific medical resources.

Anthropology and Health Practice

The role of the applied anthropologist in the field of health services continues to expand. A good example of this is the relationship which has developed between anthropology and professional nursing.

In the hospital setting, no professional has more prolonged contact with the patient than the nurse does. The nurse's role as a sort of broker between other hospital staff, patients, and family shares much with the way anthropologists often describe the service components of their profession. Like anthropologists, nurses almost invariably come in contact with a culturally diverse patient population. Effective nursing clearly requires the development of cultural sensitivity. These complementary aspects of nursing and anthropology have not been overlooked by the nursing profession, where they were noted as early as 1936 (Van Willigen 1980:30). More recently, a distinct subspecialty of "nursing and anthropology" has emerged. What is interesting about the development of this special interest is that it does not limit the role of the "nurse anthropologist" to a single activity, but rather provides an umbrella for a variety of positions. Most notably, these are

1. The professionally certified nurse with training in anthropology who utilizes these additional skills and perspectives in practice.

2. The anthropologist who directs some or all of his or her attention to teaching anthropology and the medical-nursing applications of anthropology to students or professionals in nursing. Quite often the anthropologist undertaking this role is

also a qualified nurse. The training may take place in departments of anthropology or, as is increasingly apparent, "nurse anthropologists" may be hired to teach full-or part-time in nursing schools.

3.   The anthropologist researcher who devotes attention to studying such nursing-related problems as the patient role in a clinical setting, nurse-patient relationships, and health service provision to culturally distinct peoples.

These varied but complementary career interests are represented by the Council of Nursing and Anthropology, which provides a forum for individuals to profit from communication among themselves, as well as an organized link between the professions of anthropology and nursing. These organizational activities provide a valuable example of how fully effective applied work *in any area* should be based on a tripartition of practice, teaching, and research. These varied roles are not fulfilled by a single person, but by a number of individuals working in close communication with each other.

Parallels between medical service and anthropology have also been recognized for the physician and medical researcher, although they are not nearly so well established as they are in nursing. Some medical schools offer training in anthropology and employ anthropologists in their research departments, and a few universities offer joint degrees in medicine and anthropology.

Anthropologists have also shown an interest in mental health practice, although their efforts have not been nearly as well organized as those of nurse practitioners. In recent years, the terms "clinical anthropology" and "therapeutic anthropology" have emerged as an attempt to establish a subspecialty devoted to problems in mental health care. Peggy Golde (1981) links this relatively new interest to the "culture and personality" school which developed during the 1940s and 1950s. At that time, cooperation between anthropologists and mental health practitioners was not at all unusual, although most efforts were centered on research activities rather than on the direct provision of mental health care. Moreover, as noted earlier, research-oriented medical anthropologists have for some time been equally interested in the "physical" and "mental" aspects of illness and health care, due in part to their recognition that many peoples of the world do not make the same distinction between the mind and body that Western scientific medicine normally has.

More recent interests in clinical anthropology have, however, focused on the contributions anthropologists might make to actual therapeutic practice, including the counseling of mental health clients. Golde provides an example from her own work experience:

> Clinical practice is primarily conducted from a psychological and individual frame of reference, viewed simultaneously against a background of cultural or ethnic identity. The therapist or counselor works with an individual client,

one couple, or one family, but always sees individual personality dynamics woven into the tapestry of culture, of origin, or of early training. (1981:12)

The idea that some anthropologists—with their particular experience in cross-cultural settings and small-group dynamics, and their sensitivity to ideational and symbolic spheres of human activities—might become uniquely well-qualified therapists is an intriguing one. So far, most of the practical problems of such a possibility have not been worked out. Practice in some states would require training in psychology as well as anthropology, just as practicing nurse anthropologists must be medically certified to perform in their nursing roles.

Anthropology and Aging

With their special concern for the ways in which skills and customs are transmitted from generation to generation, anthropologists developed an early interest in aging populations. Complementing their recognition that elderly persons often serve vital functions in non-Western, traditional societies has been the realization that one of the impacts of modernization has been to deprive the elderly of much of their sense of worth to society, and thus to relegate them to a special category of social isolation and neglect. At the same time, with advances in modern medicine contributing to an unprecedented rise in life expectancy, the numbers of aged persons in proportion to total populations has increased dramatically (Foster and Anderson 1978:291).

Much of the work of anthropologists interested in aging has been descriptive, basic research aimed at challenging our assumptions about the old and their place in society, and about the aging process. Other anthropologists have devoted special attention to the relationship between ethnicity and aging. Some applied anthropologists have shown concern for the institutionalization of the aged. Maria Vesperi has, for example, suggested that the physical and mental deterioration of nursing home clients may be due as much to the expectations of nursing home staff as it is to actual physical causes:

> In many cases, the aging man or woman who voluntarily enters a home has recently attempted to come to grips with the discrepancy between his/her established sense of well-being and the effects of a debilitating injury or illness. The individual feels "just a little too tired" to get out of bed; others conclude that he or she is old, sick, and incapable of continuing full independent activity. Once the possibility of "old age" has been introduced, the individual may act upon its implications in an attempt to demonstrate a capacity for continued adult decision making. Thus, the resolution to enter a nursing home becomes the "sensible" thing to do . . . . Once inside the institution, however, these concepts take on a new meaning. The "sicknesses" associated with "age" are not regarded as curable or worthy of intensive treatment by nursing home personnel. (1980:74)

The problem of what to do with the aged is in many respects unique to modern industrial societies. United States public policy regarding the aged is often subject to a bewildering array of opinion and research, much of it contradictory. Whether it is wrong to isolate the elderly in "old-aged communities" is an example of one such problem. Some recent applied research has indicated that, at least for a portion of the aged population, living in such environments may be perceived as a desirable alternative (cf. Holmes 1980:281–282). Other studies have emphasized the negative aspects of isolating the elderly from the rest of society (cf. Jacobs 1974).

As aging and its physical and cultural consequences continue to have an impact on modern societies, we can anticipate that greater numbers of anthropologists will be attracted to this specialty. The Association of Anthropology and Gerontology, established in 1979, is a sign of this growing interest. We might also anticipate (and hope) that applied anthropologists will assume greater visibility as practitioners in providing direct services to aged populations, as well as in continuing to contribute to basic and applied research in the area.

Substance Abuse and Its Treatment

There are some areas of policy concern that decision makers, along with society in general, have a great deal of difficulty in learning about. This is especially true regarding activities which are identified as illegal or deviant, where participants cannot be expected to expose themselves to public scrutiny. In these cases, ethnographers have proven particularly valuable sources of information. They have also contributed to our understanding of clinical settings where the problems of deviant behaviors such as substance abuse are subjected to various "cures."

As with research in many other areas of application, one of the greatest contributions of ethnography has been to point to discrepancies in the ways in which treatment specialists and their clients or patients perceive each other and their participation in a clinical program. Michael Agar has described how his study of heroin addicts assigned to a treatment center led to a series of recommendations for further research into the interaction between patients and staff. Agar's work was based on taking the patient's view of the institutional setting, which he gained in part from voluntarily playing the patient role for a period of time. On this basis, he was able to suggest that the effective treatment of addicts was being hampered by breakdowns in communication. While a staff therapist might, for example, consider increased cooperation on the part of the addict a sign of therapeutic progress, the patient might view the process in a strikingly different light:

> Patients sometimes defined therapeutic interaction as a *hustle*, more specifically, a *confidence game*. The therapist is the *mark* or target of the hustle. The

therapy game, as many patients call it, proceeds as follows: The patient acts uncooperative or withdrawn or hostile initially; gradually he opens up; just before he wants something from the therapist, he produces some kind of "insight" into his problem. This gratifies the professional ego and disposes the therapist to grant requests. (1973b:39)

The effective treatment of the heroin addicts also seemed to be limited by the way in which patients typically perceived the staff, as Agar explains:

Patients described staff as mostly young, inexperienced medical personnel who had moved from one sheltered, middle- or upper-class environment to another. Consequently, patients felt that treatment staff could not adequately understand life in urban slum or ghetto areas, and that they (the patients) were superior in the sense of being able to survive by their wits in the streets where the staff could not. (1973b:39)

Anthropologists have also sought to explain the epidemiology and treatment of substance abuse in cross-cultural and ethnic terms. Aron, Alger and Gonzales (1974), for example, have indicated how drug abuse treatment for Chicanos can be hampered when such programs are modeled after programs designed to serve Anglo patients. And in the past decade, cross-cultural studies of research on alcohol use and abuse have proliferated.

Specialization in Medical Anthropology

Medical anthropologists have specialized in a number of other areas, including population and birth control, the treatment of terminal illness, ethnopharmacology, and the relationship between stress and disease. In most cases, specialization has coincided with significant public interest in particular areas of health care. Since health and illness are matters of considerable concern to all of us, and since national governments around the world have come to assume a high level of responsibility for the health of their populace, these specializations should enjoy continued support and popularity.

It is interesting to note that *equitable* health care is a high priority of most developed nations. For lesser-developed countries, on the other hand, *effective* health-care programs are often seen as a primary indicator of progress. In either case, the applied anthropologist now plays a significant role in helping expand our understanding of the causes of illness, as well as in identifying many of the problems inherent in delivering effective health care.

APPLIED ANTHROPOLOGY AND DEVELOPMENT

Many of the specialty areas discussed elsewhere in this chapter and the next include a strong interest in problems associated with development. We have seen, for example, that a major focus in applied medical anthropology has been on improving health care in lesser-developed regions of the world. In this section, we will consider development and modernization from a somewhat narrowed perspective. I take the term *development* to mean deliberate attempts to alter human interaction with the natural and built environment—through innovations in agriculture, new energy exploitation and conversion, the construction of modern transportation systems, improvements in housing, and so on. I use the term *modernization* in a somewhat larger sense, to refer to the ultimate stated objective of development projects, which is usually to improve the overall quality of human life in a region.

Anthropology and Agriculture

Anthropologists have come to an interest in agricultural development through their long experience in working closely with the horticultural and peasant communities of the Third World. This involvement coincides with a national interest in improving the agricultural productivity of "food poor" countries, although the objectives of agricultural assistance programs may vary from project to project. For example, some programs have as their goal the elimination of rural poverty through the introduction of farming technology and technique, new plant varieties, commercial fertilizers, and similar innovations. Other programs are developed around attempts to improve the nutritional status of a people. Still other programs might be directed to deal with problems related to capital improvement in lesser-developed countries—such as encouraging agricultural self-sufficiency and reducing the need for food imports, or helping a country develop foods for cash export.

In some cases, the two goals of aiding overall national development and aiding rural populations are at odds, as we saw in the preceding section with Marchione's study of subsistence farmers and agricultural wage earners in Jamaica. When such a problem occurs, the question is whether this potential for conflict is actually based on differing development needs (either national versus regional needs or different social class needs) or is only based on differing *perceptions* of those needs. In her evaluation of a large-scale agricultural program in the Chingleput district of India, Joan Mencher (1977) argues that an attempt to increase foodgrains production in the region was hampered by too-close attention to a model of development which had evolved from principles of Western agricultural economics. As part of a "Green Revolution" ideology of agricultural development in the Third World which became popular during the 1950s and 1960s, the pilot project in the Chingleput district stressed aid to relatively well-established farmers, often at the expense of poorer, more marginal farmers. While some of the project's goals for increased agricultural yield were met, the development goal of responding to the conditions of poverty among marginal farmers was not satisfied.

Importantly, Mencher found *no* evidence that improvements in agricultural production within the district were the result of the project planners having favored the wealthier, resource-rich farmers. Equal or higher yields might have been expected had the government focused attention on marginal farmers and cooperative marketing strategies. Mencher argues that the project planners did not anticipate such a possibility because their perception of the marginal farmer led them to assume that these people could not be expected to adapt to the agricultural innovations being introduced into the area. However, no clear evidence supported this view.

Development strategies are often based on short-sighted or erroneous ideas about the populations they will affect. Anthropologists frequently challenge such ideas. Is it true that traditional, small-operation farmers cannot be expected to embrace modern farming innovations? Or is this simply a self-fulfilling prophecy resulting from the past systematic exclusion of these farmers from such opportunities?

By the same token, anthropologists have sometimes challenged their own cherished notions of the development process. Most early research by anthropologists working in traditional rural communities tended to emphasize the conservative side of the peasantry, arguing that traditional farmers are likely to reject changes in subsistence practices on the basis of deep-seated value orientations (see, for example, Foster's 1967 and Van Zantwijk's 1967 critique of a rural development project in Mexico). More recent studies, such as Frank Cancian's *Change and Uncertainty in a Peasant Economy* (1972) and Billie R. Dewalt's *Modernization in a Mexican Ejido* (1979) have argued against this perspective. In some cases, lower-class and poorer farmers are found to be more receptive to innovative practices than middle-class farmers who are financially secure.

The contributions of applied anthropologists to problems bearing directly on agricultural practice and innovation have been limited (as have contributions by anthropologists in many other policy domains) by the tendency for anthropologists to be utilized solely as "trouble-shooters" by change agents and government researchers. In this mode of practice, described more fully in Chapter 1 in terms of the "consultant" role, the anthropologist is called upon to explain why a development scheme went wrong, or to anticipate the potential for conflict and misapplication in a newly planned agricultural development scheme. When anthropologists have had an opportunity to work closely with other agricultural specialists over a long period of time, their contributions have usually been impressive. One such example involves the International Potato Center in Peru (Rhoades and Rhoades 1980).

Two characteristics of the work of the Potato Center stand out. First, anthropologists engage in full-time research with the Center, working alongside a wide variety of other professionals. Second, the Center is devoted to mounting an intensive effort in research and technical assistance for a limited range of problems related to crop production—most notably, to the agriculture of the potato, an important subsistence and export crop in much of the world.

One study sponsored by the Center and conducted by the Mexican anthropologist Enrique Mayer (1979) illustrates these characteristics. Mayer sought to place his research within the social context and ecological niches in which potato farming occurred in Peru's Mantaro Valley. He identified three ecological zones of potato production, which corresponded to some extent to social class differences in the area. Farming practices varied within each zone. As many such studies have suggested (including Dewalt, discussed above), Mayer argued that a single approach to improving potato production would be inadvisable because it would ignore the social and ecological realities of the region. For example, large-scale commercial potato agriculture, practiced in the "low zone" of the valley, would not be appropriate to the ecological conditions of the "intermediate zone," where peasant farming strategies prevail. Mayer pointed out that the labor-intensive agriculture practiced by peasant farmers in the intermediate zone not only supported a larger population of farmers, but also produced yields equal to those of the commercial zone.

Much of the recent work of anthropologists interested in agricultural development has centered on problems of farm management. This work attempts to match formal models of economic development with a greater understanding of the ways in which farmers make crucial agricultural decisions (Bartlett 1980). In this light, John Bennett (1980) has introduced the concept of "management style" as a way of describing differences between "active" and "inactive" farm managers. Bennett's long-term, ethnographic study of family farmers in western Canada compared the different management styles of farmers with other characteristics of farm families and of the economy. The study demonstrates the importance of household variables in farmers' decision making. The management styles of farmers corresponded not only to changes in exterior variables (such as the condition of the agricultural economy) but also to changes in family composition (such as the size and developmental stage of a household).

While anthropologists have conducted much of their work among agrarian peoples, it is only recently that a clear potential for applied specialization has emerged in this area. Much of the earlier work, to the extent that it had applied implications, can be subsumed under the somewhat broader category of community development discussed later. Recently, however, a number of anthropologists have called for concerted efforts in these areas. Robert and Vera Rhoades (1980), for example, have argued that anthropologists should be encouraged to specialize as agricultural scientists and to seek employment with government agencies and firms involved in agricultural development. The recently established bulletin *Culture of Agriculture*, published by the Anthropological Study Group on Agrarian Systems, serves as a vehicle of communication for anthropologists interested in such matters.

Natural Resource Development

Large-scale efforts to develop a region or a country are often linked to attempts to improve an area's ability to capitalize on its natural resources—whether through the construction of dams, the exploitation of forests and rangelands, the mining of precious minerals, or the development of fuel. Almost invariably, these projects affect prior uses of the land where the resources are found and have a significant impact on people who live in the area. In many cases, as in the construction of dams, human populations will have to be resettled before resources can be effectively exploited. In other cases, as in the development of fossil fuel resources, an area that was previously only sparsely settled may experience a radical influx of population. In still other instances, such as in the conversion of forests to agricultural uses, one population group might be replaced by another. Sometimes, the mere presence of a resource innovation, such as the construction of a nuclear power plant, might have a significant impact on nearby human settlements even though no great changes in population distribution are anticipated.

In each of these cases, anthropologists often provide a variety of services, such as assessing future human impacts, anticipating resistance to resource development, or helping create resettlement projects. Involvements of this kind have increased in the last decade or so as a result of a number of closely related factors. First of all, both private and public decision makers have become increasingly sensitive to the human costs often associated with resource development. In many countries, government regulations and laws require that an assessment of project impacts on human populations be included in the process of deciding whether to proceed with a particular development scheme. The current vogue in policy and planning often favors multipurpose development, and requires that consideration be given to how a particular effort can best serve a variety of economic and social, national and regional needs. The scarcity and high international market value of energy resources has resulted in increased exploitation of existing fuels and the sometimes problematic introduction of energy alternatives. In many countries, including the United States, indigenous peoples are establishing their claim to natural

resources and to the regulation of land use within areas under their jurisdiction, thus providing added incentive for cultural sensitivity on the part
of major resource developers.

As a result of long-term research in Zambia's Gwembe Valley, Thayer
Scudder and Elizabeth Colson (1979) have had several opportunities to
note the often essential relationship between basic and applied research.
With a background of early ethnographic research among the people of
the Zambia Valley, Scudder and Colson returned to the area in the
mid-1950s to study the people's response to a forced relocation caused by
the construction of a dam in the valley. This early experience led to the
opportunity for Scudder to participate in policy-related studies in other
regions of Africa where similar events were occurring. From these several
applied projects, Scudder was able to generalize a "relocation theory." He
argued that "rural communities undergoing compulsory resettlement
respond in the same general fashion irrespective of their sociocultural
background and of the policy of resettlement authorities" (Scudder and
Colson 1979:246). The response Scudder observed was one of "extreme
stress." Scudder and Colson argue:

> In coping with this stress, relocated communities behave as if they see
> sociocultural systems as closed systems, a response which greatly facilitates
> prediction by the anthropologist. They cling to familiar people and familiar
> institutions, changing during the initial years following removal no more than
> necessary to come to terms with the new habitat including its prior habitants.
> Presumably because the level of stress is close to a critical threshold, radical
> changes from within (revitalization movements, for example) and from with-
> out (including attempts by planners to change social organization) are
> rejected. (1979:247)

Scudder and Colson suggest that resettlement schemes, no matter
how culturally sensitive or imaginative, will probably not have much impact
on the way people respond to forced removal from their homeland. This
may seem like an extremely negative conclusion with little value to the
decision maker faced with implementing a resettlement program; but we
need to consider that a major objective of public decision making is to
arrive at accurate assessments of the relative benefits and costs of particular
plans of action. Scudder and Colson's conclusions respond to this level of
policy articulation. Decision makers must consider such evidence in their
planning, and the human cost of any projects involving such resettlement
should be calculated at a higher ratio to its assessed benefits. By the same
token, we can see how the promise of a rational and humane resettlement
plan could erroneously be added to a calculation of benefit and used to
underestimate the actual human costs of forced relocation. In either case,
the knowledge base on which such assessments are made has the potential
for tipping the scale as to whether dams are built, highways are con-

structed, or other resource innovations are attempted.

Relocation is not the only way a community might be affected by natural resource development. And research is not the only contribution applied anthropologists might make to the identification and possible solution of problems related to development. As director of the Wyoming Human Services Project, anthropologist Julie Uhlman headed a multipurpose "action" approach to the problems faced by local communities experiencing heavy in-migration as a result of the development of fossil fuel resources.

The project combined training, research, and direct community service goals. A multidisciplinary faculty and professional team from the University of Wyoming sought "to train students to view services delivery from an integrated perspective before they become locked into a single disciplinary perspective" (U.S. Department of Health, Education and Welfare 1977:6). Student and faculty teams not only provided aid for direct service to public agencies, but assisted two impacted communities in assessing their new service needs and planning appropriate responses to problems resulting from radical population shifts. A final goal of the project was to produce research results which could be generalized to similarly impacted communities.

Community service teams were sent to two Wyoming "boomtowns," both of which were experiencing the impact of extensive coal-mining operations. Uhlman (1977) and her coworkers found that the human service needs of these communities not only increased as a result of rapid population growth, but that the *types* of services required changed as newcomers brought different lifestyles and long-time residents were faced with adapting to new stresses. While Uhlman presumably had hoped that her experience might provide the basis for offering procedural guidelines for dealing with the impacts of population increase in other regions, her analysis of the project emphasizes the differences between the two communities and underscores the need for flexibility. She argues that the *method* of implementation developed by the Wyoming Human Services Project teams should have wide applicability, but that it requires a keen appreciation for the unique characteristics and needs of individual communities.

We can take advantage of these examples to observe how applied anthropologists can respond to different stages and levels of public policy, and to understand how important it is to recognize the level at which a particular effort ought to be scaled. Scudder and Colson's work reaches its potential on the basis of their willingness to try to generalize—a necessary step in the formulation of policy. Uhlman's efforts are more clearly directed to program-level planning and implementaion, where the experience of how specific projects relate to particular settings is a vital component of success. Both approaches are equally tenable contributions to applied work.

Community and Regional Development

Most of the projects discussed in the preceding two sections are problem-specific. They can be stated in terms of a single goal or a few closely related goals—such as improving potato production in a region or advising the planners of resettlement schemes. Anthropologists may respond to such problems in a holistic manner, but the goals of the projects are strictly limited. Other projects are holistic from their inception. These approaches typically articulate problems of development in terms of how they relate to a community or region as a whole, and as they reflect the influence of larger political, social, and economic spheres of influence which impinge on a community's development.

The Vicos project, discussed briefly in Chapter 1, provides an example of a large-scale and long-term community development project in which applied anthropologists played a major role. Vicos was a cooperative project between the government of Peru and Cornell University. When Cornell, under the project directorship of anthropologist Allan Holmberg, assumed the lease for the Vicos hacienda, it was with the intention of combining research with social and technological change and political action goals designed to encourage the people living on the hacienda to seek autonomy and become a "free community" (Mangin 1979). Cornell University was formally involved in the project for more than a decade (1951–1964).

One of the major objectives of the Vicos project was to establish community decision-making skills among the Indian population (Holmberg 1965). This could not be done, however, without addressing several related problems. The anthropologists had to establish their own roles carefully if they were to avoid being treated by the Indians in the same manner of dependence and hostility as their previous "patrons," who had leased the hacienda primarily for their own economic advantage. Before decision-making skills could be effectively applied, the Indians at Vicos had to achieve some degree of economic self-sufficiency. Thus, much of the early work of the project was devoted to introducing new agricultural techniques, searching for innovations in marketing strategies, and providing the incentive and training to encourage the Indians to diversify into other occupational trades and professions. Throughout the project, the experiment at Vicos met with varied responses from surrounding communities, the local non-Indian population, and the Peruvian national government. The Indians had to be supported in their brushes with the outside world and encouraged to develop effective strategies for building a power base of their own.

Few projects in applied anthropology have been so carefully scrutinized over as long a period of time as the Vicos project, partly because of the large numbers of anthropologists and anthropology students involved.

From an action perspective, Vicos is often described as a qualified success. It did not prove to be a miracle cure to the problems of underdevelopment. The Indians of Vicos improved their lot in life considerably, although there is debate over the extent to which this was due to the careful guidance of project staff or to the initiative of the Indians themselves (Mangin 1979:82).

Although Vicos became a "free community," it has remained dependent on the vicissitudes of Peruvian national policy. Mangin indicates, for example, that the government's new land reform law has threatened the basis on which land tenure in the community was founded. He also reports that the Indians' attitudes toward change and the outside world continue to be based on feelings of suspicion and distrust.

These qualifications do not mitigate the importance of Vicos, either as a focus for research into community development or as an action project. As in most social interventions, it is next to impossible to determine how the people of Vicos would have fared had there been no project. (Comparable studies conducted in similar communities which did not benefit from the outside effort expended at Vicos would have helped in this regard, but they were not attempted.) On the other hand, the project serves as an important demonstration of how the intentions of particular community development projects are woven into the fabric of the larger world, and are subsequently accountable to complex structures of heritage and authority.

Similar observations can be drawn from a later development project in Peru which closely followed the Vicos model. Directed by Peruvian anthropologist Oscar Nunez del Prado (1973), the project at Kuyo Chico demonstrated that large-scale, holistic development programs can be effective responses to the problems of regional underdevelopment. What is more, events in Kuyo Chico influenced other Indian communities in the area, particularly in their dealings with non-Indians and in the successful development of public works projects. Like Vicos, the project at Kuyo Chico was also influenced by Peruvian national policy and, according to Nunez del Prado, threatened the established order of land tenure in the region to a degree that was sufficient to encourage the government to withdraw its support.

Although the work undertaken at Vicos and Kuyo Chico serves to highlight the contributions anthropologists might make to community development while serving as principal change agents and as administrators of development projects, it must also be recognized that they are anomalies in the literature of community and regional development. In a review of Nunez del Prado's *Kuyo Chico*, Robert A. Manners (1974) complains that the study tends to overstate the contribution of anthropology and to distort the contributions that might be expected from other sectors of society. Acknowledging that Kuyo Chico was a success, Manners commits the near heresy (from the perspective of some zealous applied anthropologists) of asking, "Would the results have been any different if funding and official sanction were held constant but a couple of Peruvian social workers or a pair of civil libertarian lawyers, or two more carpenters, or an economist and an agronomist, had been substituted for the . . . anthropologists?" (Manners 1974:700).

It is important to recognize that most community development projects are *not* managed by anthropologists, and that no clear evidence exists that they should be. If anything, applied anthropologists who do assume such positions will probably be most successful when they can add to their training in anthropology the ability to envision a development problem in terms that transcend the limits of any particular discipline.

Development Anthropology and Change Agents

The literature of anthropology and development deals extensively with the role of the applied anthropologist. According to classic texts in applied anthropology, this role is primarily that of a researcher advising overseas change agents of the importance of a culturally sensitive approach to development. Such arguments are often based on examples of how a lack of cultural understanding can lead to ineffective or disastrous results, or of how an increased awareness of cultural process might have salvaged a project in trouble. In this mode, Ward Goodenough (1963) discussed the "pitfalls of cultural ignorance." Conrad Arensberg and Arthur Niehoff (1964) prepared a manual for development change agents working overseas, the purpose of which was not only to improve the agents' sensitivity to the unique cultural puzzles they might encounter in foreign countries, but also to increase their awareness of the limits of understanding imposed by their own culture. A major chapter in Arensberg and Niehoff's book was devoted to "American Cultural Values."

In most of these contributions, the line is clearly drawn between the anthropologist as a researcher or advisor and the change agent as an action specialist or decision maker. Homer Barnett (1956) went so far as to suggest that the two roles were incompatible, and that anthropologists would be best advised to maintain some distance from the processes of actual decision making.

This type of material represents some of the most systematic attempts by anthropologists to describe the development process. Still, without fully disparaging the contributions, in retrospect the genre often seems to rely too heavily on carefully selected "just-so" stories. We are introduced to the well-intentioned but misinformed and ethnocentric change agent, usually in the form of a government representative. Then we meet the recalcitrant, suspicious native. After this, we are told how the anthropologist comes in to save the day, setting the change agent straight and placating the native. The formula seems simple enough, but how close is it to reality?

One rather outspoken detractor has been Glyn Cochrane (1971), a former development administrator turned anthropologist. Cochrane criticizes the "part-time" applied anthropology summarized by Foster (1969) and others. If development change agents have sometimes been culturally inept (a conclusion Cochrane does not fully accept), applied anthropologists stand equally guilty of having been ignorant of the administrative aspects and bureaucratic niceties of development work. Cochrane calls for a new generation of development anthropologists with a keener knowledge of "organizational delivery systems." He describes these as:

> . . . general practitioners. . . who have obtained broad or specialized competence in anthropology but who do not wish to pursue a university career. It is necessary for these people to develop skills to function as members of what I term a development team in the field. Some may do staff work. Theirs is the task of supplying an anthropological dimension in the day to day activities of international agencies and governments. (1971:109-110)

Much of what Cochrane envisioned has begun to take place, not only in development anthropology but in many of the special-interest areas described here. Still, to be fair to those he criticizes, we must realize that their contribution emerged at a rare time in the histories of both the United States and anthropology. Many of these early assessments were based on experiences occurring immediately after World War II. Not only was the anthropology of that time largely either ambivalent or antagonistic toward application, but the United States had very little prior experience in overseas development. In many respects, both popular opinion and foreign policy in the United States were still clothed in the elusive veil of "manifest destiny." As patronizing and high-minded as United States anthropologists have sometimes appeared in writing about overseas development work, much of their approach seems justified as an appropriate response to the collective inexperience of the United States populace. Cochrane, on the other hand, was writing from the perspective of his overseas development work for Britain, a country with a much longer history of colonial involvement.

The Victims of Development

An advocacy perspective shows through in most anthropological discussions of international development work. This is not surprising when we consider that those people most likely to have been the favored subjects of traditional ethnographic field research are also the most likely to suffer from ill-planned or indiscriminant development. I have argued elsewhere that a tendency to advocate for the "underdog" has sometimes been a factor in limiting anthropologists' ability to understand the "privileged" (Chambers 1977), but nonetheless we must recognize that anthropologists have served important roles as witnesses for peoples who have been disadvantaged and endangered by the uneven processes of modernization.

In development work, rarely does everyone share equally in the benefits accrued from a planned technological change or social innovation. In the case of large-scale development projects, the risks for some peoples may far outweigh any presumed benefits. One objective of humane planning is to ensure that decision makers fully recognize these potential costs in human suffering. Too often they do not. In other instances, the costs might be recognized but not heeded.

One of the most pervasive problems in assessing the benefits and costs of development is arriving at a consensus of what these terms mean in any given instance. The calculation of benefits and costs is a value-laden enterprise. How does one measure the *quality* of human life? More specifically, how can we account for socially and culturally different ideals in our assessment of any particular development scheme? At what point is a particular human cost tolerable, and at which extreme is it simply too much to bear? Who will make these decisions, and what information will they have at their disposal?

In discussing the impact of Western expansionism on the tribal peoples of the world, John Bodley (1975) argues that development has always been associated with massive exploitation of a region's human and natural resources, accompanied by an attitude of ethnocentrism which permits developers and change agents to argue that their efforts are "for the native's own good." Bodley identifies several stages in the exploitation of tribal peoples. First, settlers and missionaries arrive as a part of a "frontier process." Conflicts between settlers and tribal peoples often lead to armed conflict. Western governments then step in to establish order. In the classic sense of this tale, the recognition of disorder is based upon a judgment that the "natives are restless." The relatively stable and orderly social systems often enjoyed by tribal peoples before they became a part of someone else's frontier are rarely recognized.

Government control of tribal areas leads to a colonial mentality. Western governments assume responsibility for the welfare of native peoples. Even as colonialism declines, accompanied by the rise of Third World nationalism, the effects of expansionism are often not lessened. National governments assume responsibility for their tribal peoples, along with control over the resources of whatever territories these people have managed to retain. Struggling to modernize, these new nations continue the pattern of exploitation over the tribal peoples within their boundaries. Western nations often assist with new development schemes. Seldom do the tribal peoples manage to return to the autonomy they once enjoyed.

The same observation can be applied to other groups of people who are transported from one lifestyle to another on the vagaries of someone else's ideal of progress—notably to refugees and immigrants. Efforts to assist these people, however well intentioned, often result in what Gilbert Kushner (1973) has called the "administered community." Kushner demonstrates how the administrative plans and personnel offered as temporary measures to help uprooted people adjust to a new settlement or way of life tend to remain in place long after they have fulfilled their purpose. The result can be a prolonged, if not permanent, denial of the community's right to self-determination.

The ideology of this pattern of expansionism has included the belief that the spread of Western influence represented both a technological and moral victory. Many anthropologists have been quick to point out that it was *not* a moral victory, and in the light of an increasing awareness of the social awkwardness and resource inefficiency of much of our "superior" industrialization, some have questioned whether, in the long run, it will be judged to be a technological victory. In either case, the anthropologists' close association with traditional peoples has helped encourage and maintain an advocacy perspective. Established groups such as the Anthropology Resource Center and Cultural Survival, Inc., maintain through their membership and publications a much-needed sense of vigilance. Both groups, for example, have supported research and advocacy projects addressed to the needs of Indians in the rapidly developing, resource-rich regions of South America.

Similar patterns of exploitation exist in the United States. Jorgensen et al. (1978) have described the difficulties American Indians have encountered as the natural resources on their lands have become increasingly attractive to an energy-starved nation. Jorgensen argues that applied researchers, often employed to assess the impacts of large development projects, have a special obligation to "use their special information and skills for humanity." In regard to energy development in the western United States, he writes:

> Today, neither reservation Indians nor local Whites in the West have been adequately informed about the potential effects of energy developments on their lands and lives. There is a considerable need for social scientists to analyze the potential personal, social, economic, and political effects of energy developments and to make this information freely available. (1978:14)

While the principle of advocacy can be an important part of development work, we must keep in mind that its application *always* draws on value commitments. In some instances, a strong advocacy position vis a vis a particular people may dull the advocate's appreciation of the full implications of his or her intentions. (Just as a social science researcher's blind allegiance to a particular method of research might hinder his or her ability to arrive at alternative discoveries through the use of other methodological approaches.)

In a public lecture, French anthropologist Andre-Marcel d'Ans

(1979) argued that this might be true of the strong advocacy position some anthropologists have taken in supporting a proposal that a national park in Brazil be set aside for the use of the Yanomamo Indians. While sympathetic to the difficulties the Yanomamo face as their traditional territory is lost to the vagaries of "civilization," d'Ans questioned why they had been selected for special treatment. Was it simply because, through the popular films and writings of anthropologists, most United States citizens were more keenly aware of the plight of the Yanomamo? Would setting aside such a large area (approximately one million acres) be an appropriate response to the overall social and economic conditions of Brazil? D'Ans pointed out that there were many other Indian peoples undergoing similar stress in Brazil, and there was not enough land in the entire country to provide them all with equal allotments. Neither did the park proposal address the needs of millions of non-Indian Brazilians living in poverty; in fact, the park proposal might be seen as detrimental to their welfare.

The point is that advocacy assumes the common obligation of all anthropologists to consider any interpretation of an event from multiple points of view and to constantly challenge their own perspective, maintaining a keen appreciation of the consequences of their own cultural and professional blindspots.

Modest Proposals

Development work has closely followed cycles of public opinion and intellectual fashion. The policy interests of any given time help determine what types of projects will be attempted, how much and what kind of resource will be committed to them, and where they will take place. Many current trends in development work appear to favor the participation of applied anthropologists. Even a decade ago, development work sponsored by the United States Agency for International Development was based largely on effecting economic change and measuring the results of development almost entirely on the basis of economic criteria. Policy priorities at this time favored large-scale development projects which would stimulate national economies and presumably have a "trickle down" effect of reducing poverty and disadvantage among the least privileged of a country's people.

Significant changes in the way the Agency for International Development conducted its overseas development programs began to occur during the 1970s. The "New Directions" of the Agency (Jansen 1980) turned away from the assumptions implied by the "trickle down" approach and began to focus on smaller-scale developmental projects directed where the need was the greatest.

The Agency's new guidelines included more careful attention to the impacts of development projects and required that the people who were to be most affected by the projects be consulted as to their perceived needs and preferences. Increased awareness of social and cultural obstacles to development led to a requirement that applied research (called "social soundness analysis" by the Agency) be included as a part of the process by which Agency decision makers determined whether to support particular projects. By the early 1980s, United States foreign aid policy had begun to shift back to a policy emphasis on larger-scale economic development projects. The Congressionally mandated requirement for social soundness analysis has, however, remained in place—ensuring, although perhaps on a smaller scale, the continued participation of anthropologists and other social scientists.

Despite shifts in federal policy, the notion of small-scale development directed to areas of acute need has considerable popular appeal. This approach is consistent with the idea of "appropriate" and "relevant" technology inspired in part by British economist E.F. Schumacher (1973). Schumacher's emphasis on "economics as if people mattered" relates to a sense of resource scarcity, an alarming evidence of worldwide ecocide, and the disappointing results of prior attempts to solve the world's problems through the application of large-scale technological solutions. For the time being, at least, many of us have begun to see the space we occupy in the universe as finite and in desperate need of conservation. Ethnic "power" movements and religious ferment throughout the world have taught us that modern civilization, with all its startling advances in communication and transportation, is not necessarily a "melting pot" and may be more like a stew of discontent. A growing recognition of the costs of rapid technological growth has become a part of our awareness. We can expect many of our responses to development problems to steer a course of modest proposals. It seems to be a course of respect, awareness, and tolerance which is not at all inconsistent with the anthropological perspective.

At the same time, we need to recognize that modesty and "appropriate technologies" can become a shield for a lack of commitment to the problems of uneven world development. The anthropologist Charles Erasmus noted this more than two decades ago:

> I am opposed to the notion that [large-scale] contruction projects are quixotic and extravagant compared to the inexpensive, self-help projects through which people are supposedly taught to lift themselves by their own bootstraps. Nor can I take seriously the implication of *The Ugly American* that the hope of the underdeveloped areas are retired, diamond-in-the-rough, United States millionaires who invent irrigation pumps operated by bicycles . . . We cannot preserve free society through some modern loaves-and-fish miracle by sending professional do-gooders abroad to prod people into cheap, bootstrap development while we sit at home hypnotized by our television sets and by the flashing chrome on the neighbors' new cars. We must all contribute to the necessary costs of development. (1961:320)

PERSPECTIVE

While areas of special interest in applied anthropology presume an in-depth knowledge of another field of inquiry (such as medicine or international development), other distinctions exist between the interests of applied anthropologists. These distinctions form special interests or skills in their own right. We have noted some of these in this chapter. Applied anthropologists might, for example, be specialized in a particular style of research, such as social impact assessment or evaluation research. Several major approaches to applied research will be discussed in Chapter 5 of this book. We have also seen that applied anthropologists tend to be specialized in the types of activities in which they are engaged. They may be researchers, or they may be teachers in highly specialized settings (as when applied anthropologists teach in medical schools), or they may be actively involved in the delivery of one or another kind of service.

As we review the ways in which anthropologists have contributed to other fields of knowledge, we might note another trend toward the development of special interests. While most anthropologists retain a major interest in problems related to culture process, this interest is realized in different ways. Regardless of his or her topical area of specialization, the anthropologist can express an interest in cultural activities in at least three ways:

1. *The Importance of Local or Indigenous Beliefs and Practices.* One of the contributions of anthropology is to demonstrate that most human groups have developed practical and effective ways to meet the basic needs of human existence. These practices are in turn reinforced by a belief system which helps relate individual practices to a total way of being. An understanding of indigenous belief systems and the practices which accompany them is useful in a number of ways. Farming practices which seem impractical from the vantage of Western agriculture may, for example, make more sense when viewed in their cultural context. Similarly, the persistence of indigenous practices which have become maladaptive because of the radical changes in the conditions of a people's existence may seem irrational, but can be better understood when associated with the cultural context from which those practices are derived.

2. *The Cultural Belief System of Change Agents.* Some applied anthropologists prefer to focus on the practices and belief systems of change agents, generally reflecting upon aspects of their own culture rather than upon the cultural systems of another people. An anthropologist might, for example, consider a modern United States hospital as a cultural setting, and thereby contribute insight to some of the practices and beliefs concerning health care which are unique to this institution. To what extent are the primary health-care goals of a modern hospital compatible with the status needs of doctors and nurses, jeopardized by competition between hospitals, or shaped by a biomedical belief system which may in some cases actually inhibit effective patient care? Anthropologists working in this vein have helped us understand our own institutions better.

3. *The Delivery of Services.* Some applied anthropologists have focused on the processes involved in delivering one or another type of service. This interest assumes a sensitivity to the processes of cultural exchange. It may involve situations in which there is a considerable distance between the cultural beliefs of the deliverers and recipients of the services involved. But in other cases anthropologists might focus on situations in which people share much the same cultural beliefs but occupy different roles or statuses in relation to a particular service activity. A good example is the difference in contemporary attitudes toward childbirth in the United States. On the one hand, clear differences exist in cultural attitudes toward the techniques of giving birth. Some ethnic groups, for example, rely heavily on the use of midwives, and may employ different "charms" or home remedies to ease delivery. On the other hand, a fairly standard medical model for child delivery is shared by most people in the United States. Although this model can change on the basis of new medical insight as well as changing patterns of belief, it includes such practices as the routine use of drugs to induce labor, the administration of anesthetics during labor, the preference for a supine position for delivery, the mandatory presence of a physician during delivery, the use of instruments to hasten birth, and the prolonged hospitalization of the mother after delivery. The fact that confidence in these techniques may often be shared by the deliverer and the recipient of birthing services does not negate the importance of their cultural component. Each of these practices can be traced to beliefs concerning who is most responsible for the actual process of birth: the mother or the attending physician. Many of the practices are related to beliefs concerning the relative statuses of doctor and patient, and attitudes about whose convenience is most important during the birthing process.

Anthropologists tend to take a special interest not only in specific topical areas, methods, and roles, but also in particular manifestations of cultural process. The decisions they make in regard to the latter are seldom made explicit and are sometimes based more on how they learned to relate to their field than on a deliberate weighing of the advantages of one or another possibility. As applied anthropologists become more aware of the variety of choices involved, their ability to relate their choices to the solution of particular problems is improved.

RECOMMENDED READINGS

Medical Anthropology

The areas of specialization in applied anthropology discussed in this chapter and the next are represented by a large and rapidly growing literature. In addition to the sources in medical anthropology cited earlier, the interested reader will find dozens of texts and readers offering an overview of the field. Especially recommended as general texts are Ann McElroy and Patricia K. Townsend's *Medical Anthropology in Ecological Perspective* (Duxbury, 1979) and George M.Foster and Barbara Anderson's *Medical Anthropology* (John Wiley, 1978). Edited readers devoted primarily to crosscultural studies and basic research are David Landy's *Culture, Disease, and Healing* (Macmillan, 1977), Francis X. Grollig and Harold B. Haley's *Medical Anthropology* (Mouton, 1976), J. B. Loudon's *Social Anthropology and Medicine* (Academic, 1976), and Lola Romanucci-Ross, Daniel Moerman, and Lawrence Tancredi's *The Anthropology of Medicine* (Praeger, 1983). Noel J. Chrisman and Thomas W. Maretzki's *Clinically Applied Anthropology* (Reidel, 1982) is an edited volume of contributions by anthropologists who work in health science settings.

Some early readers which include a focus on applied case studies are Benjamin D. Paul's *Health, Culture and Community* (Russell Sage, 1955), Thomas Weaver's *Essays on Medical Anthropology* (Southern Anthropological Society, 1968), and L. Riddick Lynch's *The Cross-Cultural Approach to Health Behavior* (Fairleigh Dickinson, 1969). More recent edited readers in the same vein are Laura Nader and Thomas W. Maretzki's *Cultural Illness and Health* (American Anthropological Association, 1973), Eleanor E. Bauwens' *The Anthropology of Health* (Mosby, 1978), and Michael Logan and Edward E. Hunt's *Health and the Human Condition* (Duxbury, 1978).

Most of these materials deal both with physical and mental health. Joseph Westermeyer's *Anthropology and Mental Health* (Mouton, 1976) is a collection of essays, many centered on application, dealing primarily with mental health problems. Leonard D. Borman's edited volume *Helping People to Help Themselves* (Haworth, 1982) details an anthropological contribution to the development of self-help groups.

The Society for Medical Anthropology publishes the *Medical Anthropology Quarterly*. Journals of general interest include *Medical Anthropology;* the *American Journal of Public Health, Culture, Medicine and Psychiatry*; the *Health and Policy Quarterly*; and *Social Science and Medicine*.

Articles providing an overview of nutritional anthropology can be found in Edward Montgomery and John W. Bennett's "Anthropological Studies of Food and Nutrition: the 1940s and the 1970s" (in *The Uses of Anthropology*, American Anthropological Association, 1979) and Margaret Mead's *Food Habits Research: Problems of the 1960s* (National Academy of Sciences, 1964). Two recent readers in nutritional anthropology which have an applied focus are Thomas K. Fitzgerald's *Nutrition and Anthropology in Action* (Van Gorcum, 1977) and Norge W. Jerome, et al. *Nutritional Anthropology* (Redgrave, 1980). Journals include the *American Journal of Clinical Nutrition, Ecology of Food and Nutrition*, and *Nutrition Research*

Recent material devoted to health care in specific locales and under special conditions includes Norman Klein's *Health and Community: A Rural American Study* (Kendall/Hunt, 1976); John Friedl's *Health Care Services and the Appalachian Migrant* (Ohio State, 1978); Boris Velimirovic's edited volume *Modern Medicine and Medical Anthropology in the United States-Mexico Border Population* (Pan American Health Organization, 1978); Setha M. Low's *Culture, Politics, and Medicine of Costa Rica* (Redgrave, 1984); G. M. van Etten's *Rural Health Development in Tanzania* (Van Gorcum, 1976); Z. A. Ademuwagun, et al., *African Therapeutic Systems* (Crossroads, 1979); Arthur Kleinman's *Culture and Healing in Asian Societies* (Hall, 1978); and Charles Leslie's *Asian Medical Systems: A Comparative Study* (California, 1976). Journals publishing material related to health-care delivery problems include the *Journal of Health and Human Resources Administration* and the *Journal of Behavioral Medicine*.

Philip Singer's edited volume *Traditional Healing: New Science or New Colonialism?* (Owerri, 1977) is a critical review of some of the problems inherent in introducing Western medical science to traditional societies.

Madeline Leininger's *Transcultural Nursing* (John Wiley, 1978) is a collection of papers devoted to nursing and anthropology. Ann L. Clark's *Culture/Childbearing/Health Professionals* (Davis, 1978) is a discussion of anthropology and ethnicity directed to practicing nurses. The Council of Nursing and Anthropology publishes a periodic newsletter.

In the area of aging, Christine Fry has edited two volumes—*Dimensions: Aging, Culture, and Health* (Praeger, 1981) and *Aging in Culture and Society* (Bergin, 1980). *Ethnicity and Aging: Theory, Research, and Policy* (Springer, 1979), edited by Donald E. Gelfand and Alfred J. Kutzik, is an interdisciplinary treatment devoted to ethnic patterns of aging and United States public policy. The impact of modernization on traditional attitudes and beliefs surrounding aging are dealt with in D. O. Cowgill and L. D. Holmes' *Aging and Modernization* (Appleton-Century-Crofts, 1972).

Michael H. Agar's *Ripping and Running* (Academic Press, 1973) is a landmark ethnography in the study of drug abuse and its treatment. Harvey W. Feldman, et al., offer an edited volume on *Angel Dust: An Ethnographic Study of PCP Users* (Lexington, 1979). Readers about alcohol use include Michael W. Everett, et al., *Cross-Cultural Approaches to the Study of Alcohol* (Mouton, 1976) and Mac Marshall, ed., *Beliefs, Behaviors, and Alcoholic Beverages* (Michigan, 1979). More detailed recent research into alcohol use in specific societies include Mac Marshall's *Weekend Warriors: Alcohol in a Micronesian Culture* (Mayfield, 1979), Harry F. Wolcott's *The African Beer Gardens of Bulawayo: Integrated Drinking in a Segregated Society* (Rutgers Center of Alcohol Studies, 1974), and Mac Marshall's edited volume *Through a Glass Darkly* (Institute for Applied Social and Economic Research, Papua, New Guinea, 1982).

Recent contributions to population research include Virginia Abernathy's *Population Pressure and Cultural Adjustment* (Human Sciences, 1979) and David G. Mandelbaum's *Human Fertility in India: Social Components and Policy Perspectives* (California, 1974).

More detailed bibliographic references to areas of medical anthropology and application can be found in Ira Harrison and Sheila Cosminsky's *Traditional Medicine* (Garland, 1976), an annotated bibliography, and Marion Pearsall's bibliography devoted to *Medical Behavioral Science* (Kentucky, 1963). Harry F. Todd, Jr., and Julio L. Ruffini are editors of *Teaching Medical Anthropology* (Society for Medical Anthropology, 1979), which includes extensive bibliographic references.

Anthropology and Development

It will be difficult to do more than touch on the considerable literature dealing with anthropology and development. In addition to the "classic" treatments referred to in this chapter, the reader might also consider Edward H. Spicer's *Human Problems in Technological Change* (Wiley, 1965); Charles J. Erasmus' *Man Takes Control: Cultural Development and American Aid* (Minnesota, 1961); Arthur H. Niehoff's *A Casebook of Social Change* (Aldine, 1966); George M. Foster's *Traditional Cultures: The Impact of Technological Change* (Harper & Row, 1965); and Margaret Mead's *Cultural Patterns and Technological Change* (Mentor, 1955).

Recent readers in anthropology and development include John J. Poggie, Jr. and Robert N. Lynch's *Rethinking Modernization: Anthropological Perspectives* (Greenwood, 1974) and David C. Pitt's *Development From Below: Anthropologists and Development Situations* (Mouton, 1976). Hari Mohan Mathur's *Anthropology in the Development Process* (Vikzz, 1977) focuses on development problems in India and includes a discussion of contributions made by Indian anthropologists. David Brokensha and Marion Pearsall's *The Anthropology of Development in Sub-Saharan Africa* (Society for Applied Anthropology, 1969) also offers a regional perspective on development. Peggy Bartlett's *Agricultural Decision Making* (Academic Press, 1981) is an edited volume focusing on the rural farmer as a decision maker.

Material dealing specifically with agriculture includes Walter Goldschmidt's *As You Sow: Three Studies in the Social Consequences of Agribusiness* (Harcourt Brace Jovanovich, Inc., 1947); John Bennett's *Northern Plainsmen: Adaptive Strategies and Agrarian Life* (Aldine, 1969); and Horace Miner's *Culture and Agriculture: An Anthropological Study of a Corn Belt County* (Michigan, 1949).

Nancie L. Gonzalez's edited *Social and Technological Management in Dry Lands* (Westview, 1978) focuses on indigenous approaches to agricultural practice in arid regions.

Work related to resource development includes a special issue of the *Anthropological Quarterly* (1968) devoted to "Dam Anthropology: River Basin Research." George Dalton focuses on the relation between *Economic Anthropology and Development* (Basic Books, 1971). In *Pilot Project, India* (California, 1959) Albert Mayer, et al. provide an example of the involvement of anthropologists as researchers in early development projects. The Vicos project is discussed further in Henry F. Dobyns, Paul L. Doughty, and Harold D. Lasswell's *Peasants, Power, and Applied Social Change* (Sage Publications, Inc., 1964).

Anthropologists assisted in the development and evaluation of United States Peace Corps programs. Robert B. Textor's *Cultural Frontiers of the Peace Corps* (MIT, 1966) and Henry C. Dobyns's, et al. report on *Peace Corps Program Impact in the Peruvian Andes* (Peace Corps, n.d.) will provide an introduction to their work.

Within the framework of "modest proposals," interested readers might refer to Priscilla Reining and Barbara Lenkerd's *Village Viability in Contemporary Society* (Westview, 1980). Jerry B. Brown's *Rural Revitalization: A Challenge for Public-Interest Anthropology* (Anthropology Resource Center, 1977) offers a rationale for an "appropriate technology" for the rural United States.

Shirley Buzzard has prepared an annotated bibliography devoted to *Rural Development Literature 1976–1977* (Missouri, 1978) which also contains reference to earlier published bibliographies.

4

Specialization in Applied Anthropology II

"How did you get interested in applied anthropology?" someone once asked me.

"I sort of backed into it," I answered.

An anthropologist's special interests in areas of applied anthropology often develop as much by happenstance as by design. My first applied work, for example, was devoted to assisting in the evaluation of a federal low-income housing assistance program. At the time, I knew next to nothing about government housing programs; I was hired primarily on the basis of my earlier experience in field research, more for my skill as a researcher than for my knowledge of any substantive field of inquiry. My subsequent research in housing, however, sparked my interest in the housing problems of the poor, in community development and urban planning, and consequently in the field of applied urban anthropology. The work also introduced me to new applied research strategies, particularly those of evaluation research, and I was later able to apply these skills to work in other policy domains.

Specialization in an applied field generally includes the acquisition of several kinds of knowledge. These include:

1. A background in the field of anthropology, and particularly in how anthropological methods and approaches have been applied to problems in the policy domain that has been chosen as a special interest. The amount of available knowledge of this kind varies tremendously from one policy domain to another. Anthropologists have, for example, done a considerable amount of work in the areas of medicine and health, development, and education. They have done less that is clearly related to policy problems in areas like urban planning, social services, industrial development, and labor relations.

2. Specialization in an applied field also calls for a background in the policies that impact upon a particular field of study or practice—the legislation, administrative regulation, customary practices, and historical development of a policy domain.

3. Effective applied work almost inevitably leads the anthropologist into other fields of basic and applied inquiry and practice. Every area of specialization to which an applied anthropologist might aspire has been addressed by others, often from quite different disciplinary perspectives. The ability to master a healthy serving of this knowledge not only sharpens the anthropologist's insight but also becomes a necessary condition for communicating with one's fellow workers.

The major part of this chapter is devoted to specialization in urban anthropology and education. Some space at the end of the chapter will be given to discussing several other current areas of applied interest.

APPLIED URBAN ANTHROPOLOGY

Except in very special circumstances, anthropology has not maintained a long-term commitment to urban research. Only in the past two decades have anthropologists shown much interest in working in cities. One piece of professional lore has held that interest in urban anthropology was precipitated by a decline in the numbers of people available for research in rural and tribal settings. In effect, anthropologists simply followed the people with whom they normally worked as these people quit the hinterlands and made their way to the city. In some cases, this is demonstrably true and helps account for the urban anthropologist's major interest in *urbanization*—the process by which individuals and populations manage the shift from rural to city life.

However, much more is involved in the profession's current shift to urban interests. Anthropologists have consistently maintained that a "science of man" could not be limited to any particular form of human settlement. For most of the brief history of the profession, the study of traditional societies has been favored because such work seemed more urgent, offered the anthropologist a dramatically different cultural and intellectual experience, and helped fill in tremendous gaps in our efforts to catalog diverse human lifeways.

Urban anthropology, on the other hand, finds its roots in the anthropologist's concern with the ways in which human systems and institutions interact, and in a willingness to apply an anthropological approach to policy problems emanating form the rapid and often haphazard urbanization of the world. In the United States, interest in applied urban anthropology corresponds roughly to the nation's overall concern with urban problems. A very early example of advocacy anthropology in urban settings emerged during the 1880s, when the Women's Anthropological Society of Washington became actively involved in efforts to address the housing problems of the poor (Lurie 1966). These activities corresponded to a national concern for urban poverty and decline which accompanied the Progressive reform movement. The more recent growth of a coherent sense of applied urban anthropology is closely linked to national and worldwide interest in the city both as an arena for social change and as a focal point of social pathology.

Urbanization

It is puzzling that anthropologists have done very little applied research directed to the immediate problems of urbanization, the area where their basic research interests are strongest. There is no urban equivalent to the concern with rural resettlement policy discussed in the preceding chapter, although some applied urban projects have dealt in a piecemeal fashion with the long-term effects of worldwide urbanization, such as the development of squatter settlements and medical and social problems associated with rapid urban growth (Basham 1978).

This lack of involvement may have something to do with the way urbanization generally occurs and the relative lack of clear governmental policy related to large-scale population shifts. The rural resettlement programs in which applied anthropologists have been involved generally result from the deliberate intervention of government or private interests. From a policy perspective, urbanization is a much more haphazard affair, usually neither officially sanctioned (especially in regard to the migration of poor and untrained people to urban areas) nor actively discouraged. Compared to most rural settings, cities tend to be "open" settlement zones. Government attempts to limit migration to urban places have been infrequent and, where they have occurred, largely unsuccessful (Graham 1976).

Sally Kimball Makielski (1978) has addressed this problem from an anthropological perspective and has pointed out a number of research interests which anthropologists might address, including the social effects of urbanization and suburban growth. She also suggests that an effective urban population policy would require a high level of coordination among government (and, I would add, private interest) policies such as those affecting land use, urban rehabilitation, labor and industrial development, and pollution control.

In a few instances, anthropologists have had opportunities to participate in or conduct research related to large-scale, planned urbanization projects. During the early 1960s, Lisa Peattie (1970b) worked with the Harvard-MIT Joint Center for Urban Studies and the government of Venezuela as a member of a research team assisting in the planning of a new city. Ciudad Guayana was a remote Venezuelan town which was changing into a major city almost overnight as a result of a government plan to locate an industrial center in the region. The actual growth rate of this planned city was phenomenal—between 1950 and 1972, Ciudad Guayana's population of 4,000 increased to 142,000 (Garcia and Blumberg 1978:591).

Peattie's major contribution to the planning of Ciudad Guayana was to conduct an ethnographic study of life in a single working-class *barrio*. In this sense, she was well within the mainstream of anthropology—her major objective was to understand how change was taking place on a community level, and from there to offer advice pertinent to the overall planning effort for the new city.

Although Peattie was able to stay in Ciudad Guayana for only the early stages of its development, her research brought to light a number of potential flaws in the planning process. Most of these, based on her "view from the barrio," were identified as communication problems existing between the middle-class planners and the poorer segments of the population.

Peattie found these difficulties in communication to be based on three phenomena: the barrio inhabitants' lack of familiarity with the new urban power structure, their inaccessibility to the power structure, and social class differences which placed a strain on effective petitioning between the workers and the planners (Peattie 1970b: 85–90).

In light of Maria-Pilar Garcia and Rae Lessing Blumberg's (1978) later evaluation of the Ciudad Guayana project, many of the remarks in Peattie's study seem almost prophetic. These authors argue that the planners' inability to understand or anticipate the largely informal patterns of adaptation of the city's poorer citizens not only made life unnecessarily difficult for these less advantaged populations but also effectively sabotaged the entire master plan for the city.

An example of how this came about is illuminating. One feature of the master plan was to design for balanced growth throughout the new city. Industrial development would occur primarily in the sparsely populated west sectors of the city. This source of employment, along with new government-subsidized housing in the west, was meant to encourage a population shift to the west and reduce the threat of serious overcrowding in the older east sectors of Ciudad Guayana. Unfortunately, this population shift never occurred. Garcia and Blumberg offer a number of explanations based on events which the planners had not adequately anticipated.

First of all, the planners had hoped to discourage the sort of *shantytown* development that is common to much of Latin American development. ("Shantytowns" are makeshift squatter settlements, built by newly arrived migrants, usually as a temporary measure. The problem for planners is that, once established, they tend to persist. Although they may serve as a functionally adaptive strategy for migrants, planners tend to identify them as eyesores and potential troublespots.) The planners prohibited shantytown-like developments in the west sectors of the city, hoping to encourage industrial workers to move into new government-sponsored housing. However, delays occurred in the construction of the new housing, too few units were built, and even with subsidies the housing was too expensive for many migrants.

The housing problem was intensified because planners failed to account for a typical Latin American pattern of urbanization, wherein individuals who first establish themselves in a city serve as sponsors for their relatives. Since only people who were employed in the industries were eligible for government housing in the west sectors of Ciudad Guayana, many migrants who anticipated the sponsorship of their kin decided to settle in the east sectors.

The cycle of migration also contributed to employment problems which the planners had not anticipated. Although the industrial jobs were located in the west, only a small proportion of the migrants actually ended up working there. Most found work in more typical Latin American lower-class occupations, such as service jobs and unskilled or semiskilled labor. Most of this work was to be found in the densely occupied east sectors of the city.

As a result of these and several other factors identified by Garcia and Blumberg, the anticipated population shift to the western sectors of Ciudad Guayana did not occur. Instead, shantytown developments flourished in the crowded eastern sectors of the city.

Before we accept this as another "just so" story, we should keep in mind that it is not at all certain that anthropologists, working from prospect rather than retrospect, could have saved the day for the planners. We can see the possibility of failure early on with Lisa Peattie's study. Why, then, did her warnings and advice go unheeded? There is no simple answer, although we will have an opportunity to reconsider this and similar cases in Chapters 5 and 6.

Urban Planning and Design

Plans and their design components are important artifacts of contemporary societies oriented to change and committed to the possibility of improvement. Plans and designs reflect whatever levels of technical knowledge and cultural sensitivity their authors can bring to bear on a planning situation. In part, they mirror the idealized intentions of a society. In some equal measure they contain important clues to the way intentions are scattered and compromised as a complex society's differing social and political realities come into conflict. All these elements of a modern society's struggle with its growth and preservaton can be interpreted from the texts and elaborate drawings of formal plans.

Architect Christopher Alexander (1965) also believes that plans and designs reflect the *structures* of human thought. The only problem, he suggests, is that the way people organize abstract plans is often different from the way they actually organize their lives. Plans are convenient ways to put complex ideas into a discrete kind of order, where each idea (part of a plan) stands clearly apart from the others and where the relationships betwen ideas are simply, even if inaccurately, diagrammed and understood. Most planning, Alexander argues, takes on the graphic appearance of the familiar tree diagram. One of the nice things about tree diagrams is that they are not messy; they appeal to our sense of order. But how well do they reflect reality? Writing primarily about city planning, Alexander suggests that the reality of how people actually live in cities would be diagrammed more like a "semilattice" than a tree. In a semilattice, functions overlap. The formal, idealized functions of a structure like a city, such as might be described politically by a tree-like table of organization or spatially by an urban land-use plan, are actually interspersed with a fine lattice of informal and ever-mutable patterns through which individuals and groups go about their business. These latter patterns do not always conform to the rigid ideal and partly imaginary structures represented by tree-like thinking.

Much of the danger lies in assuming that the structure and economy of thought afforded by thinking of cities along the lines imposed by the tree diagram actually represent the way cities are. Alexander is passionately opposed to this temptation:

> For the human mind, the tree is the easiest vehicle for complex thoughts. But the city is not, cannot, and must not be a tree. The city is a receptacle for life. If the receptacle severs the overlap of the strands of life within it, because it is a tree, it will be like a bowl full of razor blades on edge, ready to cut up whatever is entrusted to it. In such a receptacle, life will be cut to pieces. If we make cities which are trees, they will cut our life within to pieces. (1978:402)

Wesley Nakajima (1979), a planner and anthropologist, has offered an example of how tree-like thinking can influence a planner's sense of urban realities. Planners are often content to approach urban problems in terms of discrete and formally defined units, such as census tracts. Unfortunately, these units do not always conform to social realities, or to the way residents in a particular area define their neighborhoods. Working with a planning organization in a southeast United States city, Nakajima sought to improve upon the organization's ability to plan for development within a single census tract. He asked residents of the area to map their neighborhoods as they saw them, and also conducted an ethnographic survey and key informant interviews within the census tract.

As a result of this work, Nakajima identified four distinct neighborhoods within the single census tract. Identification of the unique characteristics, lifestyles, and needs of each neighborhood helped the planners respond to local needs, and dissuaded them from basing their perceptions of those needs on a single demographic profile of the entire census tract.

In pointing out the dangers of "census tract planning," Nakajima describes an instance where the planning organization sought to locate a recreational center in an abandoned school. The resulting opposition to this plan from nearby residents might have been anticipated if the planners had recognized earlier that the school was located in a neighborhood of retired persons who were almost certain to object to any plan which would attract children and change the character of their neighborhood. The planners had recognized the need for recreational facilities within the larger census tract, but their failure to realize the importance of local neighborhood boundaries and uses within that tract resulted in a poor decision.

Social class and cultural differences between the planners and those for whom they plan often result in misunderstandings. Since planning nearly always requires making policy decisions concerning the application of limited resources to specific problems, the potential for conflict is ever-present. Michael Pardee (1981) offers an example in which a group of advocacy-oriented planners and architects came into conflict with the residents of a lower-income neighborhood in Tampa, Florida. The planners had been working on a "revitalization plan" for the neighborhood. Their backgrounds were heavily oriented to the preservation of historic structures, and their recommendations for community revitalization clearly reflected their aesthetic and cultural values. Many residents in the declining neighborhood, on the other hand, were concerned with the economic vitality of the area. Their immediate response to the ideal of preservation was negative; they would rather have seen the old buildings torn down and replaced with new shopping and business facilities.

It should be noted that a conflict does not necessarily exist between the economic development of an area and the ideal of historic preservation. The problem Pardee points out is primarily one of communication. The effectiveness of the planners' revitalization plan was reduced by their inability or unwillingness to negotiate their sense of policy priorities with those of many of the neighborhood's residents.

Pardee's example emphasizes the sociocultural aspects of planning. One of the conflicts he identifies between himself as an applied anthropologist, and the architects he worked with, centers on the architects' tendency to see community revitalization as primarily a problem in the physical design of neighborhoods, while Pardee saw physical design as one aspect among many others. Urban planning, along with many other development activities, is complicated by the fact that it is often addressed in a unidimensional fashion—either from a particular professional point of view, such as we see here with architecture, or on the basis of limitations defined by government agencies or others. For example, restrictions on how federal community development funds are to be spent are often imposed on the basis of priorities established at the federal level of government. Thus, it becomes difficult on the local or regional level to establish priorities which might better address local community needs but which are also not in conflict with federally defined priorities.

Applied anthropologists, with their tendency to approach a problem in holistic terms, are often frustrated by such funding restrictions. Communities, experiencing their lives as a whole rather than as parts, are also often frustrated. On the other hand, clearly established funding policies often have good reasons for their existence: They direct resources to a particular problem area rather than scattering limited funds to the wind; they increase accountability for the use of resources and help ensure that funds are not misspent; and they can help encourage long-term planning efforts.

Advocacy planning is one (although certainly not the only) way to renegotiate policy priorities on a community level. Lisa Peattie (1968; 1970a) points out that the urban poor and minorities are often left out of the planning process. Applied research directed to trying to understand the needs and preferences of a poor community helps compensate for the omission but may not be enough. Peattie describes the planning process as a sort of "theatre" in which various "actors" attempt to come to terms. This theatre may be informed by knowledge about people, but the most significant element of "drama" is *participation*. Advocacy, Peattie argues, cannot be limited to providing information about those left out of the planning process; it requires encouraging those people to become actors.

To some extent, recent public policy in the United States has encouraged the staging of such dramas. Federal and local regulations requiring "citizen participation" in public decision making provide the stage. Advocacy and community organizations provide the actors, often with the encouragement and financial support of both public and private institutions. Such efforts have made professional planners, commercial developers, and locally elected officials more aware of and responsive to the human, neighborhood-level consequences of their activities. On the other hand, organized neighborhood and community groups do not appear to be the full answer to effective or even equitable planning. Delmos Jones (1979) has argued that such groups often function as highly conservative forces in a city, organized to serve their special interests and sometimes unsympathetic or antagonistic toward larger social issues. As much as community organization has the potential for correcting inequities in the planning process, it may also foster other social inequities, as when a community organizes to oppose the racial integration of its neighborhood. Such opposition is not limited to middle-class communities. It might in specific instances be even more intense in low-income but ethnically homogeneous neighborhoods.

Applied anthropologists have participated in a variety of projects related to community development. Some, like Peattie, have identified a low-income neighborhood as their clientele. Others, like Nakajima, have worked for city planning agencies. Some have found employment with state and federal agencies, and others have worked with the private sector. Someday there will be a public meeting at which an anthropologist working with a neighborhood group stands up against an anthropologist working for a developer who is about to build a high-rise apartment in the neighborhood. Perhaps the city planner will also be an anthropologist. We will learn more about our profession at such a point than we will learn from any number of "just so" stories.

Applied anthropologists have also worked directly with architects and designers in efforts to ensure that designs are sensitive to the environmental, social, and cultural preferences of their users. Amos Rapoport, a professor of both architecture and anthropology, epitomizes an ideal of interaction between the knowledge and intentions of anthropology and those of architecture. In his book *Human Aspects of Urban Form* (1977), Rapoport advises that one difficulty in achieving an effective level of communication between social scientists and urban designers is that the practitioners of both professions seldom know much about the other. The "man-environment" approach to urban design that Rapoport advocates requires a knowledge of how people perceive and react to cities *and* an understanding of how cities are built (1977:383).

Such knowledge cannot always be expected in a single individual such as Rapoport. Teamwork is an essential component of many effective responses to unusual design problems. Joe Harding worked with a team of anthropologists who were assisting a group of architects in the design of a Navajo community school. The anthropologists' work was done in two phases. First, they conducted a survey and needs assessment to determine how the Navajo used their present school facilities and what features and uses they wanted incorporated in the new structure. Then the anthropologists worked with the Navajo to determine priorities among the needs that had been identified. The research identified several needs and preferences which could be served through proper design:

> . . . certain aspects of traditional architecture were desired for the new center, while others were not. The general hogan shape was desired, although traditional materials were not. Traditional hogans, for example, are seen as having

rough interiors. For their school/community center, the Navajo wanted soft, smooth textures and surfaces plus the latest in equipment. Preferences for windows were fairly complex. In general, people wished to have windows in the buildings, in contrast to the hogan style of no windows—they wanted to enjoy what could be seen outside, but they did not wish to be viewed by persons outside the building. Whether there was any resemblance to what were perceived to be pueblo characteristics was also important. Some animosity still exists between the Navajo and pueblo peoples and it would appear to be a big mistake to incorporate any features which might be construed to be pueblo-like in developing a building for Navajos. (1979:23)

Harding notes that the collaboration was successful on two counts. The architects utilized the anthropologists' recommendations in their design for the school, and the Navajo accepted the design without any substantial modifications.

The Urban Poor

The elimination of poverty, and of the pathologies that we associate with being poor, has been a major policy goal of most contemporary governments. Indexes related to poverty, such as unemployment statistics, percentages of populations below the "poverty level," per capita incomes, and measurements of housing standards, are often selected as important indicators of a nation's social and economic health. While poverty is not limited to the urban experience, it is certainly more visible in cities than elsewhere, and hence is a prime target of government policy. The historian Sam Warner (1973) has argued that the growth of poverty programs in the United States is linked to improvements in modern transportation and to the development of suburban living. When the urban middle class began abandoning their inner city neighborhoods for "streetcar suburbs," their daily commutes from work to home carried them through their cities' poorer sections. These daily reminders of poverty stimulated greater interest in improving the living conditions of the poor.

One reason that urban anthropology lends itself so easily to applied interests is that, as they begin to show increased interest in the urban scene, most anthropologists choose to work among the less advantaged. There are a number of reasons for this. We have noted that many anthropologists seem to feel most comfortable working among a society's politically and economically marginal populations. Poverty is often associated with ethnically rich and culturally distinct lifeways, the sorts of things anthropologists have been accustomed to dealing with, whereas middle-class urban life is often (and quite incorrectly) associated with "sameness" and conformity. The poor often seem more accessible than the privacy-conscious middle class. Moreover, growing concern over the conditions and causes of poverty has led over the past several decades to a steady if somewhat sporadic pattern of increased government support for research in this area.

Any discussion of anthropology and poverty must include Oscar Lewis and his concept of the *culture of poverty*. Lewis based this concept on research he had conducted in rural India, in rural and urban Mexico, and in urban Puerto Rico and the United States. His well-written and appealing life histories of people living in poverty—such as *Five Families*, *The Children of Sanchez*, and *La Vida*—have had a wide and mostly appreciative reading outside anthropology. On the other hand, Lewis' (1968) attempt to generalize from these experiences and arrive at a description of the culture of poverty has sparked a considerable amount of criticism.

Lewis argued that the culture of poverty has had a pervasive influence on the lives of most of the world's poor. In essence, he claimed, the conditions of poverty, wherever they might occur, often encourage people to adopt a range of psychological characteristics and social-environmental responses which become agonizingly difficult to alter. Included in the list of traits Lewis offered are a sense of resignation and fatalism, a lack of motivation to plan for the future, a sense of inferiority, and a lack of effective political organization. Lewis argued that these traits are culturally fixed, learned through generations of living in poverty situations, and consequently are not easily remedied or changed.

Lewis' critics (and there have been many) have argued that his concept underplays the importance of the structural conditions bearing on poverty—it places the blame for poverty on the poor (they are poor because they *think* poor) and inappropriately relieves society of the responsibility for the extent to which poverty arises from and is maintained by middle-class social and economic institutions which deny opportunity to large segments of a society. Valentine (1968) argues that the *culture of poverty* concept also limits our ability to consider the importance of ethnic differences in the ways people respond to poverty.

The controversy offers a good example of the extent to which the notion of *culture* (when it is seen only as an enduring, stable, and difficult-to-change force in peoples' lives) can have serious policy implications. Edwin Eames and Judith Goode (1977:319–320) have pointed out two such implications as they apply to Lewis' point of view. First, the *culture of poverty* concept encourages policy makers to favor programs "designed to change the behavior and values of the poor," rather than programs which would change the larger social and economic system which discriminates against the poor. Second, the failure of misguided poverty programs can conveniently be blamed on the attitudes of poverty clients rather than on the poor planning or implementation of the programs.

Another policy implication of the *culture of poverty* concept, not specifically identified by Eames and Goode, is that it offers a handy justification to delay accountability for correcting the conditions and causes of poverty. If we believe that the attitudes of the poor have to be changed before progress in alleviating poverty can be made, then policy decisions will favor long-term programs of change (such as early childhood education programs) at the expense of programs which might produce a more immediate return (such as programs to enforce equal opportunity in hiring).

While these are important points to be made, it is also possible to argue that Oscar Lewis has been treated a bit unfairly by many of his colleagues. First of all, many of the critics of the *culture of poverty* concept argue as though Lewis' brief remarks on the subject were responsible for a significant change in the United States public policy. Indeed, the example has been used to demonstrate how strongly the work of anthropologists can influence public policy—in this case, in a negative way. The story goes something like this: Lewis' term *culture of poverty* was borrowed by the social critic Michael Harrington, whose book *The Other America* (1963) added fuel during the 1960s to Lyndon Johnson's "War on Poverty." The tremendous federal resources deveoted to the programs of this decade favored activities which sought to change the attitudes of the poor, rather than programs which advocated radical economic change.

This sort of unilinear argumentation might be remedied by a better grasp of the uses of policy. First of all, the arguments inherent in the *culture of poverty* concept were being enacted in United States public policy long before Lewis' time. They can be traced partially to the impact of Social Darwinism on United States social reform movements (Mencher 1967:248–250), and more explicitly to the work of popular scholars and social commentators such as John Dewey and Charles H. Cooley. Interestingly, although Harrington did use the term *culture of poverty* in his description of the poor in the United States, his evidence for the existence of such a culture was derived from other sources, including Hollingshead and Redlich's (1958) respected study of *Social Class and Mental Illness* and Cornell University's report on *Mental Health in the Metropolis* (Srole et al. 1962).

But the greater disservice, if we carry criticism of the *culture of poverty* concept to its conclusion, might not be to Lewis but to the idea of culture itself. The response to Lewis is in part a reaction by anthropologists to the way in which rigid adherence to a static concept of culture can lead to the notion that cultural values and traits are bound to endure. Such a configuration, arising in large part because the concept of *culture* was developed by anthropologists in their study of small-scale and relatively isolated societies, leads us to considerable difficulty as we try to figure out how culture might be manifest in complex urban societies. Unfortunately, many anthropologists appear to have reacted by giving up the quest altogether, seemingly content to search the paradigms of other disciplines for new roads to travel.

We will return to this problem. For now, however, it is worth noting that problems with the way Lewis used the concept of *culture* to explain poverty do not negate the important consideration that poverty is intimately linked to cultural processes. A better understanding of how the connections are made is part of the contribution that applied anthropologists can make to policy issues affecting the poor.

Many of the cultural links associated with poverty extend well beyond the environs of the poor. Laura Nader (1974) is among those anthropologists who have criticized the profession's tendency to focus on the study of the poor and to avoid research among the advantaged. Nader encourages anthropologists to "study up" in order to understand "the processes whereby power and responsibility are exercised in the United States." The policy implications of her recommendations should be clear from the following:

> What have been the consequences of social science research on crime? By virtue of our concentration on lower-class crimes, we have aided in the public definition of the "law and order" problem in terms of lower-class or street crimes. Let's assume that the taxpaying public in a democracy, after listening to a presidential speech calling for more tax money for enforcement and protection from street crimes, decides to see for itself. No matter what library they went to, the most they could get is some information on crimes committed by the lower class. They would have no way of evaluating, given present descriptive materials, whether, in a situation of limited money, they would do better to put their money on street crime or on white-collar crime, both of which, after all, imperil the lives of all taxpayers everyday in many ways. (1974:290–291)

The major concepts discussed here—those of Oscar Lewis, Lewis' critics, and Laura Nader—have had a significant impact on the way applied anthropologists view their work. In many respects, they are still hotly contested issues.

The Delivery of Urban Services

Compared to that given to other areas of special interest, such as education and medicine, applied anthropologists have shown little independent interest in the actual delivery of urban services. For the most part, interests in urban policy formulation and planning have not extended to involvement in implementation and evaluative research.

Neither has the applied anthropologists' approach to the city proceeded in an even fashion. A city represents a complex whole of services, ranging from fire protection to human services to waste management. In modern cities, each such service represents an area of increasingly specialized expertise, susceptible to much the same limitations of a professional "subculture" as are the specialized fields of medicine and education. The distance between service providers and their clients—whether it is based on differences in class, ethnicity, or some other realm of experience—can lead to serious misunderstandings.

Where anthropologists have become interested in the delivery of urban services, it has usually been in reference to the poor. Most basic research in this vein has been descriptive, with very little direct application. However, some ethnographic studies, such as Carol Stack's *All Our Kin* (1974) and Joseph Howell's *Hard Living on Clay Street* (1973), do offer useful portraits of how the poor and ethnic minorities move through the "welfare" delivery system.

Stack's study is based in part on a survey of case records for black recipients of Aid for Dependent Children (AFDC) in a Midwest city. The objective of the survey was to demonstrate the extent to which social workers identified the kinds of problems they imagined their clients to have on the basis of biases they held rather than on observed facts. This survey was accompanied by ethnographic research, which described how poor black families (mostly single females with dependent children) adapted to the conditions of poverty. Stack emphasized positive "strategies of survival" rather than negative or pathological traits of a "culture of poverty." Importantly, she was able to describe poverty as being not simply a condition of the poor, or a result of large-scale exploitation of the poor by an industrial society, but as a *delivery process* where two different senses of reality met. The one sense of reality was provided by the social workers, who struggled to fit their AFDC clients into the expectations of "mainstream" life. The other sense of reality was anchored in the experiences of the black female heads of households, who found that they could not survive on the basis of other people's expectations.

Stack's study of the lives of the AFDC clients described patterns of adaptation which the social workers had failed to understand. These patterns were based on a family and residency structure in which unrelated persons were often called upon to act as kin:

> Black families in the Flats and the non-kin they regard as kin have evolved patterns of co-residence, kinship-based exchange networks linking multiple domestic units, elastic household boundaries, lifelong bonds to three-generation households, social controls against the formation of marriage that could endanger the network of kin, the domestic authority of women, and limitations on the role of the husband or male friend within a woman's kin network. These highly adaptive structural features of urban black families comprise a resilient response to the socio-economic conditions of poverty, the inexorable unemployment of black women and men, and the access to scarce economic resources of a mother and her children as AFDC recipients. (1974:124)

As revealing as her work is, Stack's study still focuses primarily on the poor as an object of study. In the past decade, a number of applied anthropologists have had an opportunity to work on large-scale evaluation projects which centered on those who administer and implement programs designed for the poor. Frank Vivelo (1980) has described the evaluation of an experimental employment program in which anthropologists were employed as fieldworkers, partly to study the interaction between service providers and their clients. Michael G. Trend (1978c) has described a similar project based on the evaluation of a work-incentive program. I have elsewhere (1977) offered a description of the evaluation of an experimental housing allowance program which stationed observers in eight administrative agencies across the country.

Each of these projects involved long periods of field research (from six months to more than two years). The housing program will be described in greater detail in Chapter 6. For our present purposes, one outcome of the research is worth noting. The experimental housing program demonstrated considerable regional variation in the way different agencies responded to delivering essentially the same services to the urban poor (Abt Associates, Inc. 1976). Some of the variability can be attributed to the local housing market, economic conditions in the cities involved in the experiment, and so on. But most of it must be attributed to differences in the value orientations of those who administered and implemented the programs. Unfortunately, these differences were never fully documented. Although each of the observers prepared case studies of the sites where they worked, there was little attempt to "tease" out the value contrasts which were described in individual reports. (Instead, as is often the case in such projects, the differences were largely attributed to variables which could more easily be described and analyzed in quantitative terms.)

The important point is that the high degree of variation in value orientation reported in the housing allowance study contrasts sharply to the lesser amount of variation normally reported by anthropologists studying poor people. There are at least three possible explanations for this. First, the middle-class professionals who administer and implement human service delivery systems have, in general, a wider range of opportunity to express their value options than do most poor people. They do not share a single condition of poverty, and a public agency is likely to be staffed by individuals with diverse backgrounds and varied lifestyles. This helps account for some of the individual decision-making variation described in the site case studies.

Much of the regional variation might, on the other hand, be attributed to the fact that public agencies control resources which are valuable to the cities in which they operate, and are thus influenced by local social and political value systems. Thus, a human service agency in Texas might be expected to operate quite differently from one in Minnesota, although both are funded by the same source and have inherited identical policy goals. The differences between local agencies might be so great as to reveal radically different program goals. In the housing allowance experiment, for example, the objective of obtaining standard housing for black clients was met in strikingly different ways. Several local agencies actively pursued a legal course of action, threatening equal opportunity suits against landlords and rental agents who discriminated against blacks. However, at least one agency (located in a highly segregated city) met its "quota" for black clients by soliciting the cooperation of landlords who already rented to blacks, while assuring landlords who did not rent to blacks that they could enroll their poor white tenants in the program without fearing that the agency might also send black clients to them.

A third possible explanation of the variations in value orientations found among and within the administrative agencies is that the anthropologists might simply have been more sensitive to the differences among people who appeared to be more like themselves. Anthropologists working among the poor, on the other hand, might be more alert to those patterns of culture and behavior which help explain why the poor seem so different from them.

I suspect that each of these explanations has an element of truth. Together, they help indicate the extent to which applied anthropologists need to direct their attention to the *total* contexts of public policy.

Urban Pathologies

City life has often been associated with social pathologies such as alienation, stress, mental illness, and criminal and deviant activity. In the United States, some of these associations may simply be the result of a bias against the urban setting. North American intellectuals have often exhibited such a bias (Sennett 1970), sometimes to the detriment of our understanding of the positive aspects of city life. Social scientists and others have, for example, often described the city as a *cause* of the erosion of traditional values and rules of social control.

Some anthropologists have argued against this bias. In his article "Urbanization Without Breakdown," Oscar Lewis (1952) demonstrated how Mexican villagers managed to effectively maintain their values and social networks after migrating to the city. Carol Stack's *All Our Kin* (1974), discussed above, argues that those very features of the lives of the poor which scholars and social workers often regard as signs of social disintegration are actually positive adaptations to the conditions of urban poverty.

Of course, urban pathologies do exist and they are troublesome, as might be expected in any setting where the lines between the advantaged and disadvantaged are visible on a daily basis, where the mechanisms of social control are highly specialized and may favor the interests of one class of people over another, and where large numbers of peoples with strikingly different backgrounds live in close proximity.

Most of the urban pathologies with which applied anthropologists have dealt are conditions of social rather than individual deviance. Anthropologists have devoted little attention to trying to understand discrete criminal activities—such as murder, robbery, or sex-related offenses—which are not customarily sanctioned by strong or enduring peer group behaviors. On the other hand, considerable attention has been paid to deviant "subcultures" which arise from such activities as drug and alcohol abuse. Much of this work, such as Michael Agar's *Ripping and Running* (1973a), Richard Weppner's (1973) research into the "street addict's world," and James Spradley's (1970) ethnography of "urban nomads" effectively combines the special interests of urban and medical anthropology.

James Spradley has described how his study of Seattle "tramps" led him to later participate in a range of applied activities. First of all, Spradley's research was easily translated into policy concerns because much of his work was devoted to understanding how the tramps had adapted to the local legal system in dealing with being arrested for public drunkenness. Spradley identified strategies the tramps used to "beat the system" or at least to minimize its impact on their lives. He pointed out how Seattle judges and police who dealt with the tramps were influenced by their preconceived notions of tramp life and of what happened when these individuals entered the judicial system.

Shortly after his research, Spradley had an opportunity to participate in an applied reseach project under the sponsorship of a local alcoholic treatment center. One of the goals of this project was to determine how more effective treatment could be offered to the tramps. Later, Spradley accepted an opportunity to work with a local citizen committee which was concerned with the way the Seattle judicial system was dealing with the problem of public drunkenness. The advocacy activities he engaged in at this level primarily involved the "strategic use of information," which required that Spradley make use of his knowledge about tramp culture in a manner that would best suit the purposes of reforming the judicial system.

Spradley identifies three components to using information in an advocacy setting:

> First, *the advocate anthropologist seeks to write for the layman.* If research is to benefit informants, the results must be translated into terms that the general public can understand and appreciate. . . . Second, *the advocate anthropologist seeks to publish his findings in a manner that will give them the widest circulation.* Instead of restricting his writing to professional journals or scholarly books, the advocate anthropologist will call press conferences, release information to the local media, write articles for popular magazines, speak to groups of interested public citizens, and write books for the general public. Third, the advocate anthropologist *tries to release information at the most appropriate time for implementing change.* He may withhold some data from publication until after change has occurred; other findings may be distributed early in order to influence the course of change. (Spradley and McCurdy 1975:638–639)

Spradley's move from basic research to applied research for a public agency and then to an advocacy role helps illustrate that the different uses of anthropology are not necessarily incompatible. Neither is the particular order of events he describes inviolable; an anthropologist might move just as easily from an advocacy role to one of basic research, or from applied research in an administration setting to more basic research. Roles might also interchange within the career of an applied anthropologist—individuals have, for example, moved from research positions to the actual administration or implementation of public programs, and vice versa.

ANTHROPOLOGY AND EDUCATION

The anthropologist's interest in education arises from an early concern with how children are socialized to the ways of their society and how such phenomena as cultural constructs, technical skills, and community values are passed from generation to generation. Understanding the manner in which knowledge is passed on, either through formal instruction or informal means, is a crucial step in understanding how a society operates. This interest in education had an influence on early work in applied anthropology. In advising rural development agents, for example, anthropologists often emphasized the importance of designing educational programs to help introduce technological innovations in a way that would be compatible with a people's prior educational experience. The failure of developmental schemes was often laid to a failure of overseas development agents to demonstrate techniques and communicate skills in a culturally appropriate manner.

Over the past two decades, applied anthropologists have expanded their interests in education. A significant amount of their concern has been directed to urban settings and work in the United States. As is the case in other areas, much of their interest is consistent with larger public policy priorities and citizen concerns.

Cultural Processes and the School

A cross-cultural perspective has helped educational anthropologists make two important observations concerning the processes of schooling and education: first, that all education does not occur in schools, even in complex industrialized societies which have highly specialized institutions for formal schooling; and second, that institutions of formal schooling often "teach" much more than their curricula indicate. For better or worse, schools are mirrors of the society in which they are established. They are important mirrors because the images they reflect are bound to have a critical impact on youth.

If education is the major goal of schools in modern, complex societies, the kind of education that is expected to occur is a matter of serious policy debate. What is more, as major social institutions, schools are subject to important policy decisions which are only partially related to problems of education. In the United States, for example, schools have become the proving ground and center stage for policies encouraging better relations between ethnic groups, racial equality, and the provision of health care and adequate nutrition to the disadvantaged.

Many of the educational and extracurricular policies affecting schools in the past couple of decades are concerned with problems related to the school as a "multicultural" setting. Educators have generally been sympathetic to the fact that students come to schools from a variety of backgrounds, and that cultural differences among students affect both the amount and kind of education that occurs in these settings. In the United States, the term "culturally disadvantaged" gained widespread popularity in public schools during the 1960s, setting in motion a tremendous variety of programs designed to assist minority students in adapting to an educational system which had been developed primarily for white middle-class students. Similarly, terms such as *cultural pluralism, bicultural* and *multicultural education,* and *bilingual education* have become a part of the professional language of educators.

In many respects, no other professional group in the United States seems to have so thoroughly embraced and, to some extent, co-opted the concept of culture as have educators and educational researchers. While this is largely desirable, it has also led to significant misunderstandings. Theodora St. Lawrence and John Singleton have pointed out that basing the idea of educational disadvantage on cultural differences can lead policy makers to the same errors as have occurred in linking the concepts of culture and poverty.

> While multi-culturalism in schools is often a response to the problems of inequality faced by minority children within the schools and the larger society, the problem is not necessarily one of changing school experiences for *minority* youngsters. The position of minority groups in our society is an artifact of the values and structure of dominant groups in the society. No amount of enriched schooling for minority children is going to change this larger structure; that can only come from changes in the public culture of the dominant groups. While we would expect little direct influence on these groups from schooling for cultural pluralism, it is essential that schooling proposals acknowledge the sources of social disadvantage and direct our efforts towards the larger society as well as its victims. (1976:22)

Cultural ideas can also be applied in an overzealous manner by educators, as Jacquetta Hill-Burnett (1978) discovered in her work with Puerto Rican youth and school teachers in a midwestern city. A major goal of the project on which Hill-Burnett worked was to provide teachers with cultural background information that would help them adapt their teaching to the specific needs of their Puerto Rican students. The effectiveness of initial attempts to impart this knowledge was called into question as Hill-Burnett and her colleagues discovered that the teachers were beginning to use the generalized cultural explanations the researchers provided as reinforcements of their stereotypes of Puerto Rican behavior. As Hill-Burnett explains:

> Early in our work we often presented the cultural point of view to teachers by reinterpreting, in cultural terms, student conduct that teachers described but interpreted as bizarre, strange, abnormal, or deviant. To illustrate, one teacher described the "odd" behavior of two Puerto Rican boys who fought in the shop class. It was not the fighting but the incident which precipitated the fight that puzzled her. Carlos was very attracted to Antonia, Mrs. Berger reported to me. And Carlos had begun to pursue Antonia's attention with notable ardor. In shop one day, as everyone was working on their lamp-shades. Carlos, who was seated next to Antonia, engaged her in attentive, admiring conversation, when a messenger, Renaldo, Antonia's brother, walked in. As he started toward the teacher, he suddenly turned aside and physically attacked Carlos. After the teacher separated the combatants, Renaldo's only explanation for his action was that Carlos was talking with Antonia, who had been told by her parents not to talk with Carlos. In the eyes of the teachers, the physical attack was far too extreme for the explanation. We began to interpret the event in terms of Puerto Rican parental concern with the chaste reputation of their unmarried teenage daughters, and the role of brothers in guarding the reputation of the family. The family's reputation would be undermined should a daughter—like Antonia—compromise it by arousing suspicion about her proper conduct with a boy. Carlos was well known as a charming, sometimes ardent "ladies' man," but he was also a member of a street gang, The Latin Disciples. He was a "danger" to a daughter's reputation.
>
> Our good intentions were frustrated when the teachers fitted this perspective into the general stereotyped picture of amorous Latins and Don Juan exploits. It reinforced their notion that Puerto Rican parents cared only about their daughters' marital status rather than their schooling and future employment. This inference was not true . . . it was contradicted by our family interviews. (1978:120–121)

This understanding led Hill-Burnett to adopt a "situational view" in subsequent attempts to work with the teachers. It had not been enough to simply provide cultural interpretations of the students' behavior; to avoid the possibility of stereotyping these explanations she had to include information about the "contingencies, variable conditions, and contextual constraints" which helped shape the students' behavior.

As these and other examples illustrate, it is seldom enough for the applied anthropologist simply to find a cultural explanation for practical problems. Applied work often requires the anthropologist to be alert to possible misinterpretations of his or her position. Often, the significant problem in application is not how to interpret the cultural activity of one group of people, but to understand and explain how culturally based misunderstandings between groups come about.

The School Community

In policy terms, schools are interesting centers of public decision making in the United States because much of their funding is provided from a local tax base and considerable authority is maintained at the local level, usually through an elected board of education. Schools also exhibit a strong tradition of public participation, through parent advisory committees and local parent and teacher associations. At the same time, the federal government has had a considerable impact on local schools, especially through funding allocated to education programs for minorities and other special education needs. With such a considerable array of input into local school decision-making processes, the possibilities for conflict and misunderstanding should be obvious. It is little wonder that applied anthropologists have found more than enough to occupy their interests.

A major contribution of anthropology to the solution of problems in education has been to demonstrate the extent to which educational policies are often based on inadequate or erroneous information concerning the school community. John Ogbu's (1974) study of a California elementary school demonstrates how the assumptions educators make about student backgrounds often go unchallenged and untested. Ogbu conducted research in a predominantly nonwhite school. He reports that the school administration and faculty often complained that their efforts to educate were hampered because the students' parents did not encourage them to perform well. Limited achievement in the classroom was often attributed to problems stemming from poverty, the welfare cycle, and the lack of male success models in many of the students' families.

But Ogbu's research revealed a significantly different view of the school community. Although unemployment was common in the area, few of the families were receiving welfare benefits. Male success models were not nearly as rare as the educators had supposed, and most of the parents had a positive attitude toward their children's learning abilities. The parents were, however, suspicious of the educational system (which had few minority teachers), and on the basis of their own life experiences cautioned their children against expecting too much success in a "white man's world."

For their part, the teachers maintained little hope that their students would show progress in school. Their negative attitude, based in part on preconceived ideas concerning their students, contributed to a self-fulfilling prophecy in which, Ogbu suggests, students adapted to the low expectations inadvertently communicated by their teachers.

Ethnic differences in school settings help account for considerable variation in the success of students. This seems to be especially true where there is considerable disparity between the ethnic backgrounds of teachers and students, as was the case in the school Ogbu studied. On the other hand, the recent popularity of ethnicity both as a policy problem in education and as a topic for social research may limit our ability to identify other potential sources of disparity. This proved to be the case, for example, in a school community in Florida. I conducted a preliminary research project in the community as a class project (Chambers et al. 1978). The project was designed to help the teachers at a local elementary school, none of whom lived in the community, develop a better understanding of how their students' participation in a multiethnic locale affected their school performance.

The objectives for our study were established by the teachers and their principal. The teachers defined their problem as one of "cultural compatibility" and set as their goal to "become skillful in the identification of culturally based behaviors that are counterproductive in terms of the students' socialization in the school setting." Discussions with the teachers revealed that the "cultural" behaviors in which they were most interested were closely linked to their perception of ethnic differences and the prevalence of low-income families in the school community.

In attempting to provide the teachers with helpful information, the university students used a variety of research approaches, including observation, community interviews, and basic demographic research. Their work quickly produced several results, some anticipated and some not.

First of all, the teachers were well aware that the community was ethnically mixed, with significant populations of white, Hispanic, and black residents. The "cultural" mix in the community, however, was considerably more subtle and not so well recognized by the teachers. The Hispanic population was further divided into descendants of Spanish families which had immigrated early in the century, more recent Cuban immigrants, and even more recent and transient Mexican migrant workers. Social and cultural differences among the Hispanic residents accounted for significant conflict within the community.

The student researchers also gathered enough information to suggest that many conflicts in the community might have less to do with ethnic differences than with differences in the degree of permanence of community residents. The community had a highly visible minority of transient residents (especially visible because the two trailer parks where most of the transient families lived were located adjacent to the school). But the teachers had underestimated the community influence of the vast majority of the residents who, although they had low incomes, were long-standing members of the community. Surprisingly, the rate of home ownership in this area was significantly higher than the median rate for the city as a whole. Although low in market value, the homes were well maintained.

In effect, the university students found a much more stable community than the teachers had described to them. Where community conflicts did exist, it was along lines the teachers had not anticipated (within the Hispanic community and between settled and transient residents). In their report, the students pointed out that the teachers' study objectives were phrased in negative terms. It was recommended that the teachers consider the positive characteristics of the community in which they worked, and discuss among themselves how a better understanding of these characteristics might help them improve their teaching.

Both this study and Ogbu's research point out how people who live and work in close proximity often understand very little about even the most basic conditions of each others' lives. Lacking this information, they often rely on stereotypes and "common sense" assessments of the others' basic living conditions. These stereotypes in turn make it all the more difficult for people to accept information which might contribute to a better understanding.

We also realize from these examples how important it is that applied anthropologists understand the ways in which different groups perceive each other, rather than simply describing one group to another. In the study I worked on with the students, we considered the teachers to be our "clients." Our major task was to provide the teachers with information about the community in which they worked. But before we could do that we had to learn how the teachers felt about the community, and what they thought were important things to know. Our clients, then, were also a part of our research.

Education and Modernization

Public education is often regarded as an important step toward modernization for lesser-developed nations. Since many of these nations have large populations of ethnic and social minorities, their problems in public education are multiplied by differences in language, custom, and values, as well as by differential access to educational resources.

Societies vary both in the amount of attention they give to public education and in their goals for educating their citizens. Edna Mitchell (1973) has contrasted educational planning in Nepal with that of its neighbor, the People's Republic of China. Both countries have adopted education plans which emphasize the relationship between public education and national development. Both plans are comprehensive and ambitious. The Nepalese plan, however, emphasizes a continuity with traditional belief systems, while the Chinese program represents a break with tradition:

> The government of Nepal has chosen to use the already established educational system as its base for reform and in that choice has demonstrated the verification of belief in the value of ideas and respect for tradition. Meanwhile, Nepal's neighbor to the north, the People's Republic of China, has chosen a very different model of educational reform which emphasizes the development of basic practical skills at the primary level rather than attempting to teach ideas and concepts as well as (and, in fact earlier than) vocational technical skills. (1976:170)

Even more significant from the perspective of planned change is the degree to which different segments of a society maintain different views and goals related to education. In her study of a predominantly Indian community in the Chiapas highlands of Mexico, Nancy Modiano (1973) identified three distinct models for education.

The *ladinos* in the community (*ladino* is a term describing Spanish-speaking persons of mixed Indian and European parentage) viewed formal schooling as a necessary step to success in later life. *Ladino* parents tended not to challenge the system of teaching offered in the schools.

Indian parents, on the other hand, were more ambivalent about formal schooling. Traditionally, Indian children learned by associating with adults in a work-related environment. Education was incorporated in practical tasks and children were encouraged to explore their environment with much less supervision than is found in the disciplined regime of formal schools. Indian parents viewed some aspects of formal schooling, such as instruction in Spanish, as necessary for "self-defense" in a world dominated by *ladinos*. But they remained suspicious of other parts of the school curriculum, as Modiano explains:

> Nothing else that the school may teach is seen as particularly helpful, although it is nice to know about the larger world. Balanced against the desirability of limited literacy and a knowledge of Spanish are strong feelings against the mixing of boys and girls in the same classroom, sending girls to work with nonrelated male teachers, and the absenting of all children from their household chores. Many a parent has said, in effect, "As long as I keep my child in school he can't learn what is really important." (1973:38)

The third model for education in the community Modiano studied is provided by the teachers, many of whom came from outside the community. The teachers viewed themselves as change agents, with a deliberate goal of "Mexicanizing" the children; education was seen by the teachers as encompassing instruction in national patriotism and culture as well as in basic skills.

Conflict in the community's educational system is viewed by Modiano as the result of an inability to fully reconcile the three different models and the social and cultural values which support each. Another anthropologist, John Kelley (1977), has argued that Modiano does not adequately account for structural differences in the community:

> The principal difficulty with Modiano's analysis is that it views social behavior as an outcome of customs or cultural values, rather than the outcome of a system of allocation of time and resources . . . Indians introduce their children to tasks that are "an intrinsic part of the family's activities" not because this is a cherished value in their style of education but because child labor is an important aspect of the family resource allocation. The child does important tasks because he has an important role in the household economy and not merely because Indians think this is how children learn . . . (1977:219)

Kelley's remarks are similar to those of the critics of the *culture of poverty* concept, although Modiano's claims are certainly not as global or ambitious as Oscar Lewis' were. In attempting to explain why people sometimes resist change, interpretations based on a value emphasis and those based on a structural analysis of society continue to vie for our attention.

Whatever interpretation we favor, it is clear that teachers working in situations such as Modiano describes are almost always called on to do more than teach basic skills. Several other applied anthropologists have examined the role of teachers as primary change agents. Harry Wolcott (1967) worked as a teacher and ethnographer in an isolated Indian village in British Columbia, Canada. His dual role as both an agent and student of change helped lead him to a particular perspective:

> A breakthrough in my own thinking about formal education at Blackfish Village came about in the metamorphosis of my original research orientation. I had proposed to investigate what it is about village life that makes Indian pupils so refractive to formal education and why Indian pupils fail in school. As I observed and participated in village life and in the classroom, I realized that posing the query in such terms narrowed the perspective of the search. There is another question to ask, one which can be considered an alternative but which is, I think, better regarded as a complement to my original orientation: How do the schools fail their Indian pupils? (1967:31)

The way in which an applied problem is formulated is crucial. The phrasing of a problem does not necessarily determine what sorts of research findings or decision-making results one arrives at, but it certainly does narrow the possible range of explanations and solutions.

Anthropology and Teaching

Anthropologists have long argued that anthropology is a valuable part of a general social science and liberal arts program. Teaching is actually a major applied activity, particularly when efforts to teach anthropology are directed to persons who are not likely to become professional anthropologists. The perspectives and methods of anthropology have wide applicability for laypersons.

In the United States, anthropology is well established as a part of the university curriculum and has begun to make significant inroads on community college campuses. As we have already noted, anthropologists have also played important roles in teaching in professional schools of medicine, nursing, law, education, and planning. During the past several years, there have also been a number of efforts to introduce anthropology in elementary and secondary schools. Many of these, such as the *Man: A Course of Study* (MACOS) project, have included the development of a wide variety of curriculum materials which can be used by social studies teachers (Joyce 1971).

While the curriculum projects have sought to develop an appreciation of the anthropological perspective at an early age (offering, for example, extensive material related to human biology and cultural variation), other projects have sought to utilize ethnographic methods in helping students better understand their immediate social surroundings. As a graduate student, Larry Goodwin (1979) worked with an elementary school in developing a curriculum for local folklore study. Goodwin's model was similar to that of the well-known Foxfire Project, which utilizes secondary school students as primary investigators in major efforts to record and preserve Appalachian folkways. A major purpose of these projects is to increase the level of communication between students, teachers, and the community.

Suzanne Spina (1980), a high school teacher with training in anthropology, used similar techniques in an urban high school. Her students were encouraged to use an observational approach to study their own youth culture. Their efforts were successful enough to merit the publication of a regularly appearing magazine.

Other projects have been designed to offer anthropological training to school teachers, with the expectation that what they learn will prepare them to deal with the cultural diversity they encounter in the classroom. This was a major goal of the Claremont project (Landes (1965), which provided culture-specific training for school teachers in California:

> The Claremont project . . . stressed comparative study of the family in different cultures; study of schooling, health care, and other institutionalized activities in diverse culture settings; study of teaching and learning generally in different cultures among native born and among immigrants; and study of relationships among race, culture, and language. Educators were led to postpone asking *why* a behavior occurs until after they could answer operational questions of *how, when, where,* and through *whom* the behavior occurs, and toward *what* ends. This is because when asked initially, *why* often begs issues with stereotypes. (1965:287)

The Claremont project was also adapted for use in a training program for social workers. Activities like these are important because they go beyond simply trying to teach others what anthropologists have learned. As Landes' comments suggest, the Claremont project also encouraged teachers to *think* like anthropologists. By altering the sequence of questioning by which people ordinarily attempt to explain values and behavior which appear foreign to them, the training program was attempting the use of an interpretative, ethnographic mode of inquiry in the resolution of practical problems associated with everyday decision making.

Other Interests in Anthropology and Education

Applied anthropologists have worked with educators and education researchers in a number of other areas in response to policy-related and practical problems in schooling. Ethnographic research has, for example, added to our understanding of school desegregation processes in the

United States. In reviewing several recent studies of this kind, Dorothy Clement (1978) suggests that observation research contributes in at least two ways to our understanding of school desegregation. First, comparative case studies have demonstrated that school desegregation is not a "monolithic process," but rather is subject to considerable regional variation. Second, ethnographic study yields important information concerning informal processes of segregation that persist even after schools are legally and structurally integrated.

Applied anthropologists have also contributed to curriculum development projects, most particularly to those related to problems in bilingual education. A major effort in this regard has been the work of the Cross-Cultural Resource Center, established during the late 1970s at California State University (van Willigen 1980). The center involved a number of anthropologists in a bilingual education training program for teachers and parents.

Anthropologists have been involved in major education policy research projects. A good example is the federally funded experiment "Project Rural," which was designed to test the effect of large-scale federal funding on educational programs in the rural United States. Again, one of the most salient points to emerge from this research, which involved extended fieldwork in 10 sites across the United States, is the degree to which each rural community varied in its response to a federal program (Kane 1976).

Another recent large-scale experimental program which employed anthropologists as fieldworkers on several sites was the Documentation and Technical Assistance in Urban Schools Project. A major goal of this work was to utilize comparative field data in a computerized program which would provide education decision makers with information about how similar administrative and educational problems had been resolved in a variety of regional contexts (Center for New Schools 1977).

As in other areas of specialization, anthropologists and others with anthropological training have found their skills to be applicable to a variety of settings other than those of university teaching and basic research. The experimental programs described above hired anthropologists as full-time researchers for extended periods of time, in some cases up to three years at a single site. Anthropology has contributed to education in this country in several other ways. For example, increasing numbers of persons with training in anthropology are working as public school teachers. So far few attempts have been made to communicate these varied interests in a mutually beneficial way, as has occurred in the area of nursing. One exception is the Bay Area Teachers of Anthropology (BATA) association, established in California in 1971. Originally founded by community college teachers, the group soon attracted a number of teachers who taught anthropology in the public schools. One of BATA's first activities was to establish a series of workshops in anthropology for teachers who felt the need to improve or refresh their understanding of the discipline (Mattson and Abshire-Walker 1976).

ADDITIONAL AREAS OF SPECIALIZATION

Applied anthropologists have been involved in numerous other areas of special interest, although those discussed above represent the most highly organized and constitute the bulk of the work currently being done. Potentially any area of human endeavor or policy interest would profit from anthropological input.

Business and Industry

It is unfortunate that applied anthropologists have so seldom chosen to work with private companies and industries. One explanation is the profession has been biased against such activity on the basis of a highly prejudiced ethical stance which associates commercial success and profit-taking with a lack of concern for human welfare. From this extreme position, *all* business and capitalistic enterprise is viewed as part of an oppressive system of exploitation and elitism. One simply cannot be in business or industry and be on the side of what is fair and good.

The limitations of this view are obvious. This is not the place to argue for or against the strengths and limits of capitalist enterprise. But participants in all modern societies (including university professors and students) are vitally dependent on complex economic systems, and we do not escape our dependency on the trappings of modern capitalism simply by trying to ignore them. Economic systems are continually transforming, for better or worse. Whatever transformations occur in any given era are primarily in the hands of those who take an active part and have a sophisticated understanding of the system.

We do not have to look far to find abuses of the "public good" in any area of human endeavor, including business and industry. But no *essential* incompatibility exists between industry and human welfare, or between business and equity. Ironically, it is areas of application such as these, that many anthropologists have seemed so anxious to avoid, which might profit most from their association.

Given the relative lack of involvement of applied anthropologists in business and industry, it is interesting to note that one of the first major applied projects in the United States involving anthropologists on a significant scale was a management and labor relations study conducted during the 1930s as a joint project between the Harvard School of Business and the Chicago Western Electric Company. The Bank Wiring Room study, which was a part of the larger Western Electric project, made extensive use of participant observation methodology and contributed heavily to the development of interaction analysis as an approach to human relations and organization research (Chapple and Arensberg 1940).

It is possible that the further involvement of applied anthropology in business and industry has been hampered in part by trends in organizational behavior research. William F. Whyte (1978) has suggested, for example, that early social science investigators (including anthropologists) might have gone overboard in their search for informal patterns of human organization. While stressing the importance of understanding the motivations of workers, these researchers have focused their attention on nonmaterial rewards and incentives and practically ignored the motivation of money. Similar trends have occurred in studying patterns of organizational leadership, as Whyte explains:

> While early researches in the field were examining the limitations of formal authority, social psychologists sought to discover patterns of more "democratic leadership." Many hoped to discover that "democratic leadership," when skillfully practiced, was not only superior from a humanistic standpoint but also led to greater productivity. Early studies along this line . . . did indeed seem to show this pattern, but later research . . . brought out such discrepant findings as to discredit the comforting view that democratic leadership or "participant management," as it was also called, necessarily resulted in greater productivity than more traditional styles of leadership. This produced a period of confusion and frustration, while the researchers searched for new hypotheses and new strategies of research. (1978:132)

Whyte's remarks are important because they point to how researchers are subject to trends and paradigmatic shifts in their work, and also because of his criticism of the study of informal social mechanisms. He argues that the social scientists' insistence upon studying informal patterns of organization to the exclusion of formal patterns resulted in a threat to their credibility and a sort of counterrevolution on the side of studying formal mechanisms of control. One of the most important contributions of anthropology to applied research has been to demonstrate the presence and significance of informal patterns of human behavior, especially as they persist within (and often despite) highly structured, formal styles of organization. At the same time, the formal rules and patterns of organizational and bureaucratic structure do play an important role in defining a social situation, in helping determine how people communicate with each other, and in influencing the success or failure of particular projects. Effective practice (either as a researcher or a manager) clearly requires an ability to understand the dynamic interaction between formal and informal patterns of value and behavior.

Anthropologists never completely abandoned their earlier interests in business and industry. Some, like Eliot Chapple (Chapple and Sayles 1961), have devoted most of their careers to the practical study of organizations and management. Others, such as Harland Padfield (Padfield and Martin 1965), have concerned themselves with labor-management problems in agricultural industries. Interest in work of this nature has seen a resurgence and a number of anthropologists are now directly employed in the private sector or with management research firms.

Cultural Resource Management

A rapid growth in the area of cultural resources management over the past decade is the direct result of federal and state policy and regulation for the conservation and preservation of prehistoric and historic resources in the United States. While the field has been dominated by archeologists and historians, cultural anthropologists have played increasingly large roles as new definitions arise of what a "cultural resource" is.

The major impetus to cultural resource management came with the National Environmental Protection Act of 1969, which required federal agencies and other groups using federal monies to assess the impact their work would have on the environment, including historic and "cultural" resources. The definition of what constitutes a cultural resource was not entirely clear in the federal regulations, although archeological material clearly fit in the category from the beginning. Archeology gained early ground in part bacause of intensive lobbying of members of the United States Congress by several archeologists.

The National Environmental Protection Act was not the first time the federal government showed an interest in the nation's cultural resources (see, for example, George Quimby's [1979] discussion of archeological research under the depression era's WPA program). However, the new act has required a much more extensive level of activity, radically increasing the number of archeologists who work as full-time cultural resource managers and researchers.

Some anthropologists have argued that cultural anthropology should play a much larger role in resource management. Richard Lerner (1980), a cultural anthropologist employed as a cultural resource manager with the Corps of Engineers, has identified 20 broad categories of cultural resources, including social organization, linguistic features, oral history, arts and crafts, music and dance, diet, and styles of dress. Supporting legislation for the NEPA is provided by the National Historic Preservation Act of 1966, which states more clearly a principle of cultural resource management that includes the preservation of intangible as well as material aspects of culture.

The definition of a *cultural resource* is difficult. Even more problematic is assessing the *value* of particular resources when decisions have to be made as to what ought to receive high or low priority for preservation in the face of planned transformations of the environment. For the archeologist, this process is relatively easy. Archeological sites which might be threatened by new highway construction can generally be rated as to their scientific and public value. This information helps, for example, in making decisions as to the final route of highway construction, what archeological resources should be left in the ground or taken out, and so on. But imagine the problems faced by the cultural anthropologist in a similar situation. First of all, there is no common agreement regarding the value of such intangibles as unique forms of social organization and linguistic expression. Second, it is not usually obvious what will happen to an indigenous craft or trait when the bulldozers arrive. In a sense, cultural resources that are invested in living peoples are far more fragile than centuries-old material artifacts. They cannot, as a last resort, be packed up and shipped to a museum.

Interests similar to those found in cultural resources management are apparent in work in applied folklore. During the 1980s, the American Folklore Society established a section devoted to applied folklore. Many of its first members were individuals who worked with state and local folklore programs. These individuals have been active in developing educational programs related to the preservation of regional cultural resources, as well as in working with state govenments in the development of projects which encourage tourism while promoting strong regional identities.

The interests of cultural resource management closely parallel and often coincide with those of social and cultural impact assessment. We will return to these concerns in Chapter 6, where we will consider the methodology of impact assessment in greater detail.

Applied Linguistics

In some respects, anthropological linguistics should be considered among the most successful uses of the profession. It is also an area where the problems of application have contributed directly to progress in the discipline. Much of the early methodology for linguistic transcription and for the study of unwritten languages was established by missionaries in the process of translating the Christian Bible. Missionary linguists continue to play a prominent role in the study of the world's languages.

In quite a different vein, anthropological linguists applied their skills to improving language instruction as a part of their contribution to the United States' World War II effort (Cowan 1979). This work included the preparation of dozens of "spoken" language courses for military personnel.

Applied interests in linguistics (which include—but are not limited to—the concerns of anthropologists) is represented by a Society for Applied Linguistics. Much of the current work is devoted to research and practice in bilingual education, although other interests have included work in deaf education, communication in work settings, and language instruction for non-English speakers. *Language planning* is described by Carol Eastman (1983) as an interdisciplinary field which encompasses public decisions concerning language use in particular speech communities. Eastman points out that language problems are not confined to school settings, but extend to a wide range of cultural and political situations. The revival of languages, for example, is often linked to political ends. A better understanding of the roots of language controversies contributes to more effective intercultural planning. Anthropological linguistics has also contributed to the growing field of intercultural training (Samovar and Porter 1982. Programs of intercultural training have been developed to serve many different needs—to train government workers and businessmen for work in other countries, to increase public understanding of cultural differences, and to equip teachers to work in multicultural settings.

Other Areas of Special Interest

The areas of interest described in this and the previous chapter represent those in which there has been some significant effort on the part of practitioners to define their specialization. It would require a better crystal ball than mine to predict what additional areas of special interest will be noteworthy in coming decades. We can be fairly certain, however, that they will be defined by parameters of broad public interest and concern, and will often be set in motion by the mandate of government bodies and private interests. Which of the coming opportunities anthropologists seize will depend partly on their abilities to envision their own futures, and partly on their talents in communicating their worth to nonanthropologists. At the same time, the areas of interest described here are not likely to wane. In many of these areas, applied anthropologists have only begun to establish themselves. The future will most likely see even greater participation in most or all of these areas of vital public policy concern.

PERSPECTIVE

We have seen that the special topical interests of applied anthropology relate to some of the traditional concerns of the discipline as well as to public perceptions of need. The last two chapters also provided some insight into the important relationships between independent and collaborative inquiry. We have observed how applied anthropologists can adopt strikingly different roles in response to a particular human problem and yet retain a sense of common purpose.

In preparing this survey of major special interests in applied anthropology, I have chosen not to minimize the conflicts and disagreements that may occur between anthropologists as they consider various cultural processes. Rather, I have tried to show that the way an applied anthropologist chooses to look at culture will have a profound effect on the recommendations he or she makes. Other anthropologists might disagree with me. I believe anthropologists have a good deal more "choice" in these matters than has generally been recognized. Anthropologists behave and think much as other people do, and they are in perpetual danger of reifying their genuine and often very specific insights to the point that they are no longer useful and may actually contribute to serious misunderstandings. It is thus with all systems of knowledge. There is no need to be discouraged, but there certainly is cause to be vigilant.

RECOMMENDED READINGS

Urban Anthropology

There are a number of recent texts and readers in urban anthropology, although few that deal explicitly with applied concerns. Aidan Southall's *Urban Anthropology* (Oxford, 1973) is a good source for urbanization studies and contains an extensive bibliography by Peter Gutkind. Interested readers should also refer to William Mangin's *Peasants in Cities* (Houghton Mifflin, 1970). Edwin Eames and Judith Goode's *Anthropology of the City* (Prentice-Hall, 1977) and Richard Basham's *Urban Anthropology* (Mayfield, 1978) include discussions of urban poverty. Recent readers are Irwin Press and M. Estellie Smith's *Urban Places and Processes* (MacMillan, 1980); George Gmelch and Walter Zenner's *Urban Life* (St. Martin's, 1980); and Thomas Weaver and Douglas White's *The Anthropology of Urban Environments* (Society for Applied Anthropology, 1972).

There are a number of interdisciplinary readers which include substantial contributions by anthropologists. These include Sylvia Fleis Fava's *Urbanism in World Perspective* (Crowell, 1968); Charles Tilly's *An Urban World* (Little, Brown, 1974); Gerald Breese's *The City in Newly Developing Countries* (Prentice-Hall, 1969); and Paul Meadows and Ephraim Mizruchi's *Urbanism, Urbanization, and Change* (Addison-Wesley, 1969). J. John Palen's *The Urban World* (McGraw Hill, 1975) offers a particularly good discussion of urban planning issues and research.

Advocacy perspectives related to urban planning can be found in Robert Goodman's *After the Planners* (Simon & Schuster, 1971) and Richard Sennett's *The Uses of Disorder* (Knopf, 1970). Jane Jacob's *The Death and Life of Great American Cities* (Vintage, 1961) is a classic in this area.

Robert Wulff offers an excellent review of "Anthropology in the Urban Planning Process" (in *Do Applied Anthropologists Apply Anthropology?*, Southern Anthropological Society, 1976). Richard Llewelyn-Davies discusses "The Role of the Social Sciences in Architecture and Planning" (in *Anthropology and Society*, Anthropological Society of Washington, 1975).

Amos Rapoport is editor of *The Mutual Interaction of People and the Built Environment* (Aldine, 1978). Constance Perin's *Everything in Its Place* (Princeton, 1977) is a largely theoretical discussion of United States land-use policies. Perin's *With Man in Mind* (MIT, 1970) is an earlier discussion of social science contributions to problems in environmental design. Other readers dealing with behavioral responses to the urban setting from an interdisciplinary perspective include Gwen Bell and Jacqueline Tyrwitt's *Human Identity in the Urban Environment* (Penguin, 1972); Stephen and Rachel Kaplan's *Humanscape* (Duxbury, 1978); and John Gabree's *Surviving the City* (Ballantine, 1973).

A large-scale, government-sponsored urbanization project in Mexico is reported on by Frank C. Miller in *Old Villages and a New Town: Industrialization in Mexico* (Cummings, 1973). Other aspects of the Ciudad Guayana project in Venezuela, in which Lisa Peattie was involved, are reported in Noel F. McGinn and Russell G. Davis' *Industrialization, Urbanization, and Education in Ciudad Guayana, Venezuela* (MIT, 1969). Readers might also refer to Morton Klass' *From Field to Factory* (Institute for the Study of Human Issues, 1978), a study of adaptation to industrialization in West Bengal.

Additional discussions of Oscar Lewis' concept of the *culture of poverty* can be found in Eleanor Burke Leacock's edited volume *The Culture of Poverty: A Critique* (Simon & Schuster, 1971). David Caplovitz's *The Poor Pay More* (Free Press, 1967) is a popular book on the economic exploitation of poor people. Stanley Lebergott's *Wealth and Want* (Princeton, 1975) is a challenging conservative critique of United States public policy related to the poor.

Fay Cohen describes her advocacy work with an urban branch of the American Indian Movement in "The American Indian Movement and the Anthropologist" (in *Ethics and Anthropology*, Wiley, 1976). Stephen Schensul has written of his involvement in a Chicago action research project in "Skills Needed in Action Anthropology: Lessons from El Centro de la Causa" (*Human Organization*, 33:203–209, 1974). An earlier Chicago-based action project is described in Sol Tax's "Residential Integration: The Case of Hyde Park in Chicago" (*Human Organization*, 18:22–27, 1959).

Journals focusing on urban study include *Urban Anthropology, Urban Life, The Urban Affairs Quarterly*, and *The Urban Interest: A Journal of Policy and Administration*. The Society for Urban Anthropology publishes a newsletter and occasionally sponsors seminars devoted to applied urban anthropology.

Education

Classic contributions in the field of anthropology and education include Solon Kimball's *Culture and the Educative Process* (Teachers College, 1974); George D. Spindler's edited volumes *Education and Anthropology*

(Stanford, 1955) and *Education and Culture* (Holt, Rinehart & Winston, 1963); and Murray L. Wax, Stanley Diamond, and Fred O. Gearing's *Anthropological Perspectives* (Basic Books, 1971), which includes a good cross-cultural bibliography of the area by Harry M. Lindquist.

Other general materials include Judith Friedman Hansen's overview *Sociocultural Perspectives on Human Learning* (Prentice-Hall, 1979) and a number of edited volumes, including Frederick Gearing and Lucinda San-gree's *Toward a Cultural Theory of Education and Schooling* (Mouton, 1979); Craig J. Calhoun and Francis A. J. Ianni's *The Anthropological Study of Education* (Mouton, 1976); Joan I. Roberts and Sherrie K. Akinsanya's *Schooling in the Cultural Contest* (D. McKay, 1976) and *Educational Patterns and Cultural Configurations* (D. McKay, 1976); and John H. Chilcott, Norman C. Greenberg, and Herbert B. Wilson's *Readings in the Socio-Cultural Foundations of Education* (Wadsworth, 1968).

There have been a great number of basic research studies of interest to applied anthropologists working in education settings. Focusing on the roles of various actors in school systems are Thomas A. Leemon's *The Rites of Passage in a Student Culture* (Teachers College, 1972); Elizabeth M. Eddy's *Becoming a Teacher* (Teachers College, 1969); and Harry F. Wolcott's *The Man in the Principal's Office* (Holt, Rinehart & Winston, 1973).

A focus on local school decision making is provided in Ray Barnhardt, John H. Chilcott, and Harry F. Wolcott's *Anthropology and Educational Administration* (Impresora Sahuaro, 1979); Wolcott's *Teachers vs. Technocrats* (Center for Educational Policy & Management, Oregon, 1977); and Charles A. Clinton's *Local Success and Federal Failure* (Abt Books, 1979).

There has been an impressive literature developing in the field of "the ethnography of communication," much of which is relevant to schooling. Interested readers can refer to Martha C. Ward's *Them Children: A Study in Language Learning* (Holt, Rinehart & Winston, 1971) and Courtney B. Cazden, Vera P. John, and Dell Hymes' edited *Functions of Language in the Classroom* (Teachers College, 1972).

G. Alexander Moore's *Life Cycles in Atchalán* (Teachers College, 1973) is a study of national education in a Guatemalan community which offers conclusions similar to those of Nancy Modiano.

There are probably no areas of policy concern for United States education that have been studied so extensively by anthropologists than those of ethnic diversity and equality in education. Murray L. Wax, Rosalie H. Wax, and Robert V. Dumont offer an early assessment of *Formal Education in an American Indian Community* (Emory, 1964). Several articles related to pluralism and discrimination in United States schools can be found in Peggy Reeves Sanday's *Anthropology and the Public Interest* (Academic, 1976). John U. Ogbu offers a discussion of *Minority Education and Caste* (Academic, 1978). Ray C. Rist used an ethnographic approach to research his *The Invisible Children: School Integration in American Society* (Harvard, 1978).

Problems in bilingual and multicultural education are discussed in

Florencio Sánchez Camara and Felipe Ayala's edited *Concepts for Communication and Development in Bilingual Bi-Cultural Communities* (Mouton, 1979). Patricia Lee Engle offers a good comparative review of bilingual education programs in "The Language Debate: Education in First or Second Language?" (in *Anthropology and the Public Interest*, Academic, 1976).

Two special issues of the *Anthropology and Education Quarterly* [7(1), 1976 and 8(1), 1977] are devoted to teaching anthropology, and a third [8(2), 1977] includes a discussion of "nonacademic" careers in education for anthropologists.

The Educational Research Inventory Center (ERIC) serves as an exhaustive source of bibliographic information and research reports related to education.

Journals which are of general interest include the *Anthropology and Education Quarterly*, the *Review of Educational Research*, the *Journal of Research and Development in Education*, and the *American Education Research Journal*.

An Anthropology for Teachers Program was established in 1979 by the department of anthropology at George Washington University and the Smithsonian Institution. The program is devoted to the interests of teachers of precollegiate anthropology and publishes a newsletter.

Additional Specializations

Felix Keesing, Bernard J. Siegel, and Blodwen Hammond offer an early appraisal of *Social Anthropology and Industry* (Department of Anthropology, Stanford, 1957). The volume includes an article by Keesing on "Anthropology and Overseas Business Enterprises." A special issue of the *Anthropological Quarterly* [50(1), 1977] is devoted to "Industrial Ethnology" and describes a number of basic research projects in the area. Eliot Chapple contributed a chapter on "Applied Anthropology in Industry" for A. L. Kroeber's *Anthropology Today* (Chicago, 1953).

The classic Western Electric Company project has been described in Fritz Roethlisberger and William Dickson's *Management and the Worker* (Harvard, 1939) and criticized by Henry Landsberger in *Hawthorne Revisited* (Cornell, 1958).

The most current discussion of applications of anthropology to human problems in business and industry are found in Elizabeth Eddy and William Partridge's *Applied Anthropology in America* (Columbia, 1978), which includes relevant individual contributions by Conrad Arensberg, Frederick Richardson, William Foote Whyte, Carol Taylor, and Burleigh Gardner.

Those interested in recent efforts to apply the study of cultural variables to international problems in business and industry might refer to Vern Terpstra's *The Cultural Environment of International Business* (South-Western, 1978) and Gert Hofstede's *Culture's Consequences: International Differences in Work-Related Values* (Sage Publications, Inc. 1980).

Material related to cultural resources management which offers a cultural and social perspective includes Carole Hill and Roy S. Dickens' *Cultural Resources; Planning and Management* (Westview, 1978) and Thomas King, Patricia Hickman and Gary Berg's *Anthropology in Historic Preservation* (Academic Press, New York, 1977). Interested readers might also refer to Thomas King and Margaret M. Lyneis' "Preservation: A Developing Focus of American Archaeology" [*American Anthropologist*, 80, 1978).

Richard Dorson's edited volume *Folklore in the Modern World* (Mouton, 1978) includes several interesting examples of applied folklore.

Issues related to language policy are dealt with in Andrew W. Mirade's edited volume *Bilingualism: Social Issues and Policy Implications* (Southern Anthropological Society, 1983). The Society for Applied Linguistics publishes a newsletter. Many articles related to applied linguistics appear in the missionary work publication *Practical Anthropology*.

5

Fundamentals of Applied Research

"There are three kinds of questions that applied researchers are typically asked to respond to," I tell my students as I begin one part of a course in applied anthropology. "Sometimes they are asked to assess a present situation. What is the actual extent or range of a problem? How many people, for example, are without adequate housing? Or, what kind of people are getting into trouble when they use drugs?

"At other times applied researchers might be asked to take a look at an event from the past. What actually happened when someone tried to change a system? Did a new nutrition program convince a significant number of people to alter their diets? Were there any unintended consequences to a new transportation regulation?

"Sometimes applied researchers are asked to determine what might happen in the future, given the deliberate introduction of some stimulus for change. This is the most difficult question of all. What will be the impacts of building a highway through a previously isolated region? How will the people living in that region respond to any attempt to alter their landscape? How will the quality of those people's lives be affected?"

At this point, in one of my lectures, a student raised his hand.

"What if anthropologists can't find out the answer to any of these questions?" he asked.

"If they want to be helpful," I said, "they'll be honest. Remember, answers are nice if you have them, but they are not an absolute prerequisite to decision making, or even to good decision making. It is better to admit that you don't know everything and be willing to enter into a dialogue on the basis of the information you have than to pretend as though you know what you don't."

Another student raised her hand. "That's fine in principle," she said, "but aren't you being paid to get answers?"

"Yes, of course," I said, "But in my experience decision makers usually look at all of this differently than researchers do. A lot of times I think they hire researchers simply to help them explore an issue, to give them another twist on something they've been thinking about. Researchers are usually trained to think about issues from another perspective. There has to be a big ANSWER. The researcher's view is usually expressed in terms of answers, even though it is acknowledged that there are no final answers. You see, it really is a different way of looking at things, but there is an interesting parallel. For a decision maker, there has to be a big DECISION, and there will always be another decision somewhere down the line."

The second student persisted. "But don't decision makers expect answers from researchers? Why else would they hire them?"

"Sure they do," I said. "And some decision makers are more savvy than others. Some expect very clear, straightforward answers, and that's it. But what I'm trying to say is that, in my experience, most people who make decisions for a living know better than that. They value research because it can help shape their thinking. It can provide answers sometimes, and partial answers other times, and sometimes no clear answers at all but a lot of useful information. The trick for an applied researcher is to let that person know what you do know, not what you wish you knew or think you ought to know."

A third student raised her hand. "I think there's more to it than that," she said. "If you give the wrong answer, you might lose your job. And if decision makers rely on your wrong answers, they might lose their jobs. And aren't you forgetting the people you're studying? If you're wrong, that might really hurt a lot of people. Isn't that a good reason for being as careful as you can and not flying off the handle just because you think you have to answer some question?"

"Then why try to answer anything?" another student chimed in.

"Because a decision is going to be made whether you're involved or not," the third student said. "Maybe you can give an answer, but even if you can't, at least you're going to leave those decision makers with more to consider than they had before."

Applied anthropology encompasses several strategies (basic and applied research among them) for responding to human problems. This distinction between applied and basic research approaches, which we first considered in the first chapter of this book, is seldom made so sharply as will be advocated in the next two chapters. The distinction has to do not only with how anthropologists respond to the questions they are given, but also with how people ask questions. It should be clear from the following discussion that no single mode of inquiry is fully responsive to the myriad ways we have of using knowledge to make decisions.

DIFFERENCES BETWEEN BASIC AND APPLIED RESEARCH

In order to understand the differences between basic and applied research, we need to look beyond the usual terms that are often offered as justifications of one or another of these approaches. Applied anthropologists sometimes describe their work as "practical" and "relevant," in contrast to the "unrealistic," "impractical," and "ivory tower" activities of their colleagues. In turn, anthropologists not involved in applied work sometimes characterize applied anthropologists as "opportunistic," confused in their methodology, lacking in theoretical perspective, and overly subjective in their commitment to "saving the world." These persons often label their own work as "pure" and "rigorous" in its methods and intentions, and as offering the only reasonable route to furthering our knowledge of the human condition.

We can easily see that these sloppy criteria are more the result of short-sighted professional in-fighting than of any significant differences in scope of work. The negative characteristics associated with either side of the argument are largely characteristics of *poor* anthropology, regardless of where they are found. Conversely, the positive characteristics claimed by either side can be associated with *good* anthropology.

A more fundamental (and more useful) distinction between the aims of basic and applied research lies in differences between applied (collaborative) and basic (independent) inquiry. To appreciate this distinction, we need to consider how the problems appropriate to either of these modes of inquiry are typically derived. Before we do this, one important point should be recalled. In the past, the terms *applied research* and *applied anthropology* have been treated by the profession as though they were virtually synonymous. But in the following discussion, applied *research* will be described as a particular type of inquiry which can be contrasted with basic research. Applied *anthropology*, on the other hand, encompasses *both* applied and basic research strategies in so far as either has a direct bearing on problems of decision making.

The objective of independent inquiry in the social sciences is to test and refine theoretical statements related to human behavior. These statements are presumably "value free," and although we generally recognize that an investigator's values and cultural conventions invariably help shape the direction of any kind of inquiry, the goal of maintaining a reasonable distance from a particular value orientation is essential to the conduct of basic science. This is what hypothesis testing in basic science is all about—an investigator does not simply set out to prove that his or her original assumption was correct, but also to explore the possibility that it might be fundamentally wrong. The aim of basic social science research is to challenge the assumptions that underlie behavior through systematic inquiry into the conditions and premises of human existence.

Applied research, on the other hand, does not generally derive from a theoretical base, but rather from those *assumptions and perceptions of need* which have been identified as having policy significance. These perceptions of need may be influenced by social science theory, but they are not dependent upon it and are typically also influenced by ideologies, political and commercial intent, hunches, and raw guesses. In these cases, the assumptions underlying a course of action are often taken for granted, and the goal of collaborative inquiry is generally to help decision makers select from alternative strategies for implementation and to measure the effects of their choices. It is important to keep this in mind—that the major objective of applied research is *not* to challenge most of the basic assumptions which underlie a policy stance, but to help figure out how to translate ideas into action and to then determine the impact of those actions on the real world. Rather than trying to prove whether basic assumptions are right or wrong, the applied researcher is generally concerned only with their operational validity—that is, with whether an expected outcome follows from a given event, even though the actual relationship between an event and its outcome may not be scientifically known.

In this sense (but only in this sense) applied research does not strive to be value free. From any of several points of departure, collaborative inquiry aims strictly to describe the results and implications of following an agreed-upon course of action. The assumptions underlying such actions are almost invariably determined on the basis of societal values. A bolder way of making this point is to suggest that collaborative inquiry is necessarily shaped and constrained by the public values and policy intentions from which it evolves. The objective of applied research is not to establish that a given value is appropriate or that a particular intention is right (that is, correctly following the premises from which it is derived), but to establish what is likely to happen or what actually happens when a specific course of action is pursued.

This is not to say that applied researchers are unconcerned with problems of objectivity. Though they accept social values (and hunches and guesses) as important premises to their work, and generally do not seek to test these premises according to the normal tenets of basic research, applied researchers join their colleagues in basic research in the struggle to achieve a high standard of observation. They share the more general concerns of scientific inquiry—how can the validity and reliability of a set of findings be assured, and to what extent is any particular discovery influenced or skewed by the peculiarities of either the observer or the observed?

Applied research deals with assumptions and perceptions of need in two ways that are different from the processes of basic research:

1. As we have noted, collaborative inquiry *accepts* assumptions based on social values and untested (or, for practical purposes, untestable) ideas which underlie a policy decision to follow a particular course of action.

2. It generally *cannot* be expected that collaborative inquiry will prove a given result has occurred for the reasons we assume it does. The central goal of applied research is to establish what results did occur, or what is likely to occur in the event of an anticipated action. In other words, applied researchers match *goals* to *outcomes*; they generally do not match *means* to outcomes (although the temptation to assume that they have justified means as well as goals is great on the part of researchers and research clients alike).

A typical applied research problem asks "what" and "who" rather than "why." This is an oversimplification, but it will help us explore the differences between collaborative and independent inquiry. As the following brief examples illustrate, every unresolved human problem leaves us with both "what" and "why" questions:

Example One.   A city council must locate a site for a new public housing project. Five neighborhoods are identified as potential sites. The council's determination of the most appropriate site will be based in part on a consideration of what is likely to happen in each neighborhood if the housing project is located there. Will existing residents object? Will the project have a positive or negative effect on neighborhood business, recreational and educational facilities, or traffic flow? Will the new public housing residents gain or lose important resources as a result of being located in one or another neighborhood? These problems are derived from a sense of anticipation, and they can be addressed with an inquiry based on *what* is likely to occur in each instance. Neighborhood surveys might, for example, help clarify the relative degrees of opposition to be expected in each potential location. Observation of existing traffic patterns and public facility uses should help fill in the picture. An investigator might also try to determine what has happened in similar neighborhoods where public housing projects have already been located.

A number of "why" questions are also associated with this same problem. Why do some neighborhoods object more strenuously than others to the placement of public housing in their communities? Why do potential tenants prefer one neighborhood to another? These are not irrelevant questions, but they do require a different style of inquiry—most importantly, they call for the ability to generalize beyond a specific case and to challenge popular assumptions concerning public housing siting. Consequently, while these are policy-relevant problems, they are best responded to from the premises of basic research.

If the profession of applied anthropology includes both basic and applied research, why is the distinction between the two so important? One reason is that some of the most enduring problems in application develop out of misunderstandings between researchers and research clients—confusion resulting from differences between what a client wants to know and what a researcher wants to find out. Clearly, where such differences exist the possibility of producing knowledge that will be used is just about nil. And why does this problem occur so frequently? For one thing, most social scientists have been trained solely from the perspective of basic research. They tend to think in the terms of independent inquiry and find it difficult to adapt their sense of how research is done to the full range of questions which are likely to concern their clients.

In the above example, the potential value of both collaborative and independent inquiry is clear, as well as the vital relationship between the two. However, deciding which approach (or what combination of the two approaches) is most appropriate for a particular inquiry can only be determined by considering the research client's expectations and resources. Thus, some of the criteria of utility discussed in the next chapter play a vital role in arriving at an appropriate research strategy—effective applied research demands that these criteria assume priority over considerations of what, given ideal conditions, would be the most interesting, richest, or theoretically fruitful approach to inquiry.

Example Two. A manufacturer of motorcycles spends a great deal every year on advertising. The company wants to know which of several advertising campaigns have successfully attracted buyers, and what segments of the population represent the most promising market for future sales. These are "what" and "who" (applied research) questions which might be answered with survey questionnaires and validated through observation, as well as by tracing company sales records. Again, there are also a number of interesting "why" (basic research) questions. Why do the motorcycles appeal more to some ethnic, age, or sex groups than others? Why do some advertisements result in higher sales than others? These can be important things to know, but they are different questions and require a basic research strategy.

This example illustrates how both applied and basic research questions can be derived from decision-making contexts. An advertising campaign is based on a variety of assumptions about what type of sales "pitch" will appeal to the public, as well as on assumptions about what part of the public represents the most likely market for a product. These assumptions may be based on theories of public buying behavior (developed, perhaps, from earlier studies of marketing behavior), but they are just as likely to develop from the advertiser's or the manufacturer's hunches, values, and personal preferences. Where the assumptions come from is not as important in terms of collaborative inquiry as the question of whether they do the job—in this case, sell the product. Finding out the results of an advertising effort does not, strictly speaking, test these assumptions. An advertisement may, for example, appeal to the buying public for reasons other than those assumed by the advertiser. Neither does applied research reveal, except occasionally as broad-based hunches, any new theories upon which further projects might be based. The basic concern of applied research is to demonstrate, as efficiently as possible, whether intended effects do (or are likely to) result from a particular course of action. If there is a connection between this and what a change agent thinks is causing a particular public reaction, that is fine. However, applied research does not rise or fall on the ability to make such connections, but only on its demonstration that a given goal has been (or is likely to be) reached. In other words, applied research demonstrates "what," not "why."

This distinction is also important because research clients are often as confused about the strengths and limits of the research they sponsor as their researchers sometimes are. If the advertiser in this example assumes that a demonstration that people are buying a product because of a particular promotion effort actually means that buyers perceive that effort in the same way as the advertiser does, he or she might be in for a great disappointment the next time around. Thus, it is doubly important that researchers and their clients realize the boundaries of any research effort they undertake.

Example Three. An international development agency has sponsored a number of rural irrigation projects in developing countries. One applied research question would be to determine the overall success of the projects according to clearly specified goals. Are rural farmers making use of the new program? Have the expected increases in productivity and family income occurred? Other important "what" and "who" questions represent further refinements of the research. Are there differences in the success rate of various projects? Who benefits most from irrigation? Does any segment of the population suffer as a result of the innovation?

Again, reasonable and important "why" questions are also associated with this example. Why do the projects result in greater increases in agricultural productivity in some countries than in others? Why, in particular locations, do some classes of people benefit more than others?

With this example we can explore some of the decision options that might derive from applied inquiry directed to the first set of "what" questions. Let us say, for the purposes of illustration, that our assessment of the outcomes of the irrigation projects reveals the following:

1. That the projects are more successful (that is, result in greater productivity) in areas where the principal crop is a fruit or vegetable and are less successful in areas where grain is the principal crop.

2. That in several project sites, benefits from the irrigation projects accrue only to the farmers who, by local standards, were already rather prosperous. Less successful farmers do not appear to benefit and their competitive disadvantage might actually be worsened by the new projects.

In either of these cases, those responsible for the success of the irrigation project might decide that more research of a different kind (independent inquiry) is necessary to answer the "why" questions. On the other hand, different but equally valid decisions can be imagined on the basis of the information that has already been acquired. For example, since the projects seem to work best for fruit and vegetable farmers, a decision maker might decide to concentrate all future efforts of this kind on this particular segment of the agricultural population. An entirely different strategy might be necessary to meet the needs of grain farmers.

The second finding seems a bit more complex and requires more speculation as to the goals of our hypothetical development agency. If a major goal is to encourage unsuccessful farmers to leave agriculture, then the project has demonstrated a degree of success. If, on the other hand, the goal is to narrow the economic gap between the most and least successful farmers, then the results suggested above indicate failure. This assessment might lead to a recognized need for basic research, to an abandonment of the project, or to a modification of the project. (In this case, one such modification might be simply to establish an upper income limit for participation in the project.)

Thus, a variety of decisions might be developed from the results of collaborative inquiry. These could include a decision for basic research into the "whys" of specific project outcomes. But other, equally worthwhile decisions can be made simply on the basis of the applied research—to continue or discontinue the project, to target the project to those conditions which seem most likely to result in the expected outcomes, or to make other such modifications as seem called for.

In reviewing these examples, it is reasonable to ask why we need applied research and its exploration of actual or anticipated outcomes of events, when basic inquiry has the potential to provide us with greater insight into the relationship between events. It is always desirable to know as much as we can about any phenomena on which our well-being depends. But we live in an imperfect and rapidly changing world, and decisions cannot always be shelved until we have a perfect and complete knowledge of a phenomenon. The real world, and our interest in various aspects of it, does not hold still. We have a certain and continual need for means by which we can quickly and accurately assess the directions we have chosen, and applied research is devoted to this end.

We can also question the extent to which a preference for independent inquiry results from the research bias to which most anthropologists are trained. Basic research may be the preferred mode of inquiry for investigators whose major interests lie in making contributions to the theory of their discipline, but it is not always the most appropriate strategy for researchers who seek a direct connection with decision making. People who make decisions have a range of choices as to how they make those decisions. Research is only one choice (and not necessarily the best one). If we look at the second example discussed above, we can see that our hypothetical advertising executives have several choices as to how to proceed with a decision. Basic or applied research could be helpful, depending upon what the advertising executives want to know, how much time they have to figure it out, and how valuable they think that information will be (that is, what they are willing to pay). On the other hand, an advertiser might rely less on research by deciding to test the market with a new product and base a decision on how well it sells in a few stores or a single location. Or, if time is at a premium and money is short, an advertiser might elect to base a decision only upon his or her prior experience with similar products and markets. Each of these represents legitimate choices, depending upon the total context in which the advertiser is operating.

Researchers trying to introduce their skills to decision makers sometimes appear foolish when they lump research and problem solving into the same basket of technique. They expose their inability to discriminate among several approaches to solving problems, and thereby reveal their ignorance of the world in which decision makers operate. This is one of the reasons that applied anthropologists can seldom afford to think of themselves only as researchers.

The fact that collaborative inquiry derives from values and ideology, from perceptions of need as much as from theories of change and behavior, does not mean that it need be unduly influenced by the vested interests of decision makers. The requirements for the conduct of applied research are no less rigorous than those governing basic research. While applied inquiry reflects our basic assumptions more than it challenges them, the knowledge it seeks can be devastating in its simplicity. Does a new plan or program work, or doesn't it? More than any other question, this is the one upon which the careers and reputations of decision makers rest, and from which we all chart the uncertain course of our future.

It is important to keep in mind that, while the profession of applied anthropology is built from the results of both basic and applied research, any particular effort must be judged first in terms of its specific objectives and their appropriateness to a clearly understood decision-making context. A number of anthropologists have attempted to reconcile the differences between applied and basic research by calling for a link or "feedback loop" between the two. In this manner, the data of applied research can contribute to new theoretical insights, and these insights in turn can guide new applied research. There is nothing wrong with this formulation, except that it can be entirely misleading if the "feedback" is taken as the *primary* objective of these two modes of inquiry. The major aim of applied research is *not* to contribute to general social science or anthropological theory. Neither can the questions of applied research be derived solely from a theoretical base. In this sense, collaborative inquiry is not only unique in the way in which its problems are derived, but also in the major ends to which its results are directed.

Collaborative inquiry will always come out a poor second when it is evaluated in terms of its contribution to theory. If, on the other hand, applied research is judged on its own merits and in consideration of its special relationship to decision making, we can see that it fills a need to which basic research cannot respond. Individual applied anthropologists frequently move back and forth between one mode of inquiry and the other throughout their careers. Research clients often require both styles of research at various stages of policy formulation and decision making. The important thing is that we develop a clear sense of when one or another approach is called for, and that we recognize the potentials and pitfalls of both:

> A prospective society, subject and committed to change, requires the means of both challenging the directions of change and of fostering the implementation of change once the basic directional signals have been decided upon. To some extent, these processes of independent and collaborative inquiry must exist independently, and perhaps often antagonistically, if we are to maintain the delicate balance between chance and predictability that a complex society seems to require (Chambers 1981:4)

Basic research is not without its practical value. Many of the studies referred to in other chapters of this book follow a model of basic research and were selected as examples of particularly useful, policy-relevant research. The difference is that, while basic research may help *inform* public policy, applied research helps decision makers *confirm* and choose from among policy and decision alternatives which have, as a general rule, been preselected on the basis of characteristics of a policy problem that are external to the requirements of science.

In this chapter we will consider several fundamental approaches to applied research and policy analysis. Our discussion will extend beyond the specific contributions of applied anthropology. Once again, it is important to recognize that applied social science has developed largely outside the paradigms of anthropology, and that the contributions of applied anthropologists must always be viewed within the larger context of a more general research approach.

THE APPROACHES OF POLICY ANALYSIS

Current policy analysis generally takes one of two points of departure, both of which modify the usual search procedures of scientific investigation by deriving models and research questions on the basis of characteristics that are at least partly outside the rules of basic scientific inquiry. In this vein, Stuart Nagel and Marion Neef (1979) distinguish between applied research which "takes policies as givens and attempts to determine their effects" and applied research which "takes goals as givens and attempts to determine what policies will maximize those goals."

This important distinction can be illustrated with a hypothetical example. Let us say that we are interested in developing a response to the problem of unemployment among minority youth. Using the first approach, we would move very quickly to the program level of policy making—deciding, let us say, that a program which provided federal government subsidies for local youth employment programs would be a reasonable response to the problem. Our analytic effort in this case would be to attempt to measure the effects of the program we had devised.

The second approach focuses on the derivation of a policy. Such an approach would be more likely to identify a range of policy options and test for the optimal policy (Nagel and Neef 1979). In this case, alternatives might include a variety of subsidy programs, different strategies for mobilizing private sector hiring of minority youth, and so on. This model for research tends to be more experimental than the other and, in many respects, more closely follows the tenets of basic scientific research, although problem areas and the range of alternative responses to be tested are still derived from characteristics that are external to the normal procedures of scientific investigation.

The external characteristics that come to bear on applied research are apparent in three distinct dimensions of policy analysis. Policies are judged on the basis of their appropriateness, their cost-effectiveness, and the extent to which they actually respond to the expectations of citizens or consumers. It is important to recognize how these dimensions can be integrated into a research design.

Appropriate Policies

The selection of public policies and of programs for implementation are best preceded by a considerable amount of forethought as to what kinds of policies and programs will be appropriate given the social and cultural settings in which they will be enacted. The differences between an ideal policy position and a realistic, appropriate response to a policy problem can be considerable. The historical, social, and cultural characteristics of a policy setting need to be considered in judging any attempt to change or modify existing approaches to problem solving. To take an extreme example, we might argue that an optimal approach to eliminating child abuse would be to strengthen a local government's authority to remove children from *potentially* as well as actually abusive family environments. But the social and cultural costs of such a policy—judged in terms of a society's tradition of independence from government control, values related to family life, different cultural ideals related to child discipline, and the possibility of error and the abuse of authority on the part of government representatives—are probably too high to justify such a radical approach, even though a "compromise" would almost certainly mean that society must "tolerate" a certain level of child abuse.

Considerations of appropriateness limit applied research to the extent that they limit the range of policy responses which are judged worth exploring. Such considerations also help determine the criteria by which policy responses will be evaluated once they are in place.

One of the problems with determining the appropriateness of policy responses is that it is often done implicitly, by decision makers who presume to "know" the limits under which they are operating. While it is important to recognize that there will always be limits to programs of change, it is equally important to accept the idea that judgments of the appropriateness of a policy response ought to be made on the basis of empirical evidence as well as experience.

Where it has been applied, the anthropological approach has been especially amenable to problems in policy formulation. Qualitative methods of research provide an exploratory technique that is ideally suited to identifying and sifting through subjective and common sense interpretations of a problem. Observational techniques, which require a degree of direct involvement with the "actors" of human situations, are capable of revealing characteristics of a social and cultural environment which should be included in the calculation of the appropriateness of any particular policy option. One of the persistent failures of many change and reform programs has been an inability to anticipate what will happen when an idea leaves the drawing board and begins to have an actual effect on the lives of people.

At the same time, anthropologists need to be sensitive to the idea that the measure of appropriateness which is sought in policy analysis requires attention to more than the likely response of the subjects of a policy. Equally practical measures of appropriateness include considerations not only of the consequences of decision making, but also of the social and cultural *"roles" and determinants* of public decision making—a society's traditions of power brokerage, the ways in which the sponsor of a policy allocates and administers responsibility, and the social and political environment in which decision makers compete for resources and justify their actions.

Costs and Benefits

Public decision making, as well as the applied research which contributes to it, is characterized by *accountability*. Efforts to promote change and instigate reform are limited by the amount of resource a society is willing to allocate to particular areas of policy concern. While there is probably no strict correspondence between how much money and human energy is devoted to a problem and how much progress is actually made, it does seem obvious that solutions to most problems require some tangible investment of a society's resources—the spending of something more substantial than good intentions and avowals of concern.

To a large extent, the allocation of resources in a complex society is a political and administrative event. Decisions as to how resources will be spent precede opportunities to plan and implement specific programmatic responses to areas of policy concern. In government, budgetary considerations play a large role in determining how an agency defines its policy goals, since the intentions and orientation of an agency come under close scrutiny when funds are allocated. Accountability continues throughout the life of a program. Periodic audits are designed to ensure that resources are being spent for the purposes for which they were allocated, and periodic budgetary review is meant to ensure that funded programs and activities are responding to public needs in an efficient and equitable manner. The "language" of budgetary decision making is predominantly economic, and budgetary and economic considerations are paramount in policy decision making. At the same time, the processes of decision making which lead to resource allocation and review are not based solely on economic criteria. Aaron Wildavsky (1974) has demonstrated the extent to which the budgetary considerations of the United States Congress are influenced by an underlying historical and political context and are negotiated in terms of a variety of noneconomic rules and procedures. Social and political alliances, for example, often act to supersede purely economic criteria for decision making.

However they are phrased, problems of resource allocation represent a major characteristic of applied social science research. As a research question, resource allocation is often represented by attempts to measure the relative cost and benefits of alternative approaches to resolving policy problems. The rationale of "cost-benefit analysis" as an analytic technique is quite simple. It represents an attempt to compare the costs of a course of action to the expected benefits of that action. To the extent that both costs and benefits can be accurately measured, these techniques of analysis provide a valuable tool for determining where resources will be allocated (often in terms of "opportunity costs," in which the cost of an activity is compared to the value of the resource if it were "invested" elsewhere), and for selecting from among a variety of alternatives to the solution of a single problem.

As we have already noted, cost-benefit analysis has been criticized because it generally requires that all the costs and benefits of a course of action be expressed in monetary terms in order to arrive at equivalent units for comparison. But how, critics argue, can one express a true monetary value for the many social and cultural costs and benefits which ought to be included in such a calculation? Let us say, for example, that a government agency is considering the adoption of a national health plan. Of the alternative plans they will consider, some will be more comprehensive than others, and they will probably require greater resources. On the other hand, the more comprehensive programs might save more lives, alleviate more suffering, and substantially reduce the personal economic crises that are often associated with major medical expenses. To compare the cost of developing a program with its benefits it becomes necessary to assign a monetary value to such things as human life and well-being. This is obviously a difficult and perilous process.

Another criticism of cost-benefit analysis is that its calculation sometimes ignores qualitative variables which are difficult to quantify. To the extent that analyses of costs and benefits guide public decision making, they also help determine the criteria for deciding what is and what is not a significant variable for comparison. Variables which have an agreed-upon procedure for assigning value often receive inordinate attention. It is easier, for example, to assign a monetary value to the loss of productive farmland than it is to attribute a specific cost to the cultural and psychological effects of rural unemployment. Those measures which are easily "costed out" are likely to assume undue significance in a final equation of costs and benefits.

As serious as these criticisms are, their proponents seldom offer other satisfactory means for arriving at a basis for resource allocation. Cost-benefit analysis is a powerful analytic tool. The problem of assigning a monetary value to measures of human well-being is often exaggerated, since the selection of a dollar unit of comparison is largely for the purpose of quantification. In this usage, dollars have a numerical meaning beyond a strict monetary meaning. No one is claiming, for example, that a human life is actually "worth" n dollars. What is being said is that, for the purposes of comparison, we will agree to *assign* this value to a human life. Otherwise, we cannot make any decision at all, because it is impossible to weigh and consider the merits of inestimable values.

Risk analysis is similar to cost-benefit analysis in that it attempts to measure the benefits of following a particular course of action against specified social and human risks. The major difference is that, while cost-benefit analysis derives primarily from concerns of resource allocation, risk analysis is focused on concerns of public safety. Risk analysis can, for example, be extended to problems in which the costs or benefits to a resource base (such as the federal government) seem negligible. How, for example, might we compare the human risks of various methods of birth control to their benefits as alternative means of effective contraception?

Anthropologists are almost bound to approach cost-benefit analysis and similar analytic techniques with a measure of skepticism. Their critical perspective informs them that any calculation of value is subject to social and cultural variation. Their relativistic view cautions them against an approach which relies so heavily on economic measures of value and attempts to compare seemingly incomparable variables. The lack of familiarity with quantitative techniques that many anthropologists suffer only increases their suspicion.

We might question, however, the extent to which criticisms of these approaches result simply because they make the criteria for decision making more explicit than they are under other conditions. Procedures such as cost-benefit analysis advise us that our search for a "better world" must stand the test of a realistic appraisal of the resources available for improvement. From this perspective, we can reason that one contribution of applied anthropologists and other social scientists should be to help (albeit still critically) in the attempt to arrive at realistic measures of social and cultural cost and benefit.

Public Participation in Decision Making

A third set of external characteristics which influence and help define applied research are those which relate to the participation of the public in policy decision making. Societies differ considerably in the extent and manner in which they encourage their populace to participate in public decision making. Even modernized, complex societies exhibit variation. For example, in many Latin American countries which have highly personalistic forms of government, the principal forms of public participation include demonstrations and the sending of delegations to meet with top government officials. While such activities are not unknown in the United States and Western Europe, other forms of participation, styled partly on the notion of the "town meeting," have been encouraged. Many countries now require by law that the planning of new policies, public programs, and major government expenditures include evidence that the public has had an opportunity to participate in the decisions being made.

Whether they are as effective as they might be, requirements for public participation affect applied social research in a number of ways. In the most obvious manner, applied research is often directed at attempting to discover what people want and how they are likely to react to a proposed innovation. In effect, such research is itself an indication of public participation. Effective citizen input into public decision making also has the potential for adding new, unanticipated aspects to a policy or plan, consequently broadening a research effort in order to address concerns expressed by the public. In some cases, social scientists might be involved in helping resolve critical disputes which have resulted in public resistance to a policy or plan.

Regulations requiring citizen participation in public decision making have led to a variety of techniques and procedures for accomplishing the task. Some of the most useful, research-based approaches will be discussed elsewhere in this chapter. At the same time, it should be noted that many government mandated citizen participation programs have been remarkable failures, or at least severely limited in their effect. Some of the causes of failure are worth exploring:

1. The term *citizen participation* has been applied to a great variety of activities, many of which do not involve actual participation in decision making at all. One popular form of "participation" is the public meeting, which more often than not is an *information* meeting in which the public is informed of the intentions of an agency or organization long after the basic blueprint for an activity has been drawn up.

2. The public meeting as a form of citizen participation often attracts a very partial segment of a populace. Either few people show up for such meetings, or the people who do come represent a particular segment of the public—usually those who feel they have the most to lose if a particular policy or plan is adopted.

3. Often a considerable amount of time expires between public meetings and the actual "start up" of projects. Sometimes several years can pass between these events, and citizens are likely to have forgotten that they had any opportunity to participate (not to mention the possibility that conditions in a community might have changed significantly in a matter of a few years).

4. Policy makers and planners are often uncertain of what they hope to achieve with citizen participation activities. Do they look for consensus, which in most cases can be achieved only by distorting or underrepresenting significant public views? Does citizen participation mean that public policy decisions must be based solely on public opinion, ignoring the fact that some people may be much better informed than others about an issue, and that a majority opinion might actually be wrong?

5. In many citizen participation activities, the public is not privy to the "language" of policy making and planning, a situation which contributes to serious breakdowns in communication. (When, for example, the United States Soil and Water Conservation Service invited the public to respond to a draft of the Service's proposed new regulations, the Service's informational brochure included discussion of a great range of alternative approaches to providing conservation services, including the possibility of offering no services at all. Citing a complete range of alternative actions is helpful to planners, even to the extent of acknowledging alternatives the planners have no intention of taking. In this case, however, the public information provided did not explain why a number of seemingly bizarre alternatives were listed—most of the public responses the Conservation Service received were from irate and worried service clients who thought the Service was seriously considering closing shop.)

These and similar obstacles to effective citizen participation activities alert us to the need for considering citizen input and public decision making from a research perspective. Indications of public opinion concerning a policy or plan should be subject to the same vigorous sampling criteria as basic research activities. Policy makers and applied researchers alike must be able to evaluate public opinion on the basis of the quality of information people have at their disposal. Applied researchers should be especially sensitive to the needs and opinions of segments of a population which are not likely to be vocal in their support or opposition to a new public activity.

At the same time, as important as the relation between research and participation can be, it is always only partial. The public responds to issues at a different level than do social researchers, largely in the context of a variety of self-interests and sometimes on the basis of radically different values. Policy makers and planners recognize that most serious policy questions are not resolved on the basis of consensus but rather, if they are resolved at all, on the basis of detente.

VARIETIES OF APPLIED SOCIAL RESEARCH

Most of the remainder of this chapter is devoted to describing three major varieties of applied social research. While these approaches employ similar research methods and strategies, they are distinguished by the kinds of research questions each is intended to address.

The term *social accounting* is used here to describe a number of procedures designed to periodically measure and assess current conditions related to an area of policy concern. A second variety of applied social research is concerned with *evaluation,* or with determining the extent to which past policies and programs succeed in responding to the goals established for them. A third variety of applied social research is that of *social and cultural forecasting,* which has been developed from strategies designed to predict the outcomes of anticipated policy-related events. In effect, these three varieties of research differ according to their occurrence in various stages of decision making—the first is concerned with current conditions, the second with past endeavors, and the third with future events.

APPROACHES TO SOCIAL ACCOUNTING

Change-oriented societies require the means of recording their progress and anticipating the possibility of setbacks in the achievement of accepted goals. Populous, complex societies impose severe limits on the ability of decision makers to gauge by experience alone whether their decisions have any impact upon an effort to alter the quality of human existence. Programs and policies are often generated on the basis of perceived or imagined needs, custom, and administrative tradition, rather than on the basis of a demonstrated need. When limited resources have to be allocated against the background of a seemingly endless array of public needs, the empirical demonstration of the existence and extent of particular needs becomes a vital concern for effective decision making.

Social accounting procedures seem to multiply as societies increase in complexity. In most modern societies, such research activities derive in large part from earlier attempts to establish reliable indicators of economic change. Indications of per capita income, poverty indexes, the gross national product, and similar measures are convenient markers of economic health. But they respond only partially to the need to provide indications of social well-being. How do we measure the "gross national product" of human happiness? Can we devise indexes of employment discrimination to match those developed to gauge poverty and unemployment? Can there be such a thing as a per capita share of human suffering.?

Social Indicators

The idea underlying the development of reliable indicators of social life is actually very similar to that of economic indicators. In both cases, the objective is to develop and maintain a data base which can be used to compare indexes of social or economic progress on a regional as well as historical basis. The social indicators movement is international and has been applied to national, state, and local levels of policy decision making. In effect, social indicators provide a controlled time series data base for monitoring and assessing changes in social well-being. Importantly, most indicators are indicative of well-being only by inference—we assume, for example, that there is a relationship between social well-being and such indicators as housing quality, educational attainment, and employment opportunity. (Accordingly, the application of social indicators for decision making is often accompanied by a considerable amount of basic research which tests for the accuracy of the inferences being made as well as for the reliability of techniques utilized in obtaining reports of well-being.)

As a decision-making tool, social indicators are meant to provide a basis for allocating resources and for planning program activities. While such data has long been available in one form or another, it is only during the past two decades that major efforts have been made to systematically collect such baseline data in a manner that will ensure its comparability from one year to the next, or from one setting to another. Because the compilation, analysis, and verification of social indicator data usually require a sophisticated knowledge of statistical procedures, few anthropologists have become deeply involved in generating such data. As their involvement in applied research intensifies, however, several points of mutual interest emerge.

Although still on a limited scale, applied anthropologists have become involved in helping develop reliable social indicators for developing nations, as Andrews and Inglehart (1979) suggest in their discussion of the international context for social indicators research. Obviously, measures of social well-being must consider the contexts of the social and cultural value systems to which they will be applied. For example, international indicators of housing quality should be developed on the basis of indigenous preferences for particular architectural styles, amenities, and the like. Similarly, the inference from housing quality to a judgment about the social well-being of a group of people should be considered in relation to the importance of shelter in each setting, family residence patterns, culture-specific values of privacy and communality, and so on.

Anthropologists have also had an opportunity to participate in the development of cognitive approaches to delineating measures of social well-being, as Roxann Van Dusen and Robert Parke have indicated:

> There is considerable interest in subjective measures of well-being . . . The research problem is to develop and refine measures of subjective well-being and relate them to measures of change in the objective environment. The experience of anthropologists in distinguishing between the informant's perception, and the researcher's reconstruction (or, perhaps more honestly, hunch) of the informant's perception is relevant here. There is growing recognition, within the social indicators community, that we are dealing with several different "realities." (1976:341)

Van Dusen and Parke also suggest that the anthropologist's experience with "small area" research should lead to an interest in the development of social indicators for local and regional level decision making. Anthropologists might contribute, they suggest, in devising cost-effective techniques for collecting community data, in helping define relevant boundaries of community and regional interaction, and in developing the potential of social network research.

Anthony Wallace has suggested that social indicators research might be improved if it were based on qualitative as well as quantitative study:

> I would suggest . . . that the census and survey type data upon which social indicators rely be supplemented by the detailed ethnographic and historical study of a small number of communities, selected carefully to represent major regional and social sectors of the United States. About any one such community, studied continuously over years both by survey research methods and by the methods of the ethnographer and the historian, a body of data of great value for the analysis of process over time would accumulate . . . The study of these *index communities* would supplement, in an important way, the cross-sectional studies of national samples now being undertaken by survey research methods. (1976:13-14)

Applied anthropologists are already beginning to work with a variety of social indicators in those instances where they have become program administrators and policy decision makers. Here, more than anywhere else, their sensitivity to cultural variability and to the subjective criteria for defining social well-being represent vital tools for interpreting the data that becomes available to them.

Needs Assessment

Social indicators are valuable because they provide data that is useful in making judgments about social needs. A number of other approaches to assessing needs can complement the systematic collection of social indicators. In contrast to the social indicators movement, which originated primarily out of a need for reliable national data bases, most of these approaches have developed from attempts to judge needs at a local or regional level. Generally, needs assessment research is undertaken at the request of a single service agency or industry, as a part of its overall planning program. A mental health agency might, for example, require an assessment of the mental health needs for the area under its jurisdiction. A housing agency, public utility, or private corporation might have similar periodic research requirements.

While there are a variety of approaches to needs assessment, most rely on one or a combination of three methodologies (Warheit, Bell, and Schwab 1977):

1. *The use of key informants.* An indication of social needs can be gleaned from in-depth interviews with selected key informants—usually persons in a community who are familiar with the delivery of services in the area under study.

2. *Conducting community interviews.* Various means can be utilized to gauge what the general public consider to be social needs in their community. The most popular approaches have been the field survey questionnaire and public meetings.

3. *The study of rates under treatment.* Some approaches to needs assessment rely entirely or in part on demonstrating the extent to which persons are presently using a particular type of service, or on other indications of "treatment" (a high incidence of police arrests for public drunkenness might, for example, indicate a need for alcohol rehabilitation and counseling services).

While needs assessment strategies might seem fairly routine—and, in fact, often are undertaken in a routine and unimaginative manner—they are subject to the same problems of method and interpretation that plague other kinds of social research. Community social needs vary with the socioeconomic and cultural composition of sectors within the community. Demographic indications of need can be misleading if researchers and decision makers do not consider the extent to which a social need might be differently defined within a community. Needs also vary according to social and cultural differences in the way people respond to problems—communities with strong family support systems might, for example, have less need for some kinds of social services than communities which lack such systems. Even the concept of *need*, as opposed to that of *demand* or *want*, is subject to misunderstanding.

One way applied anthropologists have contributed to needs assessment research has been by encouraging and participating in community research activities that are responsive to problems such as those indicated above. We have seen in the preceding two chapters that it is not at all unusual for service providers to be misinformed about important social and cultural characteristics of the communities in which they work. Community background information provides important baseline data for the development and improvement of useful needs assessment approaches.

At the same time, applied anthropologists need to be aware of the contexts in which needs assessments are made. They have to struggle, for example, with their own traditions, with the idea that it takes a long time to "know" a community, and with a strategy for field research that, at least in its initial stages, tends to encourage the researcher to collect data in a loose and almost indiscriminate manner. At least three characteristics of needs assessment research advise against such a strategy:

1.   A hierarchy of needs has probably already been established by the service agency conducting an assessment. One important contribution an anthropological researcher can make is to encourage planners to rethink the criteria they have used to establish needs. On the other hand, researchers need to be aware that many "needs" are mandated—that they are, in effect, the reason for a service agency's existence and cannot be ignored. Sorting out the legislative, administrative, and funding limitations of a service agency's mission is a first step to needs assessment.

2.   Needs assessment research must generally be responsive to strict time constraints. Service agencies conduct needs assessments as an aid in planning or to support applications for funding. In either case, agencies usually require as much information as they can get in as short a time as possible.

3.   Community service agencies have limited funds to devote to research. Needs assessments must be cost effective as well as time effective.

These characteristics, which help define the appropriate level of needs assessment research, also pertain to most of the other varieties of applied research described in this chapter. For the anthropologist, they pose research problems which require creative responses and a good measure of forethought.

Applied anthropologists have begun to play a prominent role in needs assessment research related to international development programs. For example, government legislation affecting development activities sponsored by the United States Agency for International Development has increasingly focused on strategies for determining the "social soundness" of overseas development programs, resulting in systematic attempts to establish culture-specific measures of social well-being and indications of community need (Jansen 1980).

Resource Assessment and Human Services
Information Systems

Complementary to needs assessment are strategies designed to assess the resources a community or region has available for responding to specific needs. Again, resource assessment is not as simple a matter as it might seem at first. Resources not only must be available, but they must be culturally appropriate. Culturally heterogeneous communities and large urban areas are likely to have many "hidden" resources which are not readily recognized by researchers and decision makers with backgrounds different from significant portions of the community in which they are working. These sorts of problems are multiplied in international settings. In the following example, Glyn Cochrane indicates the sorts of problems which change agents might face in Third World countries:

> Schools and hospitals are often sited near administrative centers whose locations were determined during the colonial period when concern was with the maintenance of law and order rather than with development. When assessing access and utilization data, it is necessary to make sure that the types of services offered are appropriate; for example, service by male medical technicians to Muslim women may not be acceptable. Counting effectiveness in terms of the number of doctors per thousand people, without knowing whether the usual kinds of health problems call for a doctor's skill—or if doctors will visit sick people living some distance away, or if the sick will visit the doctors—is not very helpful either. Likewise, estimating health care in terms of hospital beds, while sometimes useful is less so in cultures that consider illness a consequence of fate or that place a high value on caring for sick persons at home through use of traditional remedies. (1979:37)

Resource utilization and its assessment is complicated by more than cultural variability. Considerable complexity and variability exist within the service sectors of any sizable community, and the delivery of both government and private services is complicated by the fact that large numbers of agencies in a single locale offer similar services. In a United States urban center, for example, housing services might be provided by dozens of federal, state, county, and city agencies, as well as by any number of private charities, real estate, banking, and trade organizations. Such services might be underutilized or ineffectively utilized, either because the public is not aware of their availability or because the service providers have been unable to coordinate their activities in order to maximize the use of the total array of resources available.

A response to these problems has been the development of computerized human services information systems designed to provide a common data pool from which service agencies can draw. The value of such an approach for needs and resource assessment is clear; information systems have the potential for dramatically improving and expanding the data base from which decision makers and applied researchers work, to the extent that the data can at least approximate the true scope of the service systems from which it is derived.

Some anthropologists have suggested that the development of computer information systems represents an opportunity to adopt a holistic approach to the interpretation of the service capabilities of modern societies—an approach that is akin to the aims of traditional ethnography. In a discussion of "electronic ethnography," Alvin Wolfe and his colleagues argue that the concept of holism derived in part from the way anthropologists organized their data:

> Among the most important activities any ethnographer engages in are the preparation, collation, indexing and storing of field notes. Only if such nits and grits are done well, can the relevant information be retrieved when needed.
>
> Surely, it was such tasks of organizing the information derived from observations of hitherto unknown cultures that led anthropologists to conceptualize culture as a complex whole, differentiable into various domains and levels, yet integrated through relations among those domains and levels. Anthropologists knew systems theory intuitively before it was codified.
>
> As anthropologists took into account more of the internal variability within traditional cultures, previously thought to be simple, their informal methods of handling data were strained. The matter was still worse with respect to the differentiation and specialization of modern societies. In studies of complex societies, then, anthropologists tended to provide local color, while the major statements were derived from the macro-level data sets of economists, political scientists, and sociologists. (1980:1)

Wolfe goes on to suggest that electronic data-processing technology provides a new tool for ethnography:

> It is not just that computers can rapidly and efficiently handle masses of data, but that programs can now be written to model the more complex relations among data domains and levels. The technical phrase, Data Base Management System, refers to methods for handling large sets of data logically organized to satisfy a variety of users' requirements. Instead of relying on sequentially organized records whose relations derive basically from the fact that they draw certain attribute values from common domains, modern data bases may utilize other kinds of organization. Record structures may be hierarchical, originating in a root record and branching out in one-to-many relations, toward terminal records, as segmentary lineage systems or bureaucracies do in social life. Or record structures may have a network form, wherein each record may be related directly to several other records, a very complicated architecture that, alas, models the complexity of most sociocultural phenomena. The most complex architecture of data bases has become feasible partly because of the increasingly rapid, high speed integrated circuitry [of computers]. (1980:2)

Approaches to social accounting stress the present conditions of a society as they relate to decision making and problem solving in specific areas of policy interest. At their best, they are far removed from routine enumerations. Their effectiveness can be judged on the extent to which they accurately reflect the true conditions of the complex social settings from which they arise.

EVALUATION RESEARCH

There are several justifications for the evaluation of public programs and other human service activities. Periodic review of the extent to which a program is responding to established goals assists in planning program changes and making judgments about the continuation of funding for programs under review. In a more general sense, evaluation research helps policy makers arrive at criteria for new policy responses after having assessed the successes and failures of prior program responses. Without systematic and regular procedures for evaluation, policy and decision makers would have little empirical basis for measuring the effects of their actions.

Evaluation research tends to be program specific. An evaluator strives to determine the extent to which a program achieved the goals established for it, and possibly to trace the course of any obstacles the program might have encountered. Generally, the design and scope of an evaluation project should be as specific (and limited) as the goals of the activity being evaluated.

Although evaluation reports usually come at the end or at periodic stages of program activity, the actual research effort may begin early in the development of a program. This is the ideal case, as it permits timely observation and data collection. When an evaluation is called for at the completion of a project, the researcher is often faced with trying to compensate for lost and incomplete data.

Carol Weiss (1972) has described evaluation research as ideally being based on a partnership between the researcher, the planner, and the program implementor. The researcher should, for example, participate in the earliest stages of program planning—his or her contribution is important in helping establish clear program goals which are amenable to evaluation. At the same time, planners and program implementors should participate in the design of the evaluation effort, helping ensure a close relationship between what is being researched and what the program staff hope to accomplish. Evaluation researchers might also periodically report their early findings and impressions to the project staff, giving the staff an opportunity to make suggestions as well as to alter their program activities if these early results indicate that the staff might have difficulty in reaching their goals.

Close cooperation between the researcher and the "researched" not only helps ensure that an evaluation effort will be appropriate to the goals and program limits of an activity, but also that the observations and recommendations finally offered by the evaluator will be used in subsequent program planning.

Evaluation research efforts vary considerably in their scope. *Program evaluations* are limited to the investigation of "real world" human service activities and are generally conducted at the local level. Many government-supported programs, for example, require that local agencies periodically review and report on their activities. From time to time, private companies and industries will evaluate their efforts. The extent to which such reviews include social and cultural research (as opposed, for example, to the use of economic evaluation measures) also varies considerably.

Another approach to evaluation research is *experimental evaluation*, which generally occurs at a higher level of policy decision making. The idea underlying experimental evaluation is to test innovations in public policy by developing program activities on a limited, experimental basis, and then carefully evaluating the effort. Large-scale experimental evaluations often call for developing trial programs at several sites.

Deciding What to Evaluate

In every evaluation research effort, those involved must decide what aspect of a human service activity is most worthy of study. Such decisions depend on a number of factors. If the activity is new or especially innovative, or if it is an established program being tried out in a unique social or cultural setting, the evaluation effort should include an attempt to understand the internal dynamics of program activity and the program's relationship to the social and political environment in which it is placed. If, on the other hand, the objective is to evaluate an established program operating in a familiar setting, where the successes and failures of similar programs are well known, a simpler evaluation model which attempts only to measure the achievement of program goals might be more appropriate. This latter model is usually referred to as an *outcome* or *summative evaluation*. The outcomes of local-level human service activities are generally not difficult to evaluate, provided that program goals have been clearly stated. Outcomes can often be determined and evaluated quantitatively. If, for example, a local program has the goal of providing low-cost dental services to 600 families, determining whether that goal was reached is a simple matter of accurate record keeping and counting.

Outcome evaluation is more problematic when goals are hazy and not easily quantifiable, or where a well-tested relationship is not established between a goal and the operating procedures selected to reach that goal. Many human service activities have multiple goals, some of which may be more explicit than others. A housing program might have, for example, the goal of providing cash assistance to a certain number of low-income families seeking to improve their housing. A less explicit goal of the program might be to improve the overall economic and social position of these families. It may turn out, however, that the amount of assistance is just enough to provide for improved housing, but that attendant costs (maintenance, utilities, transportation, and so on) escalate to the point that many families participating in the program are actually at a greater economic disadvantage than they were before they entered the program. In this case, the first goal of improved housing has been met, but only at a cost that is detrimental to the overall economic well-being of many of the affected families.

The need to measure the attendant effects and more implicit goals of a human service activity depends on the level of policy decision making to which an evaluation effort is meant to respond. On the local level of program operation, many of the implicit goals of an activity are "inherited" from a state or federal funding agency. It would be of little benefit to attempt a program evaluation of these derived goals, since the staff working at this level have virtually no authority to respond to or change the assumptions which underlie such goals.

On the other hand, local agencies and other human service institutions often do have latitude in determining how they will reach set goals. *Process evaluation* is designed to measure how well a program succeeded in meeting its objectives. Such evaluations are especialy useful in instances where program goals have not been achieved. Human beings seem to have an especially difficult time explaining failure. In activities which have occurred over a long period of time (such as marriages and human service programs), the memories of participants tend to be selective and limited by personal biases. In such cases, the evaluator serves as both the memory and collective conscience of a human service program. In ongoing evaluation projects, a researcher concerned with process can often anticipate failure early in a program's history, and offer insights and suggestions which might permit a program to adapt its procedures. In effect, process evaluation moves from a basic concern with outcomes to an interest in the internal dynamics of a human service activity—focusing attention on administrative structures, interpersonal relations, and styles of service delivery.

Human service activities also operate within a larger context which includes the local political and social environment, the various levels of policy to which service providers are responsible, and so on. *Systems evaluation* attempts to consider these contexts as they relate to specific program activities. Evaluation research focused on such systems has the potential for assisting decision makers to the extent that an evaluator can point out how the community in which an activity is taking place has responded to a change effort—what are the actual or potential points of community conflict related to the program's objectives, where can decision makers and project implementors expect cooperation, and how are these factors affecting program operation? Systems evaluations might also describe the degree of competition existing between human service activities in a local area, point out how the clients for a particular service are responding to its delivery, and so on.

Each of these models for evaluation requires attention to the appropriateness of a research effort judged on the basis of factors which the staff of a service activity actually have the authority to change, as well as to limits of program resources for sponsoring evaluation research. Large-scale process and systems evaluations require more time to accomplish than most outcome evaluations, and their appropriateness should be justified both in terms of cost and the extent to which the expected evaluation results can be anticipated to contribute to effective policy decision making.

Applied anthropologists have participated in evaluation research for some time. Until recently, however, their major involvement has been as "troubleshooters" for overseas development projects. We have already discussed the limitations of this approach—for example, when anthropologists are called in to help determine why a program did not work as expected, their input usually comes too late to do much good. Fortunately, during the past decade or so, applied anthropologists have had opportunities to enter the evaluation process at early stages of project planning (Partridge 1979). Today, anthropologists participate in evaluation activities in a variety of work situations. They work as research contractors to perform "outside" evaluation research services. They work as staff for government agencies and private companies, performing "in-house" evaluations, Or they may be in a position of policy making, using evaluation research as a tool to improve the quality of their decision making.

Quasi-experimental and Nonexperimental Design

Ideally, evaluation research is comparative, following the scientific criteria for randomized controlled experimentation. The requirements for such research are that the researcher control the treatment (experimental) variable that is being tested and that the variable be tested, at a minium, in terms of its impact on an experimental group receiving treatment and a control group not receiving treatment. In practice, these conditions are often compromised. In simple outcome evaluations, for example, it may be enough simply to determine whether a program has achieved its quantitative goals (in these cases, presumably, the relationship between a treatment or service and its effect on a human clientele has already been tested at another policy level).

Most evaluation research is conducted in natural field settings rather than in laboratory or clinical settings, further complicating research procedures. Evaluations cannot, for example, always strictly control treatment variables or maintain precisely comparative experimental and control groups. A number of "quasi-experimental" research designs have therefore been adopted for use in evaluation (Campbell and Stanley 1966).

A relatively simple example of quasi-experimentation is called a *time-series design*. With this procedure evaluators attempt to measure the effects of a program or human service activity on the basis of periodic measurements before and after the activity takes place. *Multiple time series* designs add another dimension to evaluation by comparing the "before" and "after" measurements of an institution where a particular intervention occurred with similar measurements from institutions where the intervention did not take place (Weiss 1972). The assumption underlying time series design is that changes in "before" and "after" measurements can be attributed to the intervention being attempted. This assumption seems even more reliable when similar changes do not occur in institutions or among groups where the intervention does not take place.

The use of *nonequivalent control groups* is a popular approach to quasi-experimentation and is used when it is impossible to randomly select control groups. A variety of research designs have been developed to permit the nonrandom selection of control groups, primarily in terms of how well they correspond in important characteristics to an experimental group (Cook and Campbell 1979).

Many program evaluations, especially those involving the evaluation of local-level human service activities, do not rely on experimental procedures at all. The *case study* approach attempts to describe the effects of a single program or other activity, generally by a simple "before-after" comparison. Obviously, such comparisons do not test many of the assumptions underlying a particular human service activity, and it is difficult to generalize from the case study of a single, regionally based program. On the other hand, case studies provide outcome data and narrative descriptions of program processes, and this information is often useful to local-level decision makers and implementation staff.

Large-Scale Experimental Evaluation Projects

While many evaluations attempt to measure the effectiveness of established human service activities, others are developed to test innovative policy ideas before they are fully implemented. *Demonstration projects* accomplish this aim by conducting natural experiments in which a limited number of individuals receive benefits while the entire process of project operation, service delivery, and project effects is carefully evaluated.

Sometimes demonstration projects occur at a single site. The Vicos and Kuyo Chico experiments described earlier provide an example. A major problem with the single-site project is that it is difficult to account for regional factors which might affect the outcomes of a demonstration. As a result, multi-site demonstration projects have become increasingly popular. Dozens of such projects have been conducted in the United States during the past decade, ranging from two to a dozen sites and lasting anywhere from a few months to several years. Obviously, such activities are expensive and time consuming. At the same time, their costs are small compared to the enormous sums which might be wasted if a major policy innovation were implemented and failed or achieved only limited success because its effects had not been adequately tested.

Anthropologists have contributed to a number of these evaluation projects, often as field researchers assigned full-time to the regional experiment sites. One example of such a project is the Experimental Housing Allowance Program (EHAP) conducted in several sites across the United States during the early and mid-1970s. The basic objective of the EHAP was to test a new set of low- and moderate-income housing assistance policy ideas, several of which had already been implemented in a few European countries. The core policy idea was to provide *cash assistance* to families seeking improved rental housing. The program was in contrast to other federal housing programs, such as public housing, in which the government more or less served as a landlord for low-income residents. The policy ideas motivating the EHAP included attempts to encourage private housing suppliers to improve substandard housing (by creating a reliable market for low-cost, standard rental housing) and to encourage low- and moderate-income housing clients who might otherwise live in public housing to take more initiative and responsibility in meeting their housing needs. It was also reasoned that the EHAP would help disperse low-income clients throughout urban areas rather than isolate them in public housing "ghettos."

The EHAP had three major parts. A *supply experiment* was developed to test how local housing suppliers would respond to the program; a *demand experiment* was designed to determine how potential housing assistance clients would react to the program; and an *administrative agency experiment* was conducted to compare the way different types of local human service agencies might administer the program. For each part of the experiment, different sites were selected for demonstration projects. Eight such sites were chosen, for example, for the administrative agency experiment. An anthropologist or similarly trained social scientist was assigned as an observer at each site, in most cases staying for over a year as the sole local representative of the evaluation effort.

I have described the anthropologists' contributions to the administrative agency experiment in greater detail elsewhere (Chambers 1977). Although their work had much in common with traditional ethnography, it was different in a number of important ways:

1. At the sites where they worked, the observers were the most visible of the

researchers, but they were a relatively small part of the total research effort, which involved the collection of a wide variety of quantitative and qualitative data. The research effort had to be carefully coordinated, and the anthropologists had to function as team members rather than as completely independent researchers.

2.   The anthropologists worked as observers and interviewers and participated in the analysis of data, but they were constrained from participating in agency activities because their active involvement would have compromised the experimental controls imposed on the projects.

3.   The anthropologists had to learn to make judgments about the kind of information they collected on the basis of its relevance to the overall policy questions which guided the research. Many interesting occurrences noted by the anthropologists might be judged not to have policy relevance.

4.   The observers had opportunities to compare their field experiences and to visit other sites where the experiment was being conducted—a rare experience for anthropologists, but one which proved to be highly productive.

5.   The observers' daily research tasks were determined on a dual basis—both in terms of their skills as anthropological researchers and because they were the only researchers on site. Thus, they often had to divide their time between collecting qualitative information which would contribute to their case studies of the sites and assisting other researchers in carrying out tasks which had little relation to the case study effort.

6.   The anthropologists worked with several research populations. During their stay on site, they conducted research among low-income participants, agency staff, and influential community leaders. To some extent, each of these populations required the observers to adapt to different role expectations and adjust their research approach accordingly.

For the most part, the anthropologists working with the EHAP provided process data which helped the evaluation team account for program outcomes at each site and explain differences between the sites. Their daily exposure to the agencies added a depth of detail that is rare in evaluation research. In *Housing Allowances for the Poor*, M. G. Trend (1978b) offers a case study of one of the experimental sites.

Programs like the EHAP can be viewed not only as large social experiments, but also as experiments in applied research. They serve as important tests for combining qualitative and quantitative research strategies, and they provide opportunities to test the independent merits of adapting qualitative research models to policy-relevant experimentation. Such projects also serve as tests for combining site-specific data with comparative data drawn from a number of sites—an important precedent in attempting to separate the general effects of policy interventions from their impact on specific regions and sites.

SOCIAL AND CULTURAL FORECASTING

In many ways, the large-scale experimental evaluations described above border on the retrospective intent of most evaluation research and the prospective aim of forecasting techniques. In social and cultural forecasting, the emphasis is on trying to determine what will happen *before* a program or project is implemented.

In modern complex societies, the relationship between the past and the future seems especially tenuous—rapid technological change and ever-more-imaginative styles of social organization and cultural response seem to require constant vigilance. Who would have anticipated Hiroshima and the current nuclear arms race from the first impulse to try to split an atom? Who, among those who witnessed the coming of the industrial age, could have foretold widespread poverty and resource depletion in the Third World and the near epidemic proportion of pollution-related diseases in the most highly developed countries? At the center of the policy idea and the planning process is the desire to see into the future with clarity and good judgment.

In the latter half of the twentieth century, most of the world has come to recognize many of the limits and dangers that accompany rapid development. The world seems smaller, its resources rarer, and its capacity for renewal more limited than our predecessors imagined. It is little wonder that many of us feel a need to accurately foretell the future.

Social Impact Assessment

In the United States, the most far-reaching of recent government attempts to encourage more careful planning has been the National Environmental Protection Act. The Act focuses on the conservation and preservation of natural resources, requiring that the planning for government projects (and other projects using federal funds) be based upon a determination of the impact each project will have on the environment, including in most cases the impact on the social and cultural "resources." The National Environmental Protection Act has been followed by a number of other federal, state, and local regulations with similar requirements. Similar regulations have also been adopted in countries other than the United States. To one extent or another, most of these regulations count the quality of human life as a part of a country's resources. Accordingly, requirements for enviromental impact assessment often include provisions for assessing the social gains and losses that might be expected to accompany a program of planned change.

Social impact assessment is unique among forecasting approaches because it looks upon society as a resource, a characteristic which is an artifact of its close association with environmental legislation. Consequently, social impact assessment is in many respects the most historically based and conservation oriented of several social research approaches to the future. The policy questions normally asked of social impact assessments are likely to focus on how development projects can proceed with a minimum of societal disruption, rather than on interventions which originate from the intention of improving social life. Even in cases where social impact research might generate recommendations for active intervention, these result from a consideration of the potentially harmful effects of a particular course of action.

The variables of social life included in assessments of social impact differ considerably from project to project. A handbook prepared by the United States Forest Service (1977) recommends consideration of 38 social variables potentially subject to impacts related to the management and exploitation of forest lands. These range from changes in land allocation and use, to changes in population distribution, to possible disruptions in community identity and "sense of place." A social assessment manual prepared for the United States Bureau of Reclamation (1975) lists 35 broad categories of social well-being, each including multiple variables of potential impact. The categories extend to such wide-ranging considerations as family and individual lifestyle, community "culture," transportation, food production, and military preparedness.

In general, social impact assessment procedures are subject to the same limitations as other approaches to applied research. How can we be sure, for example, that the types of data chosen for the measurement of social impact are reliable indicators of the characteristics being assessed? Are the number of health-care personnel in an area or the cost of health-care services accurate measures of the quality of health care, regardless of intervening regional and cultural considerations? Determining social impacts is a particularly difficult exercise because it often implies an ability to project present social and cultural values well into the future. This, of course, is what planners and decision makers attempt to do as a matter of routine; but the extent and manner in which social research has positively contributed to the process remains an unsettled question.

On the other hand, one of the intriguing aspects of some of the most concerted recent social impact assessments is the extent to which they have encouraged a high level of interaction between researchers and decision makers. The design of social impact research is often focused from its beginning on developing decision alternatives for dealing with potential impacts.

Another feature of some of the more impressive attempts to predict social impacts is the extent to which they are incorporated into genuinely interdisciplinary research efforts. Government regulations pertaining to the assessment of the impact of development projects are not limited to a consideration of social variables. Equally pervasive environmental and economic variables must be considered. In many cases, local impacts must also be considered in relation to regional and even national or international priorities.

One problem decision makers regularly face in dealing with the impacts of development projects is the great variety of information which has a bearing on their decisions. A project may be socially sound but environmentally disastrous; in finer detail, most projects indicate a range of both positive and negative values. But how does one measure a "positive" against a "negative" when the variety of information being considered is so diverse?

An interesting response to these problems has been to encourge researchers and decision makers to work together in establishing impact priorities and in clarifying the alternatives to development projects. One such procedure, which involved the participation of several anthropologists, will help illustrate many of the points we have discussed.

The United States Army Corps of Engineers develops many of the government-sponsored public works projects undertaken in this country and overseas. Like those in many other government and private institutions, decision makers working for the Corps of Engineers have been concerned with the variety of impact assessment requirements they must satisfy before they can expect approval of their projects. By the early 1970s, most of their projects required at least four independent assessments— including projections of impact for economic development, regional development, environmental quality (including archeological resources), and social well-being. It was not at all clear how each of these assessments related to the others, or how priorities could be established among them.

In an attempt to resolve these difficulties, an agency of the Corps of Engineers developed what was later to be identified as a Water Resources Assessment Methodology (WRAM). The basic idea underlying WRAM procedures was to encourage the researchers who would normally work independently on each of the individual assessment projects to work together and arrive at an integrated and definitive statement concerning impact priorities (Solomon et al. 1977). The initial test of the WRAM procedures was later documented by anthropologists involved in the experiment (Peterson, Chambers, and Clinton 1977; West 1979). The procedures for the test can be handily summarized:

1. The test site selected was a channel improvement project for a river in southeast Louisiana. This river passed through both agricultural and forest land. Channel improvement was being considered as a means of relieving extensive flooding problems in the agricultural area.

2. Six alternative plans (including one "no action" plan) for channel improvement were drawn up by the engineers participating in the project. These plans varied in their cost, in the extent to which they would relieve the flooding problem, and in the amount of impact they would probably have on the region.

3. An interdisciplinary team, including engineers, economists, biologists, social scientists, and fish and game professionals was appointed. This team met together to familiarize themselves with the project and with the test site.

4. Members of the team then began to independently conduct impact research

in the area. They continued to meet together, however, and to discuss their findings, as well as to provide each other with recommendations for further research.

5.   After an initial period of research, the team began to systematically discuss impact variables which seemed to have a bearing on the project. This discussion required specialized researchers to explain and justify their initial findings to nonspecialists, a fruitful process which not only helped the specialists sharpen their criteria for identifying impacts related to their area of expertise, but also kept all the members of the team informed of the entire range of impacts which were being considered.

6.   After additional research in the test area, the members of the interdisciplinary team began to prioritize the impacts and to relate them to the four required impact accounts (economic impact, regional development, environmental quality, and social well-being). This stage of the experiment required the team members to reach agreement as to which potential impacts seemed more important than others—deciding, for example, the relative impacts of a threat to an endangered species of wildlife, expectations of increases in agricultural production, and the social costs of displacing families.

7.   As priorities were established, the team began to assess the degree to which each alternative plan would impact the variables deemed relevant to the project.

8.   At the conclusion of their work, the team had contributed to an integrated document which established impact priorities across disciplinary boundaries and offered an appraisal of how each alternative plan of action was expected to affect the economic, social, and environmental status of the test area.

It should be noted that the WRAM procedures, while a significant improvement over many approaches to impact assessment, are far from perfect. One of the more interesting features of the experiment is the extent to which the researcher's science is blended with the decision maker's art. The "artfulness" of making decisions is only a little less mystified by such procedures; it is not replaced.

The Cultural Analysis of Impacts

The difficulty of anticipating the impacts of development projects is magnified when researchers and decision makers are called upon to deal with considerable differences in cultural view, as might be expected in work with culturally distinct peoples. We have already noted that most of the early work in applied anthropology involved advising development specialists in colonial and Third World settings. Similar work continues on an international scale, although in most cases the focus is less on the administration of colonial and dependent territories and more on encouraging self-sufficiency and economic development among the less privileged of the world's population (an activity which, some observers are quick to point out, is often still motivated by a shade of "neocolonial" self-interest).

During the late 1960s, the United States Agency for International Development revised its assistance policies to focus on the "poorest of the poor" and to ensure that foreign development projects were designed a way appropriate to the social settings for which they were planned. The Agency's approach to *social soundness analysis* includes elements of both needs assessment and the more futuristic aims of social impact assessment.

Interestingly, as the Agency began to recognize the need for a systematic approach to social soundness analysis, several anthropologists found themselves caught up in a curious reversal of the way in which anthropologists normally become involved in applied research. As John Van D. Lewis (1981) reports, anthropologists were originally employed to participate in determining how social soundness analysis could be developed and applied to typical Agency projects, rather than being hired to actually conduct the research. Only later did a significant number of applied anthropologists become involved in field research, while the number of anthropologists working in decision-making and administrative positions within the Agency grew rapidly. This is one of the best examples of the willingness and ability of applied anthropologists to take advantage of career opportunities which are not primarily devoted to research but which offer an opportunity to significantly alter the course of public policy.

In general, applied anthropologists have begun to show a much greater sensitivity than many of their predecessors to the problems of administering foreign development projects. Along with this sensitivity has come a willingness to adapt traditional anthropological methods to the policy needs and resource limitations of decision makers. Anthropologist Glynn Cochrane's (1979) recent guide to the *cultural appraisal* of development projects was written in part with such an end in mind.

Cochrane's efforts are directed to a particular stage of decision making. How, after a development agency has determined the type of development program it will favor, do project managers decide upon the best locations for carrying out their activities? To what extent can a consideration of regional, social, and cultural factors assist in making a reasonable decision? Following the selection of a project site, to what extent should social and cultural factors be considered in planning and implementing specific projects?

One major, often subtle, difference between social impact assessment and techniques such as social soundness analysis and cultural appraisal lies in the kinds of impacts being considered. Social impact assessments tend to focus on how development projects will affect a local social and cultural setting. While not ignoring this dimension, social soundness analyses and cultural appraisals tend to devote considerably more attention to how the social and cultural responses of a group of project "beneficiaries" will impact upon a program. To some extent, this difference can be attributed to the policy environment from which these approaches to applied research have been derived. In the United States, requirements for social impact assessment developed from public and Congressional concern with the preservation of a resource—in this case the social well-being and cultural vitality of people. On the other hand, social soundness analysis and cultural appraisal originated with the concern of development agencies for the success of their projects. While the well-being of people is still of considerable importance in such settings (serving, in effect, as a significant measure of "success"), people are also more likely to be perceived as potential obstacles to development—which, in fact, they often are.

Scenarios for the Future

Sometimes an applied research project is not so concerned with impacts as with future human needs and expectations. How do the residents of a community want their living space to be twenty or fifty years hence? What are the implicit ideals of progress and development being used by the managers of a business enterprise to plan for the future of their company? What kinds of human services will be required of a government in the next century? How should a new product or innovation be presented to the public? These are all vital policy problems to which anthropologists, despite their long interest in understanding how humans adapt to and stimulate change, have so far contributed little.

A variety of forecasting techniques have been developed to respond to the needs of decision makers. The most popular of these are attempts to duplicate decision-making processes through a variety of panel discussion and "gaming" situations. In effect, participants are asked to respond to a given set of policy problems. Their responses are carefully recorded and become the basis for further discussion and additonal prioritizing. The strategies can be fairly informal (as in the Nominal Group Technique) or highly sophisticated (as in Delphi and Synetics approaches).

The most common use of forecasting techniques has been in work with "expert" committees, such as citizen advisory committees, task forces, and management groups within business and industry. Many of the procedures were first devised for use in business management, and only later adapted to government decision making. Where conditions permit, forecasting techniques have also been utilized in citizen participation meetings and workshops. They have been employed in needs assessment research as well as in attempts to anticipate future needs.

Although applied anthropologists have participated in the use of forecasting techniques, they have contributed little to their development. One exception is the work of Robert Textor, who has advocated the use of *ethnographic futures research* in building culturally based scenarios of the future (1979). Through intensive interviews, Textor and his students ask informants to provide a variety of scenarios focusing on what they want for their future. Although most of the work Textor describes is based on developing scenarios on a national scale, his techniques of elicitation could be applied as well to a variety of decision-making situations.

OBSERVATION AND ETHNOGRAPHY IN APPLIED RESEARCH

The day when most anthropologists trained solely in qualitative research techniques and avoided statistical aproaches to data collection and analysis is, fortunately, nearly buried in our past. For applied anthropologists, the ability to work with both qualitative and quantitative research strategies has become essential. After all, the research *problem* ought to suggest the method most appropriate to its resolution, rather than the researchers' preferences for one or another method.

All the same, anthropology enjoys a special relationship to the techniques of qualitative research. While increasing numbers of anthropologists have become adept at utilizing sophisticated statistical techniques, the value placed on first-hand experience gained through being "where the action is" has not appreciably lessened. Observational and ethnographic techniques originally developed for research in small, isolated communities have been adapted for use in modern, complex societies and are increasingly being introduced into applied research settings. These transitions are due not only to the initiative of anthropologists, but also to the interest of decision makers. Moreover, while anthropology's link to qualitative research is based on a long-standing tradition, anthropologists can no longer claim exclusive rights to its methods. In both basic and applied research, the familiar terms of "fieldwork," "participant-observation," and "ethnography" are gaining currency in nearly all the disciplines of social science.

What Is Ethnography?

The increasing popularity of qualitative approaches to applied research has increased the variety of research opportunities available to anthropologists and other social researchers. At the same time, problems and misunderstandings have arisen along the way. Many of these relate to the terms we use to identify qualitative research techniques.

First of all, the idea that it is valuable to observe how people behave in natural settings is not unique to anthropology. Decision makers have probably always accepted the idea that some types of information and insight can only be learned from first-hand experience, and that poring over reports and figures is a poor substitute for "getting out in the field." Hence the necessity evolved for "inspection tours" in business and industry and "site visits" in the management of government programs. Much of the qualitative research conducted in applied social research is something like a site visit—it is based simply on the need to gain first-hand information about how a program works or how an activity is being carried out. *Observation research* has been used extensively, for example, in studying education processes and in urban planning research (the "windshield survey" is an often-used preliminary technique for becoming acquainted with a neighborhood). *Open-ended and informal interview techniques* have been applied to a great variety of research settings where responses to standard surveys might be suspect or where the researchers do not know enough about a problem to even phrase a sensible question. *Unobtrusive measures* (Webb et al. 1966) have been used in a number of practical problem-solving situations.

All these approaches employ methodology familiar to anthropologists—looking, probing, and looking again. In applied research, anthropologists have proven themselves adept and resourceful at employing such techniques, regardless of what they are looking for. But misunderstandings arise when a distinction is not made between the *information-gathering* and *interpretative* skills normally associated with anthropology. This distinction is made clear in Harry Wolcott's discussion of the relationship between applied research and *ethnography*. While not discounting the value of any approach to qualitative research, Wolcott insists that ethnography, distinct from the specific techniques of fieldwork, has a special meaning which is often misunderstood by applied researchers and decision makers.

> Specific ethnographic techniques are freely available to any researcher who wants to approach a problem or setting descriptively. It is the essential anthropological concern for cultural context that distinguishes ethnographic method from fieldwork techniques and makes genuine ethnography distinct from other "on-site observer" approaches. (1980:59)

Wolcott is correct in insisting that the term *ethnography* be reserved for work which attends to the anthropologist's special concern for cultural symbolism. At the same time, we should recognize that observational techniques can be fruitfully applied to a great variety of other problems, and that the special information-gathering strategies associated with fieldwork have considerable value apart from their use in ethnography. As in so many other cases, the important thing is that all the parties of a research project understand the character of the work in which they are engaged—confusion and disappointment can easily result when researchers and their clients fail to make a clear distinction between the information-gathering and interpretative aspects of any kind of research endeavor.

Ethnography, strictly defined, has special utility in applied research which transcends its value simply as a technique of inquiry. Michael Agar (1983) has described ethnography as "an encounter among different traditions." In his view, ethnographers deal with problems in understanding between different traditions which result in communication "breakdowns":

> A breakdown initiates a process of "resolution" where knowledge needs to be changed—perhaps trivially, perhaps in a fundamental way—before under-

standing can occur. Resolution is a dialectic, emergent process resulting in some new knowledge that bridges the original gap between the traditions. When it is accomplished, the social action that originally elicited the break-down becomes "coherent." The original diffference is adequately connected to the similarities among the traditions so that understanding can occur. (1983:53)

Another way to state this is to argue that ethnography has the poten-tial of mediating understanding and resolving essential points of cultural conflict by explaining the occurrence of misunderstandings and providing clues to their resolution. In this manner, ethnography is not simply descriptive but is also actively involved in transcending conflict by provid-ing a new basis for understanding. A similar point has been made by Charles Reichardt and Thomas Cook (1979), who argue that ethnography contributes to applied research through its emphasis on "discovery," as opposed to the emphasis on "verification" that is normally associated with quantitative research approaches. Reichardt and Cook demonstrate how this difference applies to problems in evaluation research:

In the early days, it was assumed that programs could easily be designed to produce desired results and that the purpose of evaluation was merely to verify these anticipated effects. Quite naturally, then, evaluation was drawn toward quantitative methods with their traditional emphasis on verification. Of course, later it was found that amelioration was not so simple and that programs might have a wide variety of unsuspected side effects. The empha-sis of evaluation thus began to shift away from the verification of presumed effects toward the discovery both of how a program might be devised so that it would have a desired effect and of what effects either suspected or unsuspected these programs might actually have. Consequently, some fields of evaluation (most notably education) have shown a growing interest in qualitative methods with their emphasis on discovery. (1979:17)

One especially promising avenue of social research design has been the use of both quantitative and qualitative methods as independent tests of the reliability of both approaches. The term *between-method triangulation* (Denzin 1970) has been used to describe such procedures. The logic under-lying triangulation is that, since methods of research have different epis-temological roots and often imply different assumptions about data, agreements between the methods should increase our confidence in the reliability of the overall research effort. A triangulation of methods can also assist applied researchers in maximizing the utility of their work—output data can, for example, be considered alongside process data in order to give a clearer view of both the *what* and *how* of program activities.

But what happens when method triangulation does not result in agreement? These findings can be even more significant, as they suggest that there might be serious limitations to each of the methods brought to bear on a problem. The "reconciliation" of such problem cases provides an interesting commentary on the extent to which single-method approaches to social research can often be held hostage by the limited disciplinary scope of their practitioners (Trend 1978d).

PERSPECTIVE

The fundamental approaches to applied research can be described in terms of how they relate to different stages of program activity and whether they are meant to reflect present, past, or future circumstances. Differences also exist between experimental and program research. Experimental research more closely approximates the aims of basic (independent) inquiry than does program research, where the aim is generally to help a single institution assess its effectiveness in responding to particular human needs.

Most applied research activities have some common characteristics which help shape and motivate the direction of inquiry. We have discussed some of these characteristics in this chapter as they relate to policy formulation and decision making. Policies must be appropriate to the circumstances in which they will be enacted. They must be sensitive to problems of accountability and ideals of effective resource use. Increasingly, they must also reflect some degree of public participation in decision making.

The issues of accountability, often described in terms of the measurement of relative costs and benefits, have been especially troublesome to many anthropologists, some of whom have argued that we simply cannot measure the well-being of individuals or societies in quantitative terms. In a sense, they are correct. Nothing can be wholly measured in terms of its quantity. A thousand oranges grown under poor conditions and thus low in sugar content are not the same as a like number of oranges produced under ideal conditions. Critics of cost and benefit analysis also have a point when they argue that current approaches to the measurement of human well-being generally reflect a bias toward material comfort and tend to discount other values. So long as this remains true, the techniques of measurement will disproportionately favor those segments of a society or region which hold material well-being in high regard, especially those groups which have the resources and inclination to take advantage of opportunities to improve their economic position.

RECOMMENDED READINGS

Useful introductions to policy analysis include Stuart S. Nagel and Marian Neff's *Policy Analysis in Social Science Research* (Sage Publications, Inc., 1979) and Robert R. Mayer and Ernest Greenwood's *The Design of*

Social Policy Research (Prentice-Hall, 1980). "The Policy Analysis Explosion," published as a special section of *Society* (16(6), 1979) is a particularly helpful guide.

Of the many discussions of cost-benefit analysis, I have found Mark S. Thompson's *Benefit-Cost Analysis for Program Evaluation* (Sage Publications, Inc. 1980) especially helpful.

Readers interested in the development of social indicators might refer to *The Journal of Social Indicators Research*. Discussions of national social indicators research in Canada and the United States can be found in a special issue of *The Annals of the American Academy of Political and Social Science* (435, 1978).

George J. Warheit and co-authors offer a clear and practical guide to needs assessment in *Needs Assessment Approaches* (National Institute of Mental Health, 1977). M.J. Grinstead describes the involvement of a team of anthropologists in a major needs assessment in "Poverty, Race and Culture in a Rural Arkansas Community" (*Human Organization*, 35, 1976).

Gerald M. Britan has discussed "The Place of Anthropology in Program Evaluation" (*Anthropological Quarterly*, 51, 1978). James N. Kerri described the evaluation of a Canadian Housing Project in "A Social Analysis of the Human Element in Housing" (*Human Organization* , 36, 1977). The evaluation of an overseas evaluation project conducted by anthropologists is described by Tarig Husain in "Use of Anthropologists in Project Appraisal by the World Bank" (in *Development from Below*, Mouton, 1976).

Recent large-scale experimental evaluation projects have resulted in two published case studies by anthropologists. These are M.G. Trend's *Housing Allowances for the Poor: A Social Experiment* (Westview, 1978) and Charles A. Clinton's *Local Success and Federal Failure* (Abt Books, 1979).

Discussions and descriptions of the involvement of anthropologists and other social researchers in social impact assessment can be found in Sue-Ellen Jacobs' *Social Impact Assessment* (Mississippi State, 1977); Roy S. Dickens, Jr., and Carole E. Hill's *Cultural Resources: Planning and Management* (Westview, 1978); and Kurt Finsterbusch and C.P. Wolf's edited *Methodology of Social Impact Assessment* (Dowden, Hutchinson & Ross, 1977).

More specific contributions can be found in Mim Dixon's *What Happened to Fairbanks: The Effects of the Trans-Alaskan Oil Pipeline on the Community of Fairbanks, Alaska* (Westview, 1978) and William Millsap's "New Tools for an Old Trade: Social Impact Assessment in Community and Regional Development" (in *Social Science Education for Development*, Tuskegee Institute, 1978).

Readers interested in social assessment can also refer to the monthly newsletter *Social Impact Assessment*, which includes brief case study material.

A general discussion of social forecasting can be found in Daniel P. Harrison's *Social Forecasting Methodology* (Russell Sage, 1976). The most helpful introduction to the maze of current forecasting techniques that I am aware of is John W. Dickey and Thomas M. Watts' *Analytic Techniques in Urban and Regional Planning* (McGraw-Hill, 1978).

Approaches to the use of observation research and ethnography in applied research are described in Richard N. Adams and Jack J. Preiss' edited volume *Human Organization Research: Field Relations and Techniques* (Dorsey, 1960); in a special issue of *Practicing Anthropology* (3(1), 1980) devoted to "ethnography and observation research in policy study"; and in Marion Lundy Dobbert's *Ethnographic Research: Theory and Application for Modern Schools and Societies* (Praeger, 1982).

Qualitative approaches to evaluation research are discussed in Michael Quinn Patton's *Qualitative Evaluation Methods* (Sage Publications, Inc. 1980) and Thomas D. Cook and Charles S. Reichardt's edited volume *Qualitative and Quantitative Methods in Evaluation Research* (Sage Publications, Inc. 1979). The latter book includes several discussions of method triangulation and an article by Donald T. Campbell devoted to tests of validity for qualitatively derived data.

William J. Tikunoff and Beatrice A. Ward edited a special issue of *The Anthropology and Education Quarterly* (8(2), 1977) devoted to "Exploring Qualitative/Quantitative Research Methodologies in Education." Joan Cassell has prepared *A Fieldwork Manual for Studying Desegregated Schools* (National Institute of Education, 1978). Qualitative research methods are also discussed in Christine L. Fry and Jennie Keith's *New Methods for Old Age Research* (Center for Urban Policy, Loyola Univ. of Chicago, 1980).

Pertti J. and Gretel H. Pelto offer an overview of applied research in chapter ten of their *Anthropological Research* (Cambridge, 1978).

6

The Cultures of Policy

"What do you find the most interesting about applied anthropology?" a friend once asked.

"The feeling that there is so much more to learn," I answered.

Much of the work I have done in applied research has seemed on the surface to be mundane and routine. But it has always carried with it a sense of surprise and an underlying current of intellectual excitement. In a way, applied research is like coming back to anthropology through a rear door. Your focus has to be first on the immediate needs of your client. But, at least in my experience, every response to a client's expectations has left me with a renewed sense of profession. It has encouraged me to think of anthropology not only in terms of what it has been, but also in terms of what it might be in the future. When I say that applied work interests me because it impresses me with how much there is left to learn, one of the things I am suggesting is that every project I have been involved in leaves me with a sense of how much remains to be accomplished simply to understand what I have just done.

Thus far in this book we have been guided by two very general observations. First, although it shares much with other social sciences, anthropology remains unique in the amount of attention it gives to problems of cultural analysis and interpretation. I have argued and suggested through examples that the concept of *culture* is central to the discipline, whether an anthropologist chooses to explore the kinship categories of an isolated and primitive society or the unemployment patterns of a modern industrial work force. This is not to say that culture is the only phenomenon anthropologists attempt to understand, but it is normally the focal point of their interests.

The second observation, made in several ways throughout the preceding chapters, is that applied anthropology is a unique expression of the anthropologist's skills and insight—unique because it derives so much of its momentum from outside the discipline and because its practitioners possess a special knowledge that is not necessary for the practice of other approaches to anthropology. This special knowledge is based on an understanding of policy settings and decision-making processes. The practice of applied anthropology requires specialized training and experience equivalent to that which delineates other major subareas of anthropology (that is, archeology, linguistics, physical anthropology, and ethnology). An individual anthropologist is no more prepared or qualified to act as an applied anthropologist on the basis of his or her general background in anthropology than is, for example, an anthropologist trained primarily in ethnology professionally equipped to direct the excavation of an archeological site or pass expert judgment on human fossil remains.

I emphasize this latter observation because the tendency has been to describe applied anthropology solely in terms of its uniqueness as a *career opportunity* rather than as a *specialized approach to understanding*. This tendency derives, I suspect, from those earlier periods of application when anthropologists seldom brought specialized knowledge of the policy contexts in which they were working to bear on their (usually short-term) applied assignments. The general ineffectiveness, rarity, and early demise of this style of application is testimony to its limitations.

This chapter is devoted to describing some of the relationships between culture and policy. In some respects, it is more exploratory than the earlier chapters. We are approaching the point where the idea of application and its significance seems very fresh and often tentative. Yet it is clear that the kinds of issues addressed here, however they might be resolved, will increasingly command the attention of applied anthropologists.

CULTURES IN POLICY SETTINGS

Culture, as we discussed it in the first chapter, is the information and the interpretation of information by people—the meanings that are passed around from person to person and from group to group. Culture process represents a struggle to make meaning from the raw material of the human imagination—to verify beliefs, to discover new insights, and to reduce the ambiguity that arises from the barrage of unfiltered and disorganized information that is routinely available to us.

The study of culture is based on an attempt to discover how people make meaning from information, to determine the significance and value they attach to their interpretations of reality, and to explore how constructed meanings and measures of significance shape behavior and social action. This concept is not especially esoteric. All it requires is acceptance (on the basis of an incredible amount of evidence) of the observation that there is seldom, if ever, a perfect correspondence between absolute reality, the information people have about reality, and the meaning that is given to this information.

In a sense, the study of culture is the study of the necessarily faulty collection, coding, and transmission of data. But we have to be careful here. What is the "fault" in a procedure that seems inevitable? Traditionally, anthropologists have been able to evade such questions on the basis of their preference for a relativistic point of view. The cultural interpretations and values of a people make "sense" because they are believed and because they tend to be adaptive to the life circumstances of the people who hold them. So long as anthropologists were content to study single and radically delimited collectivities of people, most of whom were expected to *share* their cultural constructs, these notions seemed entirely adequate.

The Problem with Culture

We have seen from several examples used in this book how anthropologists ran into difficulty when they attempted to apply the culture concept to human problems of major policy significance. Much of their difficulty can be attributed to the way they have used the term *culture* both to describe the processes of making and sharing meaning and, in a fundamentally different way, to draw parameters around the settings in which those processes occur. Thus, a *culture* is a group of people who are assumed to have similar cultural processes. Phrased in this manner, the study of culture has usually emphasized the similarities within groups of people who are distinguished by one or several characteristics, such as their subsistence technology, ethnicity, language, or geographic isolation. At the same time, when students of culture have focused on relationships between groups, they have tended to emphasize cultural differences rather than similarities. These preferences have, in turn, led to the notion that a "culture" is a highly distinctive unit which is best understood and compared to other cultures on the basis of the shared norms or standards of behavior of its members (Goodenough 1970).

There are several explanations as to why anthropologists have dealt with the concept of *culture* in this manner. Theodore Swartz (1978) rightly points to a link with the anthropologist's early preference for studying small-scale societies, which were assumed to be relatively homogeneous in their beliefs and behaviors—societies which have, in Durkheim's terms, a pattern of "mechanical solidarity" whereby their cultural processes are expected to be shared to such an extent that individual personalities correspond in most important respects to a "collective consciousness." Swartz argues that this idea is not only inappropriate to the study of larger-scale societies, but even limits the anthropologist's ability to understand cultural processes in more isolated and smaller-scale societies.

Another explanation for the anthropologist's emphasis on the cultural homogeneity and distinctiveness of peoples can be found in the development of the discipline of anthropology, and in the attraction for anthropologists of ideals of cultural relativism and advocacy. A major goal of anthropology has been to combat the ignorance fostered by ethnocentric attitudes, and the most widely accepted way to do this has been to demonstrate the logical and moral consistency that can be found in non-Western societies. What is more, the demonstration of cultural differences *between* societies is a valuable heuristic tool for convincing others of the importance of anthropology as a field of study, since it is on the basis of such demonstrations that we might explain the conflicts that occur as different "cultures" come into contact.

It is, of course, important to recognize the significance of shared cultural processes and of differences between groups. However, an almost exclusionary preference for these kinds of explanations, coupled with a tendency to identify cultural units in a traditional and often stereotypical way, has led to a number of difficulties for the study of complex societies in general, and for applied anthropology in particular.

As we have seen, applied anthropologists are generally called upon to explain cultural processes as they arise within groups and between groups. The idea of policy offered in this book can be rephrased in cultural terms. A policy setting is a situation or circumstance in which different intentions come into conflict and where some attempt to negotiate or mediate is called for. For an applied anthropologist, the significant setting that begs understanding is not a single cultural unit, it is the stage upon which a particular human problem becomes meaningful to all those groups of people who have an interest in its resolution. By virtue of their association with policy and decision making, applied anthropologists are called upon to explore the *relationships between cultural processes* and, in large part, to discover the *faults and breakdowns* of particular cultural processes.

Applied anthropologists have come to be as interested in variations within recognized social groups as they are in the differences between groups. The recognition of variation within groups is important in several respects. We can avoid, for example, the stereotypical assumptions associated with such vague and misleading social categories as "black culture," the "culture of poverty," and the "bureaucratic culture." While these categories serve as powerful heuristic and symbolic representations of the concerns of modern societies, they are seldom useful as analytic concepts. In a similar sense, delineations of "normative culture," prominent in much anthropological thinking, are not always the most useful kinds of cultural information in decision-making contexts. Change agents may be far more interested in identifying those segments of a social group who are most likely to divert from the norm—either to resist a new activity or project, or to respond positively to an innovation—than in those who will probably adhere to the norm.

Similarities between social groups are also important to applied anthropologists, since they identify points of departure for the negotiation and mediation of conflict and provide inroads for the successful implementation of social change. The meanings and values people share despite diverse backgrounds and varied life situations are often the only reasonable place from which to begin to gain perspective on the differences between them.

In many respects, cultural processes are identified in applied settings on the basis of specific problems in the formulation, planning, and implementation of policy. The criteria anthropologists (and others) have traditionally used to identify and distinguish cultural settings may still assume importance. But applied anthropologists, by the nature of their work, are often far more interested in the manner in which groups—sometimes in quite unexpected ways—form in response to policy problems.

A hypothetical situation will clarify this important point. Let us imagine a fairly diverse urban community, populated by persons of different ethnicity, education, and socioeconomic class. For the applied anthropologist, these are important but not sufficient categories of possible cultural differentiation. Finer-tuned differentiations must be based on how residents actually respond to particular activities taking place in the community. The way different segments of the community respond to a proposal to construct a low-income housing project in the area may be very different, for example, from their response to a transportation project. Similarly, the values and meanings different residents give to education and medical services may vary far more in accordance to the specific type of service offered, the way it is presented, and individual needs within the community than they do on the basis of "membership" in a particular ethnic or economic category.

In another respect, the success or failure of an innovation in our imaginary community may depend far more on the energetic opposition or support of a small minority of residents than it does on a majority opinion. Knowing the *general* characteristics of the community is often not enough.

To complicate matters further it is also important to recognize that the future of any particular change or activity in our community also rests to some extent on the manufactured meanings and value orientations of those who are introducing the activity, and on how those meanings and values mesh with the community at any particular time. Presumably the cultural responses of bureaucrats and change agents can vary as much as those of other people. Moreover, the presence of many different institutions of change in our community, representing any number of ideologies and intentions, may have a greater cumulative effect on how particular activities fare than do the intentions and assumptions underlying the individual projects.

The cultural processes that generally lend the greatest interpretative and explanatory power to the work of the applied anthropologist are those which are the most precise and are associated with clearly delineated change activities. Differentations in terms of traditional categories of cultural distinction, such as ethnicity and language, may be helpful, but they are seldom sufficient explanations for the problems attending programs of deliberate change.

Cultural Variation and Policy

If the meanings people assign their circumstances and the significance they give to those meanings are the primary concern of anthropologists, then the policy and action settings which form the stage for the acting out of cultural processes, and which contribute to the formulation of new meanings and values, are the locus of the applied anthropologist's interests. The intentions and policy ideas which provide the basis for activities of change are the cultural "texts" and "artifacts" with which applied anthropologists work. Although applied anthropologists have often centered their attention on a single group within a policy or action setting, increasing numbers of anthropologists now recognize the multi-group characteristics of each setting as a more significant problem.

I have suggested elsewhere that an anthropology which is maximally useful to policy and decision making is one that develops on the basis of the *circumstances* of policy. Taking this view, the anthropologist (whether as a researcher or a decision maker) recognizes that circumstances will give rise to unique confrontations and alliances among social groups. As I noted above, these patterns may or may not correspond to popular notions of the characteristics which set groups apart from one another or which contribute to group cohesiveness:

> What we actually study at this level are the processes by which [meanings and] values are exchanged and, in some instances, created. In other words, circumstances increase the repertoire of [meanings and] values beyond those which any individual or group brings to the circumstance. Decisions and behaviors arise out of this mix of [meanings and] values and its increase. "The whole,"

anthropologists like to say, "is greater than its parts." We might also be prepared for the whole to be significantly different from its parts. (Chambers 1981:6)

An interest in the circumstances of policy and action settings also permits us to distinguish between meaning, social norms, and values. We have seen that to work effectively the applied anthropologist must avoid the temptation to explain group characteristics simply on the basis of normative statements which describe and predict only standards of behavior. The applied anthropologist must be aware that people often make judgments on the basis of personal and group trade-offs, willingly exchanging one value for the opportunity to pursue another. Similarly, even closely knit groups usually exhibit considerable variation. As we look at how a single group responds to any particular policy initiative or planned activity, we can readily see that there are great differences in the kinds of information group members have, and in the sense they make of that information.

In much the same vein, in complex societies groups often form because of specific circumstances. Anthropologists and other social scientists have tended to focus on group characteristics which seem the most durable, such as religious affiliation, economic class, ethnicity, and so on. More transient group affiliations can be of equal or greater importance to the applied anthropologist. The circumstances brought about by attempts to direct change often lead to the formation of new groups which in turn influence the outcome of the change effort. For example, groups and individuals with little apparent common interest often join forces on the basis of different but complementary self-interests. The situation described briefly in Chapter 2, in which a railroad company and environmental groups joined together to oppose the development of a water transportation project, is not an unusual case. The ability to recognize the potential for such alliances, and to respect their temporary nature (in a different circumstance, the railroad company and the environmentalist groups could well be on opposite sides of a policy issue), is an important characteristic of applied anthropology.

Another feature of the applied anthropologist's interest in the circumstances of particular policy and action settings is that such a view helps account for significant differences between group values and behavior. Anthropologists have long been interested in discrepancies between what people say they do and what they actually do. A concern with circumstance brings this interest into sharp focus:

Different circumstances might give rise to different . . . behaviors on the part of the same individual or group. The people who participate in a particular circumstance are, in turn, a part of the uniqueness of that circumstance. Circumstances not only systematize the pre-existing meanings and values that are brought to bear on them; they also provide the impetus for creating and introducing new or previously unidentified values, or new ways of selecting from among conflicting values. Most importantly, circumstances permit people to change their minds, a luxury which (were we to take it more seriously as a condition of inquiry) might prove to be near the crux of social behavior. (Chambers 1981:8)

Applied anthropologists vary greatly in the way they deal with the specific circumstances of the settings in which they work. No doubt, as the numbers of anthropologists working in different settings increase, more far-reaching attempts will be made to generalize on the basis of like experiences, offering the opportunity to develop predictive models that will improve our ability to anticipate the effects of directed change. It is unlikely, however, that anthropologists will create such models on their own. The most useful contributions will almost certainly be the result of large-scale efforts requiring the input of a wide variety of curious and concerned participants.

At the same time, the utility of applied anthropology is not entirely dependent on the development of predictive models. Thus far, the most effective contributions of anthropologists to the resolution of policy problems have been in their on-going work as professionals equipped to interpret cultural processes as they relate to specific programs and activities of change. It may be that the most important characteristics of human response to innovation and change will never yield entirely to predictive modelings of behavior. Perhaps it is not even desirable that our existence be so thoroughly bereft of uncertainty and the potential for surprise. The ability to understand within great limits of uncertainty will always be a most important attribute of effective practice.

The Interpretation of Policy

Modern life presents us with a dizzying complexity based on the vast interdependence of people and their social circumstances. It is only because we have limited, selective, and faulty vision that we can slow the swirl somewhat and reduce the ambiguity of our lives. At the same time, we match our longing for certainty with an incredible amount of curiosity. Our access to information is well beyond our ability to keep much of it in our heads; so we have a great deal of sophisticated equipment to help us keep track of the world around us—improvements in the technology of communication, data storage and retrieval have kept pace with as well as contributed to the complexity of our surroundings. But the crux of our adaptation to the interdependencies we have created, the key to our well-being, lies in our ability to make viable decisions from a wide variety of alternative courses of action.

It is not easy to say in abstract terms what separates a good decision from a bad one. A decision does not have the same criteria of proof as a scientific statement. What we can say about decisions is that they seem to work *least well* when they disregard the interests or needs of significant groups of people, or when they assume like interests and needs where they do not exist. In a similar sense, poor decisions often seem to result from an inability to anticipate how people will respond to the future. During the 1960s, for example, United States automobile manufacturers were convinced that the demand for "big car luxury" would remain stable. As a consequence, many of the manufacturers faced serious production and marketing problems during the late 1970s, when the rising cost of energy led much of the public to reconsider their preferences.

It is doubtful that anthropologists would have had much interest in working with automobile manufacturers during the late 1960s, had they been offered the opportunity. It is not certain that they would have been able to help if they had. We have noted throughout this book that anthropologists have tended to be most interested in how people respond to circumstances over which they appear to have little control. Much of this preference is the outgrowth of anthropologists' continuing interest in research directed to groups which are outside the mainstream of the modern industrial state—peoples who clearly suffer the encroachment and often the exploitation which accompany rapid development.

Contemporary practice in applied anthropology has begun to challenge the bias inherent in this preference. If the major goal of anthropology during the past century has been to improve our understanding of cultural process on the basis of cross-cultural research, the emerging major goal of applied anthropologists is to understand how cultural process affects the circumstances of policy decision making. It is hard to imagine how this can be done without paying as much attention to those who make, transmit, and implement policy as we have given to those who are most affected by it.

Advice and Consent

Training and experience in anthropology helps shape the way anthropologists view policy problems. All anthropologists do not think alike, but they do tend to approach many issues in similar ways. Some anthropologists have been notably successful in increasing the public's awareness of the anthropological perspective, generally as teachers, popular writers, or public lecturers. Others have more directly offered their views to individuals and groups involved in policy decision making. Most notable in these respects have been the achievements of Margaret Mead, whose work on behalf of anthropology brought her into close contact with the United States Presidency, the Congress, and the federal bureaucracy (Dillon 1980). The great variety of issues in which Mead become involved reach far beyond any individual's capacity for expertise. The kind of anthropology she brought to public affairs was based less on her ability to provide policy makers with information than on her success in presenting a particular style of looking at human problems. She encouraged others to view seemingly insular problems in a cross-cultural context and taught, often by analogy, the importance of an ethnographic perspective.

When anthropologists speak to decision makers, they generally do so both as individuals and in the interest of an anthropological perspective, drawing principles of understanding from their professional experience. Some scholars have argued that such individuals cease being anthropologists during these moments (cf. Kimball 1978), noting that their contributions are not purely scientific but rely heavily on individual insight and interpretation. It would be unfortunate if we were to take this consideration too seriously. The *effective* existence of an applied anthropology depends on its being more than a science; it must also be a form of participation in human affairs. Useful participation cannot always await those levels of certainty normally required of scientific investigation.

The ways in which anthropologists speak to the public vary. When, for example, Laura Nader (1981) addressed a group of physicists concerned with energy issues, she focused on the way physicists communicate with each other. In presenting the perspective of an onlooker, her view was clearly in the tradition of anthropology. Physicists and energy analysts had, she observed, developed an inordinate "belief in numbers" which actually transcended the usefulness of quantitative measures. Nader also reported to the physicists that there were a number of energy problems and alternatives which they were not considering. During her observations of several of their conferences, she had heard little discussion of issues pertaining to energy conservation, solar energy, or the safety of nuclear power.

We should not expect every anthropologist to wholeheartedly agree with Nader's analysis of energy issues. One wonders, for example, if she could have brought the same claim of objectivity to an analysis of conferences held by advocates of environmental conservation, a position she clearly favors. For the purposes of this illustration, the importance of her participation lies in her willingness to address energy decision makers in their forum.

Some of the most eloquent public testimony of anthropologists has evolved from their interest in international human rights, a concern traditionally informed by their close association with peoples whose rights and survival seem most threatened by the impacts of modernity. When Gerald Berreman (1980) addressed a technology conference, he questioned the belief that improvements in technology invariably lead to progress. He suggested that there appeared to be no clear relationship between *technological* and *social* progress. Berreman relied heavily on the observations of his fellow anthropologists in order to claim that the human costs of unmindful technological development might well be more than our world can bear.

Regardless of their specific individual messages, when anthropologists participate in public affairs, the principle underlying their involvement is the need to underscore the importance of the social and cultural consequences of human actions. While contributions made by noted anthropologists like Mead, Nader, and Berreman are clearly important, they probably do not represent the greater potential for the participation of anthropologists in public affairs. Anthropologists of less public stature but equally valuable insight have played active roles in the communities in which they live. In some respects, these involvements may be more effective than the pronouncements of their esteemed colleagues, because they are closer to the actual implementation of policy ideas.

Since local-level activities of this kind are seldom publicized in the literature of anthropology, it is impossible to assess the extent to which anthropologists actually participate in the affairs of their communities. My impression, however, is that there has been a significant increase, especially in regions where interests in applied anthropology have flourished. On a personal level, I have observed how my interests in training students for careers in applied anthropology have led me to closer contact with the communities in which my students work. This involvement has in turn led to opportunities to consult with local government and private decision makers, invitations to serve on local boards and committees, and so on. The extent of public involvement can become intense (Schensul 1981). For some individuals, such activities may become a vital part of their continuing education and contribution as an applied anthropologist. I have learned, for example, that one of the modest but important contributions an applied anthropologist can make to help a community gain perspective on any human problem is to serve as a resident reminder of the importance of considering cultural process in assessing situations. This often involves encouraging others to look at the obvious and familiar as a cultural problem and to consider a wider range of explanation and action than they might otherwise take into account.

Some anthropologists have made notable contributions in this regard. For example, Conrad Arensburg and Arthur Niehoff have published a guide designed to help United States development agents prepare themselves for overseas assignments. Their *Introducing Social Change* (1964) includes a chapter describing anthropological field methods and cultural problems which development agents might find useful in assessing the way they approach their jobs. A more recent contribution is James Green's *Cultural Awareness in the Human Services* (1982). Green's background includes considerable experience in training social workers, and his book is an effective demonstration of the ways in which an ethnographic approach to human problems is useful not only as a research tool, but also as a framework for providing counseling services and strengthening relationships between people from different backgrounds.

THE IMPORTANCE OF BASIC RESEARCH

While applied research is significantly different from basic research, it is important to remember that the approaches are complementary and that both contribute to the development of the profession of applied anthropology. One way in which basic research adapts well to the interests of applied anthropologists is in the description and analysis of how decisions are made. Social scientists have long recognized that important differences can exist between the formal and informal organization of administrative and policy settings, and that these differences often have profound effects on how the actors in each setting respond to each other (Blau 1956). Recognizing the "hidden agendas" which often underlie policy statements and programs is an important skill for any applied researcher.

Policy Formulation

Aaron Wildavsky's (1974) *The Politics of the Budgetary Process* is a classic in political science research and merits equal attention from applied anthropologists. In effect, Wildavsky's book is an ethnography of federal policy formulation as it relates to budgetary decision making. To my knowledge, there is no better example of the strength of qualitative research in describing major policy processes.

In many respects, budgeting is the backbone of government policy. The decision to fund a program, and the level at which it is funded, has more practical impact on how government services are distributed than any other single activity. "Budgeting," Wildavsky contends, "deals with the purposes of men." One of the more interesting aspects of his book is the way in which he deals with the complexity of budgetary problems. Viewed from the outside, the national budgeting process for any major society assumes monstrous proportions, not only in terms of the amount of money to be expended, but also in relation to the number of decisions which have to be made. The persons responsible for making such decisions are not authorities in most or any of the areas on which they pass judgment, and they cannot expect to be. If every member of the United States Congress had to, for every appropriations committee he or she sat on, decide each expenditure on the basis of a thorough understanding of the facts of each case, the processes of government would come to a halt. Even the expertise of Congressional staff is not sufficient in most cases to respond to the great variety of issues represented in modern government.

Federal appropriations in the United States are aided, Wildavsky claims, by several mechanisms. One of these is for Congressmen to simplify their decision making by concentrating on those relatively uncomplicated budget items with which they are most familiar. A casual observer of the policy process might wonder, with some skepticism, why a particular Congressman spends a great deal of time picking to pieces a relatively minor feature of an agency's budget, while seemingly paying almost no attention to a much greater and more complex item. Wildavsky explains, however, that the Congressman's implicit intent is to test the overall budget of a government department on the basis of his or her superior knowledge of a few small parts of the total program.

The major aid to simplifying the awesome complexity of federal budgeting is the incremental nature of the budget. Present budgeting decisions are made on the basis of a legacy of prior decisions. The vast majority of past decisions are allowed to stand simply because they have weathered past years of appropriation. Only a few of these decisions, which for one reason or another have caught the attention of the public or of decision makers, are likely to be questioned.

Both of these "aids to calculation" are useful in interpreting the decision-making processes of a wide variety of policy settings. It has long been fashionable to be critical of the blundering inefficiencies and gross inequities of "big government" and "big business." Some of the criticism is warranted. But as observers of any policy process, we must also remember that appearances can be deceiving. Anthropologists have made a profession of demonstrating how the seemingly irrational behaviors of distant peoples are underlaid with a reason and purposefulness unique to their circumstances. On the basis of numerous examples similar to those cited here, Wildavsky has done the same for an important aspect of policy formulation in United States government. It can be hoped that anthropologists will take up his challenge.

Program Planning and Administration

When anthropologist Gerald Britan evaluated an experimental federal government program which was designed to assist government agencies in encouraging the development of technological innovations, he discovered that the agencies were more interested in activities which helped them improve the administration of their programs than they were in activities which might help them formulate better policies on a grand scale. Britan's *Bureaucracy and Innovation* (1981) offers a rare (for anthropology) look at the "middle level" of public policy endeavor. In describing the informal patterns of organization underlying the program's formal structure, and by describing this single program in relation to its place within the federal bureaucracy, Britan was able to account for the limited success and eventual demise of an important policy experiment. He also pointed out an important gap in the literature of applied anthropology.

When anthropologists concern themselves with issues of policy, they almost invariably chose one of two vantage points. They might, on the one hand, prefer to discuss policy formulation, usually in highly abstract terms. How are we going to save the world from starvation? How can we better educate, clothe, feed, or employ minorities? On the other hand, some anthropologists elect to deal with policy problems on the level of implementation. What happens when a new program designed to offer employment training to female heads of households is carried out in Tulsa, Oklahoma? What is it like to try to learn a foreign language (English) if you are a Southeast Asian refugee newly arrived in Sacramento, California? Britan provides insight into a way these two perspectives are mediated. We might summarize this as a *bureaucratic* level of policy activity, in which an agency or organization's concern for survival assumes major importance. A better understanding of the ways in which bureaucracies adapt to policy initiatives and often orchestrate program implementations to suit their perceived needs would help explain much of the distance between plans and their realization.

While both these approaches—and especially the latter—have merit, we must recognize that a lot of activity transpires between the initial formulation of a policy and its implementation. Is it any wonder that anthropologists sometimes (fortunately, less often than in the past) seem naive when they try to compare the initial impulses of a policy idea with the realization of that idea in a single setting? Britan's book offers a glimpse into the middle ground of public policy and provides valuable insight into the relationships between different levels of decision making.

Implementation

The distance between a policy formulated, a plan devised, and a policy implemented can be great. One area of basic and policy-relevant research to which anthropologists have contributed has been the study of what happens when a policy idea "hits the hard ground," striking that arena of action and reaction where someone's ideas begin to make a difference in the lives of others.

Donald Kurtz' (1973) study of *The Politics of a Poverty Habitat* uses concepts of ethnicity and ecology to describe the failure of a "war on poverty" program of the 1960s. The study, based on the development of a Community Action Council in a southern California community, demonstrates how rapidly a radical change program can become "bureaucratized" and co-opted by the mainstream society. One of the greatest problems such change programs face, Kurtz suggests, is the rapidity with which indigenous leaders of a poverty community accept their newly acquired middle-class status (which they achieve by being hired to direct poverty programs), and how they consequently tend to act more in the interest of their new-found status than on behalf of the community concerns they represent.

The problem of the co-optation of minority group leaders is wide-spread in development work. Processes similar to those described by Kurtz have, for example, been noted in Latin American peasant organizations (Landsberger and Hewitt 1970) and elsewhere.

Kurtz identifies several other factors contributing to the demise of the federally funded poverty program he studied. These included conflicts for resources among different ethnic groups, conflicts with existing community agencies, and communication difficulties between the community activists and their federal sponsors. Despite its seemingly radical intentions, Kurtz found the poverty program to be organized like a mainstream "American middle-class institutional structure." It rewarded those few who could most readily understand the structure and secure themselves a place within that structure, and it eventually alienated most of the rest of the community.

In *Teachers Versus Technocrats,* Harry Wolcott (1977) offers another anthropological study of the local implementation of federal policy in the United States. Wolcott focused on the development of a pilot project in a single school district. The project was intended to test the effectiveness of a new education planning and budgeting procedure known as The School Planning, Education, and Communication System (SPECS). The SPECS system was related to the then-popular PPBS budgeting programs supported by the federal government (see Chapter 2).

The first part of Wolcott's study provides a natural history of the SPECS pilot project, from its early planning to its "de-implementation" several years later. As a major government policy initiative designed to increase accountability in government and public service, SPECS and its parent the PPBS were a bureaucratic nightmare; despite its good intentions:

> The underlying problem that SPECS tried to address, however awkwardly, was the problem of finding ways for educators to demonstrate their accomplishments, both within their own ranks and to the public. Educators need evidence of the educational accomplishment resulting from their endeavors, but "Mickey Mouse in triplicate" is not the kind of evidence they need. SPECS bogged down under the weight of a system that seemed to become an end in itself and a threat to those who bore the brunt of the effort.
>
> The major problem with SPECS, with PPBS, and other specific accountability systems is not that they have failed to address a critical problem. Rather, they have promised a panacea to the problem without regard for the complexity of the issues and without sufficient understanding of the internal dynamics of educator subculture. (1977:241)

A major cause of the decline of the SPECS program was, according to Wolcott, conflict between those who plan and direct educational activities (technocrats) and those who conduct the activities (teachers). Wolcott uses the anthropologist's concept of moiety to describe this conflict. A moiety is a division of society (in this case what Wolcott identifies as an educator "subculture") into two groups, generally based on a rule of descent. Although there are no descent rules defining the "moieties" of technocrat and teacher, Wolcott finds the general characteristics of moieties (such as the existence of an exchange of goods and services, conscious recognition of duality, and a principle of recruitment) helpful in his analysis. He also finds the moiety concept useful in describing the types of interaction which occurred between technocrats and teachers involved in the SPECS project.

It is interesting that Wolcott chose to rely so heavily on a concept which draws a clear and certain line between the intentions of different groups of people, a line which he ultimately used to account for the failure of the SPECS program. Like Kurtz' study of a poverty program, *Teachers Versus Technocrats* provides an ethnographic account of the way in which particular policy settings delineate groups and, to a large extent, come to define the terms of interaction between groups. Similar characteristics can be seen in other anthropological studies of program implementation. In his *Local Success and Federal Failure*, Charles Clinton (1979) describes the impact of an experimental federal education project on a rural community in the southern United States. The twist to Clinton's study is his demonstration of the extent to which the community managed to adapt a massive government education initiative to their singular advantage without making concessions to federal expectations for large-scale institutional change.

M.G. Trend's *Housing Allowances for the Poor* offers another useful example of basic research applied to the study of program implementation. On the basis of his research with one site of the federal government's Experimental Housing Allowance Program (see Chapter 5), Trend describes a policy experiment that worked without major conflict between the federal sponsors, local implementors, or beneficiaries of the program. Trend accounts for these happy circumstances on the basis of shared expectations. The EHAP was designed to encourage independence and self-reliance among the low-income beneficiaries of government housing assistance. These ideals happened to fit well with the ethos of the North Dakota community Trend was studying:

> In retrospect, it seems that the key to the North Dakota operations was a set of shared expectations and adequate performance by those on both sides of the agency's desks. The agency's job was to explain the program and to give help only when needed. The participants' task was to meet the requirements and to ask for assistance if difficulties were encountered. While the AAE represented an individualistic and independent approach to subsidized housing, the North Dakota agency pushed this to the limits that the regulations allowed. By and large, the recipients responded by filling the void of lessened agency interference with their own initiative. (1978b: 324–325)

In many respects, the study of local patterns of policy implementation, and of the cultural processes bearing on such patterns, is not far from the more traditional concerns of anthropologists. The studies often permit, for example, a community focus that would be difficult to duplicate in research devoted to planning or policy formulation at higher levels of decision making. At the same time, there are limitations to the present studies, not the least being their short supply.

Limits and Potentials of Implementation Case Study

The study of how policy ideas become implemented through specific program activities is probably one of the most important areas in which basic research can contribute to our understanding of decision making in complex social settings. It is also an area of research clearly suited to the talents of anthropologists. The studies summarized above, despite their limited range, permit us to make a few useful observations about the policy process as it relates to the filtering down of federal government initiatives in the United States:

1.   The research by Clinton and Trend point out the consequences of allowing for local initiative, at least in the implementation of some types of program activities. The work of Kurtz and Wolcott point to the disastrous results that might follow programs which do not allow a great deal of local initiative. (Local initiative might be especially important in new, untested, or experimental programs, such as those described above.)

2.   Program success might be linked to achieving a correspondence in values between those who formulate policy, those who implement programs, and those who will presumably benefit. Athough the programs described by Trend and Clinton both allowed for considerable local initiative, the results were quite different. The community Clinton describes managed to subvert many of the policy goals of the sponsoring federal agency.

3.   In communities where change programs are implemented, several different strategies might develop for coping with the change. The existence of such varied strategies are explored in some detail by Kurtz and Clinton. Program activities may reinforce community factions or create new ones. The success and direction of implementation programs will surely be affected by the outcomes of various community coping strategies.

4.   While the study of planned innovation and deliberate change has often focused on the causes underlying resistance to change, evidence from several of these studies suggests that change agents sometimes unnecessarily interfere in community decision-making processes to the point of jeopardizing program activities (Wolcott 1977:245). The "resistance" of change agents to the communities in which they work may be an important factor in program implementation.

For the most part, these observations are only suggestive. One of the serious limits of the case study approach is the difficulty of ascertaining the extent to which results obtained in one setting can be generalized. It is unfortunate, for example, that each of the studies cited above was based on research with experimental programs. The reason for this bias is not hard to discern—the researchers were hired to do the work because policy makers are more interested in following the course of untried activities than in sponsoring research devoted to programs which have stood the test of time. This special concern must also influence the way change agents respond to local program implementors and beneficiaries. Some of the "interference" noted in the studies might simply be a residue of the special investment of energy and career risk involved in new program activity.

Another limitation of most existing case studies of policy activities is the lack of follow-up studies. The need for such research is again especially apparent in studies of experimental programs. Without follow-ups, it is difficult to determine the extent of "experimental effects" on program activities.

Perhaps the most important contribution case study research could make to our understanding of policy implementation would be to help account for regional and cultural differences which result in different implementations of the same policy, thereby contributing to the varied success and failure of program activities on a national basis. As a rule, major policy activities tend to be planned with very little consideration of regional differences. The result is that they tend to work reasonably well in some places and not at all in others, with very little understanding of why. For example, the housing assistance program described by Trend worked well in North Dakota but was barely functional at another site where it was attempted (Chambers 1975).

A greater recognition of the reasons underlying differences in policy implementation could result in adjustments in the planning and formulation of policies. Different responses to specific human problems might be required for different regions of a country. In some cases, giving local program implementors maximum discretion in determining and adjusting specific program activities might be advisable.

Demonstration of the need for such flexibiity, and of the direction it might take, awaits more serious application of a comparative case study approach to the study of policy implementation. Similarly, a more balanced view of the dynamics of policy implementation will require research based on how established programs have managed to sustain themselves, and less reliance upon a small collection of data pertaining to experimental programs.

The Ecological Approach

Many of the characteristics of cultural process described earlier in this chapter relate well to the principles underlying ecological research. Human ecologists are interested in the way people adapt to their place (econiche) in a larger social and environmental setting (ecosystem). The ecological approach has been applied to basic research in a variety of areas of practical interest, including the study of population dynamics, environmental control, nutrition and health research, problems related to human adaptation to poverty, housing research, and urban design. One important lesson of ecological anthropology is that, while an understanding of cultural process is important, it is rarely sufficient to provide a complete explanation of how humans adapt to their circumstances. The environments in which people operate, and the biological and natural resources available to them, impose hard limits on their activities.

Ecological studies also offer a basis for judgment that is lacking in much anthropology and absolutely necessary in policy research. As John Bennett (1976) notes in the *Ecological Transition*, the concept of adaptation evokes the possibility of maladaptation. The criteria for adaptation supplied by Bennett is the ability to maintain a *sustained yield* of resources; that is, to utilize the environment in such a way as to ensure immediate survival without depleting those resources on which continued survival depends.

The ecological model of inquiry centers on the practical limits of resource use and consequently can be fruitfully applied to policy issues pertaining to environmental preservation and conservation (Hinkley 1976). Anthropologists have contributed to ecological research primarily on the basis of their interest in small-scale societies, where the relationships between environment, technology, and local decision making are relatively easy to demonstrate. Clifford Geertz (1971) has gone a step further in describing how large-scale patterns of ecological change affect the development processes of modern state societies. Other anthropologists have attempted to account for the alarmingly disproportionate scale of resource use and environmental exploitation accompanying the growth of industrial societies. The sense of imminent disaster that pervades much of the writing of these anthropologists leaves us with an important warning. Unfortunately, their either/or catastrophic interpretations provide little practical guidance for allocating or reallocating resources amongst the complex and competitive claims of modern society.

THE USES OF KNOWLEDGE

A distinction will be helpful in the discussion that follows between information and knowledge. *Information* is the raw data of inquiry, the "facts" from which analysis might proceed. *Knowledge*, on the other hand, is the analytic and interpretative stage of research; it is the "sense" we make from data. In basic research, the distinction between information and knowledge is generally of only passing importance, since the usual strategy of inquiry is for an investigator to be responsible both for the collection of data and for making sense from it. But in applied research there is often considerable distance between the processes of obtaining information and those of analysis and interpretation. This is partly because different people, frequently trained in different research "paradigms," might be responsible for different stages of applied inquiry. It is also because the *kind of sense* required of applied research is generally different from that required of basic research.

In their work, applied anthropologists might be called upon to supply information or contribute knowledge, or both. Knowing what is expected from a particular inquiry is important. When researchers are called upon to produce only information, they have to be content to leave the interpretation of that information to others, and be prepared for the possibility that others may draw different conclusions than they might have. When researchers assume responsibility for analyzing and interpreting data that is not their own, they need to be especially sensitive to the possibility that the methodological and theoretical assumptions underlying the collection of that information may be different from theirs.

Information Utilization

The clients of applied research are not always familiar with either the full potential or limitations of social inquiry. It is as possible to expect too little from research as to expect too much. Michael Pardee (1981) offers an example based on his research with a community revitalization project (see the discussion of Pardee's work in Chapter 5). It was only after he was well into his research that Pardee discovered that he and his client had quite different ideas about what he was supposed to be doing. Pardee had assumed that he would be attempting to evaluate possible alternatives to community revitalization on the basis of what he was learning about the community. He was conducting his research in anticipation of this task. As it turned out, the planners Pardee was working with had not anticipated that he might be able to provide information *and* analysis that could actually help them decide what to do. They had only expected Pardee to provide a relatively simple assessment of the physical and social conditions of the community and a survey of community needs. This misunderstanding contributed to the underutilization of both the information and analysis Pardee later offered the planners.

Major applied research projects, employing large numbers of researchers with different disciplinary backgrounds, pose special problems in the utilization of information. This is especially true in cases where both qualitative and quantitative data sources are developed. We have noted some of these problems elsewhere in this book. Where fieldworkers are used as "site persons," they are often called upon to provide information and to perform tasks that are not closely related to their major research efforts (Clinton 1975). Research analysts, usually not trained in qualitative research, often must try to make sense out of the data supplied by field-workers. As analysis proceeds, information needs often change, but when fieldworkers are not privy to the reasons for the changes, they often fail to provide the new types of information required (Chambers 1977). In anthropological fieldwork, written research reports often provide only a portion of the information actually collected by a fieldworker—that portion which the anthropologists *think* is most relevant to the overall problem being addressed. This partial information is especially prone to misinterpretation by others (Almy 1977).

The problems noted above can be attributed primarily to a lack of communication among researchers and between researchers and their clients. An indispensable part of any applied research project should be intensive preliminary discussions between researchers and research clients. In cases where it is clear that a researcher is being employed solely to provide information, the type of information expected should be clearly anticipated. Wherever possible, applied researchers who find themselves headed for such a role should try to ensure that they will at least be consulted as their data is subjected to analysis.

Making Social Knowledge from Information

The bridge between having information and making decisions is largely composed of processes of knowledge construction. Two helpful concepts in thinking about knowledge are those of *analysis* and *interpretation*. Analysis in social thought is the deliberate and systematic sifting of information in order to discern patterns of thought or behavior. Interpretation is the process of assigning significance to those patterns.

All of these activities—collecting information, analyzing and interpreting data, and making decisions—conform to the description of cultural process offered earlier in this chapter. It is a part of the bane and the intrigue of the anthropology that we have no choice but to reflect on our data with the same cultural processes we are attempting to discern in others. Social science is, of course, a relatively precise and self-conscious way of managing one's thinking, but it can be as partial and limited as any other mode of apprehension.

For our purposes, what is important to keep in mind is that making decisions generally involves using different kinds of knowledge. First of all, *public* decisions are seldom made by a single person; they require the collective input and feedback of a variety of people, each of whom possesses information and knowledge that is partly unique. What is more, individuals trying to arrive at decisions do not rely solely on formal knowledge or systematically gathered information. It is not difficult to understand why this is so. The very nature of decision making requires the ability and willingness to make choices in the face of an uncertain future on the basis of partial information. Decisions which affect a great many people are most likely to have a varied impact on different segments of a population. For nearly all practical purposes, the knowledge we can bring to the understanding of a human circumstance is always imperfect.

What this implies is that decisions also bear the strain of imperfection. The relationships between knowledge and decision making are complex and are not as direct as we sometimes assume. Paradoxically, poor decisions can be made on the basis of reliable information; and decisions that work can be made on the basis of poor or inadequate information.

Edward Spicer (1979) provides an example from his work with the War Relocation Authority. Anthropologists working as researchers in United States relocation camps for the Japanese during World War II were asked what to do about relocating the internees when the war was over. According to Spicer, the anthropologists advised retaining the internees and gradually reassimilating them into United States society. Their argument was essentially that the internees and the non-Japanese population would have a difficult time overcoming their wartime experiences. However, the War Relocation Authority decided such an alternative was politically unfeasible. Political expediency and legal considerations encouraged officials at the War Relocation Authority to disregard the advice given by the anthropologists. The internees were released and, as it turned out, appeared to have little difficulty in readjusting to post-war American society. Had a decision been made solely on the basis of the knowledge provided by the anthropologists, it would have almost certainly resulted in unnecessary detainment of the internees contributing further to the hardships imposed upon them during the war.

This experience presents a fairly complex problem. The anthropologists working with the War Relocation Authority did not provide their clients with "wrong" information. No one at that time had any idea what would happen when the Japanese returned to their communities. There was simply no direct precedent for forming a recommendation. The anthropologists presumably relied upon their knowledge of similar cultural events in arriving at their conclusions, knowledge which included a considerable amount of information as to the adjustment difficulties and severe stress experienced by people when their lives are radically altered in a short period of time. In this case, valid though imperfect knowledge would have led to a poor decision if the War Relocation Authority had followed the counsel of the anthropologists.

In Chapter 4 we have considered the Bank Wiring Room Experiment conducted during the 1940s as a part of a series of management studies for the Western Electric Company. The experiment involved the collection of both qualitative, observational data and quantitative information. In this case, however, the qualitative data was relied upon heavily in the analysis and interpretation of the experiment. Interpretations based on observations of supervisor and employee relationships formed the basis for much of the "human relations" approach to management which the study advocated. As a landmark in organizational research, the study contributed substantially to the development of more humane approaches to management. But in a recent article, in which Richard Franke and James Kaul (1978; see also Wendel 1979 and Franke 1979) report on their reanalysis of the quantitative data from the experiment, the earlier results have been placed in jeopardy. Using statistical techniques that were unavailable when the research was conducted, Franke and Kaul can find no collaborating evidence from the quantitative data for the interpretations first drawn from the study. Rather carefully, the researchers conclude that, while there may have been great justification during the 1940s for advocating management practices that were more sensitive to employees' needs, the original scientific evidence used to advocate such a position was spurious.

This is also a remarkable story. Allowing that the issue is not yet settled (to my knowledge, participants in the wiring room experiment have not responded to this critical assessment of their work), it is still possible to observe how flawed knowledge might serve perfectly reasonable ends. It is not idle speculation to suggest that the working environments of hundreds of millions of United States workers were improved at least partly as a result of this important study. To this end, the possibility that the study might have been seriously flawed is almost irrelevant.

What Makes Knowledge Useful?

Recognizing the complex relationships between knowledge and decision making, it still makes sense to suggest that the more knowledge that can be brought to bear on a problem, the more likely it is that "good" decisions will be made. While it is important to recognize the limitations of the kinds of knowledge applied anthropologists and other social scientists might be able to contribute, a far greater concern should be the number of public decisions which are made without the benefit of any effective participation by social researchers. Two major reasons explain this lack. First, social researchers might not be invited to participate, either because their contribution is not considered to be pertinent or because it is not wanted. Secondly, social researchers might be invited to participate, only to discover that their contribution has had little or no effect on the outcomes of a decision.

Let us consider the latter possibility first. We can begin with some fairly practical observations. In a survey among federal decision makers of attitudes toward the utilization of social science knowledge, Nathan Caplan (1975) and his colleagues have identified a number of factors that contribute to the likelihood of social research being used:

1.   There must be a receptivity to social science on the part of policy makers.

2.   Social science knowledge tends to be underutilized where there are significant "differences in values, language, reward systems and social and professional affiliations" between policy makers and social scientists.

3.   Policy makers must be able to accept the ability of social scientists to conduct their work in an objective manner. This is a difficult factor since, as Caplan notes, criteria of objectivity may vary considerably among policy makers. Some of the respondents for his survey cited "irresponsible and shoddy program evaluations" as evidence for lack of objectivity. Others appeared to reject as biased those research results which "contradict what they considered to be true."

4.   Social research must be "politically feasible" if it is to be used.

5.   The utilization of social research varies with the "information-processing style" of the decision maker. Caplan and his colleagues suggest that decision makers vary among themselves in the way they use information, and this affects their receptivity toward social research.

Some of these observations indicate the need for a special effort on the part of an applied researcher—such as making sure that information is presented in a way which is familiar to the decision maker. Other observations simply offer a challenge. The knowledge that a decision maker might dismiss a research product as biased because it is not compatible with his or her common sense assessment of a situation does not suggest that the researcher should yield to the decision maker's common sense. On the other hand, the effective applied researcher is aware of the persuasiveness of common sense in others and is sensitive to the possibility of his or her own biases.

The use of social research in public decision making has many dimensions. Our concern extends not only to conditions which favor the utilization of research, but also to factors which account for the rationales underlying research use. Carol Weiss (1980) has described several such justifications:

1.   Social research can be used to conceptualize and redefine policy ideas.

2.   Social research can contribute directly to the solution of specific policy problems.

3.   Social research can also be used by decision makers to further their self-interests. Weiss points out that decision makers sometimes use research as "political ammunition." They may also use social research to "delay action or to avoid taking responsibility for a decision."

Applied researchers need to be alert to the *actual* uses for which their work might be intended. The only way the researcher can do this is by understanding the context of a research effort. Too often, researchers discover such contexts only after they are deeply committed to a research effort. Their response is often outrage, based on a feeling of having been misled. It might as well be a sense of embarrassment arising out of their own impatience and credulity.

As Weiss points out, it is not necessarily wrong for decision makers to have a hidden agenda for social research. Nor does the existence of such agendas invariably mean that research will be misused. In cases where decision makers' intentions seem counterproductive to the research effort, a researcher is well advised to carefully consider his or her decision to become involved. In other situations, an awareness of both the explicit and implicit factors underlying a research effort will equip the researcher to produce a product which responds effectively to a variety of potential uses, possibly including those of social purpose and the self-interest of decision makers.

In some respects, the anthropologist is especially well prepared to deal with these multiple contexts of research utilization, as long as he or she is willing to approach each context with the same sensitivity and pragmatism anthropologists have traditionally brought to the settings of field research. In the field anthropologists generally try to obtain background knowledge about the people with whom they will work. Anthropologists enter the field with a set of personal as well as professional goals. Experienced fieldworkers recognize that their success will largely depend on their ability to create an atmosphere of mutal trust. They are often willing to accommodate their subjects' desires to derive personal benefit from participation in a research effort. Fieldworkers accept the likelihood that their research subjects will not fully understand or share their faith in the research process. And they learn quickly to recognize situations in which they might be taken advantage of, or in which their subjects might use their association with them for nefarious purposes. Applied researchers need to acquire the same characteristics, and then go one step further to extend their sensitivity to both the clients and subjects of their research efforts.

Criteria of Utility

The unique characteristics of applied anthropology which have been discussed in this book—the often ambiguous relationship between knowledge and judgment, the vagaries of a client orientation, and the wide range of activities in which anthropologists participate—all point to a vital concern with utility. The assumption underlying our discussion has been that an adequate description of applied work requires a direct concern with the processes involved in making knowledge useful. In pursuing this interest, we must not think that good knowledge will necessarily be useful without an effort to make it so. The notion that right-minded people will naturally make their decisions on the basis of the best and most valid knowledge available is a misleading and dangerous idea. The utility of knowledge can only be evaluated in terms of specific uses; in every case, knowledge has to be deliberately shaped and molded to particular needs through a continual process of search and interpretation. People use knowledge for specific purposes—they salvage it, mess with it, twist it, elaborate upon it, add to it, and subtract from it. This is their prerogative, and it is a privilege shaped of necessity. The means and standards of any particular conversion of knowledge are as essential to the utility of that piece of knowledge as the standards of inquiry by which it was originally obtained.

A sense of utility, even a "science" of utility, is a prerequisite to effective application in any field. Just as basic science proceeds from criteria of validity and reliability, so must applied work recognize and adhere to clear criteria of utility. But what should such criteria be? The following considerations represent a few minimal characteristics of effective applied work:

1. A major criterion of utility is *accessibility*. Even the best of knowledge, from any profesion, will go unused if it is not accessible to decision makers. Most of the knowledge of anthropology, and of social inquiry in general, falls in this category. As a rule, anthropologists have been more interested in communicating among themselves than in sharing their knowledge with those outside the profession. The criterion of accessibility underscores the need for persons trained in anthropology who are especially equipped to serve as knowledge brokers. A profession which has as its sole criterion of success the production of knowledge is bound to have problems in making knowledge accessible, since its practitioners will almost inevitably have a vested interest in new knowledge and little concern with making existing knowledge more accessible to decision makers.

2. Central to any notion of utility is the criterion of *relevance*. To be relevant, knowledge must address the goals and prescribed activities of decision makers. It must also be produced in a way that is appropriate to the resource limits (such as time and money) imposed on decision makers. Anthropologists have sometimes described these considerations as arbitrary and negative limits on effective research; in fact, they are the *necessary* conditions of effective applied work. A research project which takes five years to complete will not be very useful to a decision maker who must come up with a solution in five months. Similarly, a proposal for a course of action which might cost several million dollars to implement will have little utility to a public agency with a total budget of a few thousand dollars. While these are extreme examples, problems of relevance are among the most common snags to effective utilization.

3. The criterion of *significance* is also central to our concern for utility. Useful knowledge almost invariably has to respond to different claims upon the significance of a particular course of action. Unfortunately, knowledge is often produced solely from the frame of reference and sense of significance of those who produce it. On the other hand, people who use knowledge generally have to account for their decisions from several different and competing criteria of significance. Because people determine the significance of things from different perspectives, and often with considerable self-interest, criteria of significance are necessarily embedded in political, commercial, bureaucratic, social, and personal considerations of worthiness.

Archeologists have, for example, recognized varying criteria of significance for some time. As more of their number become involved in applied work, they have been forced to acknowledge that archeological resources have significance that extends well beyond their usual criteria of scientific evidence and worth. Applied archeologists have begun to recognize that judgments as to which sites are most worth preserving must include considerations of public and even political interest in particular types of archeological material. In making their recommendations for the preservation of archeological resources, they have learned to appeal not only to science but also to measures of national and regional pride, community cohesion, and corporate responsibility. Useful knowledge helps mediate the claims and competition for significance that are inherent in society.

4. A fourth criterion of utility is that of *prospect*. Useful knowledge generally blends an empirical grounding in *what is* with a sense of what *could or should be*; it is, in other words, responsive to the goal of reforming what is into what we want it to be. Anthropologists and other social scientists are often trained to develop their observations solely from empirically derived evidence, and this sometimes creates problems in transferring their knowledge to applied settings, as well as difficulties in communicating with policy and decision makers. A simple rendering of what we are seldom gives us the most appropriate image of what we can be.

Problems of prospect are common in applied work. In any given project, are we trying to encourage people to remain as they are, or are we trying to change and perhaps even presuming to "improve" their behaviors? Researchers and decision makers often disagree as to the prospects of a common endeavor. One goal of effective applied work is to make implicit ideas of prospect more explicit and to acknowledge the ideals and expectations which underlie nearly every effort of deliberate change.

5. The criterion of *credibility* is a fifth measure of utility. Useful knowledge exhibits awareness of and builds upon the standards of evidence and credibility that are familiar to those who use it. What this means is that, however good a piece of work is, it must also be *believable* to those who will use it. This does not, however, suggest that the criterion of credibility requires that knowledge be distorted to conform to the beliefs of others; if that were the case there would simply be no need, at least no ethical need, for knowledge. A credible translation of knowledge is deliberately sensitive to the milieu in which it will be used. Despite similarities, the criterion of credibility is set apart from that of relevance. To be relevant, knowledge must be appropriate to the limits of practicality imposed on an idea or program of change. These limits may (and generally do) transcend the local or regional settings in which they are enacted. The requirement of credibility, on the other hand, is derived diretly from a policy or decision-making setting. Credibility is achieved by being responsive to the social and cultural context in which knowledge is to be utilized.

The applied anthropologist who bases large portions of his report to the Tribal Chairman of an American Indian community on data collected through the collection of oral histories is responding on the basis of his assessment of a standard of evidence routinely employed by his client. In the same manner, the anthropologist who is reporting to a Midwestern school district on her evaluation of a local experiment in bilingual education might find numbers more convincing than anecdotes. These are only the most obvious of examples. Credibility extends to the most subtle nuances of communicating with clients. It is achieved only on the basis of a clear awareness of the settings in which work has been undertaken. It can rarely be faked.

These five criteria of utility—accessibility, relevance, significance, prospect, and credibility—offer a preliminary basis from which we can judge the effectiveness of most applied work. They are, as I have suggested, as essential to successful application as the scientific criteria of evidence by which we normally evaluate the quality of social inquiry.

The Institutionalization of Applied Social Research

Although the value of applied research is better established now than it was in the past, much of the utilization of social research remains haphazard. The mere acceptance of the idea that human problems have social and cultural components does not ensure that these aspects of the problem will be addressed in decision making. Often the decision to do applied social research depends upon the ability of researchers to convince decision makers of the value of their participation, or upon the presence of decision makers who are prone to consider the need for such participation. More consistent utilization requires the institutionalization of a recognized need for applied social research.

In the United States, two phenomena have accounted for increased utilization of applied social research over the past several decades. One of these has been the tendency for potential research clients, both in government and private enterprise, to establish the need for social research as a matter of policy. Some government agencies and private foundations, for example, set aside portions of their "research and development" budgets for social research. On the local level, considerable variation exists in the degree to which project administrators and other managers perceive a need for social inquiry. Differences in political ideology also affect both the kind and quality of social research which agencies at all levels are likely to sponsor. The politically conservative administration of President Ronald Reagan, for example, heralded a decline in funding for many kinds of social research.

Another approach to ensuring the utilization of applied social research is through government legislation. We noted in Chapter 2 that much of the recent impetus for social research results from governmental interest in accountability, which has led to regulatory and legal requirements for documentation, evaluation, and forecasting research. During the 1970s, much of this sort of legislation was directed to areas of environmental concern. More generally, the government has experienced a need to justify its growing public expenditures both by demonstrating their need and evaluating the effectiveness of government responses.

Both these approaches to institutionalizing the use of applied social research in decision making are important. Both also have their strengths and weaknesses. When an agency decides to contract for social research as a matter of policy, the advantage is that such a decision indicates a receptivity to the use of social research. The disadvantage is that policies change with the personalities and conditions from which they evolve. During the 1970s, for example, the National Institutes of Mental Health sponsored a wide variety of social research programs. In the early 1980s, many of these concerns were sharply curtailed.

The advantage of a legislative approach to research utilization is that it affords greater long-term commitment. Laws requiring social research are as difficult to change as they are to institute in the first place. Legal requirements for applied social research are not immune from the impact of subsequent changes in government, but they do appear to be relatively stable. A disadvantage of legislation is that it often does not represent a genuine commitment on the part of decision makers to actually use the results of social research which they are legally required to procure. In such cases, contracting research is sometimes merely a formality and the potential for abusing the good intentions of researchers is great.

Applied anthropologists need to be sensitive to issues concerning the institutionalization of social research. They should be willing to participate in the legislative process and in "public relations" to ensure that concerns for social and cultural process are well represented. The benefits of applied social research are not always obvious to decision makers. At the same time, applied anthropologists need to avoid thinking of and promoting their efforts as a panacea for all the world's ills. Decision makers know better, and applied researchers should, too. The effective institutionalization of applied social research rests on a clear demonstration of specific needs and benefits rather than simply on a moral and professional commitment to conduct research.

ANTHROPOLOGISTS AS DECISION MAKERS

Although the advancement of research and the experience of cultural process remains the backbone of anthropology, few anthropologists spend their entire careers as researchers. In the past, teaching has been the dominant practitioner role for anthropologists. Presently, increasing numbers of anthropologists are choosing roles related to the transfer of knowledge and to decision making. In a sense, these choices are a natural outgrowth of the profession's renewed receptivity to application. Just as in the academic model experienced researchers eventually expect to become the teachers of research, in the practitioner model applied researchers often find that their careers eventually lead them to opportunities to participate more directly in policy decision making.

One of the great challenges to applied anthropology is to figure out how to encourage anthropologists in these endeavors and incorporate their concerns and insights into the profession. As this is accomplished, it will no longer be necessary to offer lengthy discussions of the uses and limitations of knowledge—these practical understandings will be a part of the profession's general orientation.

We discussed roles associated with knowledge transfer at some length in Chapter 1. In this chapter, it seems appropriate that we consider the contexts of decision making—of actually managing ideas, research, and people—as another role suitable to the experience of anthropologists. Some writers have suggested that, of all the skills and insights associated with the social and behavioral sciences, anthropology might be especially suitable to careers in management and administration. Anthony F.C. Wallace (1976) and Nancie L. Gonzalez (1980) have entertained this possibility in discussing their own advancement to administrative positions in universities. J. Rounds (1981) has suggested that the holistic perspective and the "discovery methods" peculiar to ethnographic research correspond well to the analytic and interpretative skills of decision makers.

As more anthropologists elect to assume careers in management and adminstration, we can expect significantly greater demand for attention to the problems faced by decision makers. The profession will need to have the capacity to accept a greater variety of professional commitments than it has in the past. Along with the values of science, it will be increasingly important to consider the values of decision making. These are not limited to—but certainly include—the following:

1.   Policy decision making is *incremental*. Just as we noted from Wildavsky's study of the federal budgetary process, Charles Lindblom (1959) has aptly described in more general terms the extent to which policy decision making is often ruled by a process of making "successive limited comparisons" between alternative policy responses. Decisions are seldom made in one fell swoop, but on the basis of periodic incremental changes. From a background of experience and reconsideration, policy is "made and re-made endlessly," usually in bits and pieces. This approach is different from the normal aims of scientific inquiry which, while incremental in the collection of information, are generally regarded as "revolutionary" in the way theories are formulated.

2.   Policy makers value knowledge that is designed to *authenticate* decisions (Sowell 1980). In other words, the use of knowledge is closely linked to the incremental nature of decision making. Good decision are those which provide an incentive for change. Useful knowledge articulates the relationship between decisions

and incentives, recognizing that both change in gradual increments.

3. Policy decision making is intentional or *purposive*. Social purposes underlie social policies. While there is a continual need in complex society to challenge and confront the purposes which underlie policy, decision makers do not operate from a vacuum. Business managers, for example, accept the profit motive, and federal health program administrators accept the principle of government involvement in health care.

4. Policy decision making is *manipulative*. Correspondingly, knowledge that is useful to policy makers describes and facilitates manipulation (Bastide 1974; Rule 1978). Decision makers have a commitment to and investment in change from which there is no easy avenue of retreat.

The full potential of applied anthropology rests with the ability to recognize and strengthen the links between inquiry, knowledge transfer, and decision making. As these links continue to become more recognizable, the profession of anthropology will change. The foundations for many of these changes are already in place.

PERSPECTIVE

A sensitivity toward the "cultures of policy" should encourage us to consider the agents of change and human problem solving as legitimate objects of study. While the major contribution of applied anthropology has thus far been to demonstrate how people are likely to respond to deliberate interventions into their lives, increasing numbers of anthropologists have assumed an interest in understanding how programs of change are initiated and the ways in which they are administered. Ethnographic research methods have proven useful in describing the informal (as opposed to formal and idealized) structures of policy decision making. As more anthropologists choose careers related to knowledge transfer and decision making, an understanding of the cultural significance of policy settings assumes practical as well as scientific importance.

This chapter is biased in its focus on government policy, largely becuse the limited experience anthropologists have in studying decision making is almost entirely directed to the work of government agencies. An equally strong case can be made for the importance of understanding how private interests, such as business and industry, respond to policy initiatives, make decisions, and administer their affairs. Interested readers might refer to Carol Holzberg and Maureen Giovannini's (1981) review of anthropological contributions to the study of industry.

RECOMMENDED READINGS

For general purposes, readers are referred to H.B. Barnett's *Innovation: The Basis of Cultural Change* (McGraw-Hill, 1953) and Bernardo Bernardi's edited volume *The Concept of Dynamics of Culture* (Mouton, 1977).

Discussions pertaining to anthropologists' involvement in influencing government policy include a special issue of *Practicing Anthropology* (1 (3), 1979) devoted to the subject and Dorothy Willner's "For Whom the Bell Tolls: Anthropologists Advising on Public Policy" in *American Anthropologist* (82(1), 1980). Robert Hinshaw's "Anthropology, Administration, and Public Policy" in *Annual Review of Anthropology* (1980) offers an extended discussion and bibliography.

Robert Bee's *The Politics of American Indian Policy* (Schenkman, 1982) and William A. Brophy and Sophie D. Aberle's *The Indian: America's Unfinished Business* (Oklahoma, 1966) provide accounts of United States American Indian policy which should be of interest to many anthropologists.

In recent years, the literature on research utilization has grown substantially. In addition to references cited in the text of this chapter, readers might refer to Jack Rothman's *Using Research in Organizations* (Sage Publications, Inc., 1980); Michael Quinn Patton's *Utilization-focused Evaluation* (Sage Publications, Inc., 1978); and Charles Lindblom and David Cohen's *Usable Knowledge* (Yale, 1979).

Harold Orlans' *Contracting for Knowledge* (Jossey-Bass, 1973) is an account of policy research and utilization written by an anthropologist. Reviews of the use of social research in selected areas of federal policy interest can be found in Laurence E. Lynn's edited volume *Knowledge and Policy: The Uncertain Connection* (National Academy of Sciences, 1979).

The Harvard Business Review's (1979) *On Human Relations* offers worthwhile insight for readers interested in possible relationships between managerial decision making and the anthropological perspective.

An extensive bibliography on social science research utilization appears in Carol Weiss' *Social Science Research and Decision-Making* (Columbia, 1980).

7

The Profession of Applied Anthropology

"You know," I suggested to a friend, "it seems to me that we're beginning to use the word *profession* a lot when we talk about anthropology. Before, we almost always used the word *discipline*."

"Is that right?" said my friend, who is not an anthropologist but has an interest in the way people use words.

"There are two distinct ideas about anthropology implied in that choice," I said, "and I think most of us have only begun to recognize the difference."

Anthropology is necessarily both a discipline and a profession. A *discipline* can be described as a way of approaching understanding, based on at least partially distinct rules of inquiry and the maintenance of an accumulated body of knowledge. A *profession* should be seen as a group of people with particular skills, services, and insights to offer others. To some extent, the concerns of discipline tend to be internal, while the interests of profession tend to look outward. Thus, the professional concerns of anthropologists generally have to do with such seemingly mundane things as employment, ethics, the public image of anthropology, and the training of new anthropologists.

The rapid development of interest in applied anthropology since the 1970s has added considerably to an interest in the professional status of anthropology. During the late 1970s and early 1980s, the profession began to show evidence of substantial change not only in the varieties of work anthropoligists engaged in, but also in the way anthropologists thought of themselves and their place in society.

PROFESSIONAL ORGANIZATION IN ANTHROPOLOGY

Professional and disciplinary organizations exist for a great variety of purposes. They often serve as a forum for the publication and presentation of knowledge pertinent to the profession. Most professional organizations also serve to legitimize a profession, both by "policing" the activities of its members and by trying to prevent or limit practice on the part of unqualified individuals. Additional functions of professional organizations include providing their members with information concerning job and research opportunities and serving the special interests of their members in responding to public issues.

The Roots of Professional Organization in Anthropology

The somewhat curious beginnings of organization in anthropology are important in helping us understand the field's current trend toward professionalism. It should be recognized, for example, that most of the early societies representing anthropological issues were not professional organizations at all, but were assemblages of professional and amateur anthropologists, gatherings which had been originated to advocate for issues of interest to their members. These issues included the protection of "aboriginal" peoples and archeological resources. As we have noted elsewhere, the tendency toward advocacy continues to be an important aspect of the professional ethic and concern of anthropology. At professional meetings, members often introduce and vote on motions or resolutions designed to encourage the protection of minority groups under siege. The ethical principles developed by anthropologists continue to place considerable emphasis on the protection of the subjects of research. In recent years, the advocacy concerns of many anthropologists have been underscored by the development of new organizations, such as Cultural Survival International and the Anthropology Resource Center, designed to publicize and represent the plight of indigenous and minority populations.

Most of the early anthropological organizations included a great many people who had avocational rather than career interests in the discipline. When anthropologists finally did begin to organize both as a discipline and a profession, it was against a background in which most were already employed or were expected to work in academic settings. The newly constituted professional organizations came to serve primarily the needs of basic researchers and teachers. Professional meetings and publications were given over to communicating and debating the results of basic research. These are important functions, which continue to receive considerable emphasis within most contemporary anthropological organizations.

On the other hand, many of the seemingly mundane characteristics of a career in anthropology received little attention in the profession's formal organizations. Newsletters might advertise teaching posts, and universities seeking to hire anthropologists often interviewed at professional meetings; but instruction in the mechanics of getting and keeping a job was much more informal, generally passed by word of mouth from professor to student. There was no essential problem with these procedures so long as serious education in anthropology was almost invariably seen as leading to a college- or university-level teaching position.

The Reorganization of a Profession

An account of the changes that have occurred in anthropology's professional organizations since the early 1960s or so is in part a testimony to the growing influence of applied anthropology. Like many movements of revitalization, many of the changes have occurred as a result of the energies of anthropologists who were at one time marginal to the profession's formal leadership.

The Society of Professional Anthropologists (SOPA), established in 1973 by a group of anthropologists based in Tucson, Arizona, was an early sign of the profession's newly emerging needs. SOPA was founded primarily to represent the interests of anthropologists located in the Tucson area who were not employed in academic settings. Soon to follow was the Washington Association of Professional Anthropologists (WAPA), based in the United States' capital. A number of other local practitioner associations have since developed.

In the past few years, WAPA has become the most visibly active of the regional groups. The organization has established an employment referral service for its members, published a newletter and a guide to practicing anthropologists in the Washington, D.C. area, and in cooperation with the American Anthropological Association and the Society for Applied Anthropology has conducted workshops to aid anthropologists in developing applied research and career skills.

One of the motives for the founding of local practitioner associations has been the perception on the part of their members that the major anthropological organizations have not responded to their professional needs. Although the national organizations, such as the American Anthropological Association and the Society for Applied Anthropology, have recently shown considerable interest in the concerns of anthropologists who are employed outside academia, their efforts have been hampered by dissension within their ranks. All anthropologists do not agree that the major associations should assume responsibility for the careers of anthropologists who choose to work outside academia. Many of the detractors, their own careers relatively secure, argue that the major organizations should be constituted primarily as scholarly societies representing the *discipline* of anthropology. Some of them continue to regard anthropologists who work outside academia as a very small minority who, in their view, have settled for alternative employment while waiting for an opportunity to secure an appointment in a university.

In effect, anthropology is engaged in a dilemma of cultural process. As late as the mid-1970s, it was still not clear how many anthropologists were engaged in full-time applied work. It was not until 1980 that we learned that a full one-fourth of the membership of the American Anthropological Association were in that category, making anthropologists working outside academia the largest-interest minority in the profession. But it has not been clear, then or now, that practitioners are actually a *minority*. Considering that anthropologists working outside academia are among the least likely to join professional organizations that have a reputation for favoring the interests of academics, it is not too farfetched to guess that practicing anthropologists employed outside university settings will soon—or have already—come to represent a majority.

During the past several years, the major professional organizations have made notable efforts to better represent the interests of practicing anthropologists. In 1978, the Society for Applied Anthropology began publishing *Practicing Anthropology*, a publication devoted in large part to the work and interests of anthropologists working outside academia. The *Anthropology Newsletter*, published by the American Anthropological Association, has recently devoted much of its space to the career concerns of practitioners. In 1979, the membership of the American Anthropological Association passed a *Resolution in Support of Anthropologists Working Outside Academia*, which among other considerations, required the association to publish a directory of its members who were not working in universities. Prior to that time, the only directory published by the association was devoted almost exclusively to a listing of the faculty of university anthropology departments. In 1984, the American Anthropological Association created a unit of its organization devoted to the concerns of practitioners.

The Limits of the Profession

The professional organizations of anthropology face a future which will continue to require adaptation. One of the major problems lies in the diversity of anthropological practice. Many other professional organizations serve an important function in certifying and giving credentials to their members to practice. It is hard to imagine how anthropologists might be certified. The specific activities of applied anthropologists are not only diverse, but most of them are also claimed by practitioners with other professional backgrounds. Anthropologists cannot, for example, lay exclusive claim to the ability to perform social impact assessments or conduct evaluation research.

When the great majority of anthropologists aspired to college level teaching positions, their credential was a Ph.D. in anthropology. But most of the positions outside academia which could be filled by anthropologists do not require such a degree. Presently, a number of anthropology departments in the United States are offering training in applied anthropology designed to prepare students for employment at the master's degree level. No one has yet dared to predict the impact this development is bound to have on the profession in coming years.

The major professional organizations continue to have difficulty in responding to the information needs of their diverse memberships. As a result, the number of specialty organizations established to meet these needs has increased notably. Whether these smaller organizations will be incorporated into the larger associations, or will actually begin to compete with them for membership, poses a question of considerable importance to the profession.

Perhaps the best way to define a profession is as a collection of individuals and special-interest groups with unique interpretations of a common goal. In anthropology, the common goal revolves around a shared concern with cultural process and adaptation. The diversity is generated from the personal experience, training, and careers of anthropologists. As anthropologists exhibit a greater willingness to involve themselves in a wide variety of professional activities, we can expect even more diversity within the ranks.

PROFESSIONAL ETHICS AND APPLIED ANTHROPOLOGISTS

Anthropologists work with people in a variety of role relationships. As a rule, a large part of their information and insight comes directly from human involvement with research *subjects*. Applied anthropologists frequently engage in team research efforts which involve them with *colleagues* of their own and other disciplines. They generally work for a *client* or, if they are directly involved in decision-making activities, for an *employer*. When they write or speak to larger, general audiences, or when they claim that there is particular social value to their work, applied anthropologists are also working for *society* as a whole.

In each of their relationships with others, anthropologists represent themselves *and* their profession. The practice of anthropology is ultimately judged by nonanthropologists on the basis of their interactions with individual anthropologists. One reason that it is important for anthropologists to conduct themselves in an ethical manner is because the larger reputation of their profession is at stake in each of their dealings with others.

Another rationale for concern with the ethical behavior of anthropologists is the realization that their work has the potential to harm people. Information and knowledge about people represents a kind of power, and the use of information is rarely neutral. To the extent that anthropological knowledge is useful, so is it subject to misuse.

Anthropology and Ethics

Professions differ in their approach to ethical behaviors, depending at least in part on the nature of their work. The ethical statements of the planning professions, for example, tend to emphasize ethical responsibilities to the clients of research. Anthropologists have traditionally placed greater emphasis on the protection of the subjects of research. In the medical profession, the provision of health care is considered a basic right. Physicians, for example, generally agree that they should avoid making decisions as to whether their patients deserve medical attention. Many anthropologists, on the other hand, would accept the idea that there are potential clients who should not be afforded the benefits of anthropological work.

Anthropologists have recognized that it is not always easy to make sound ethical decisions from the competing claims of modern society. This attitude is reflected in the preamble to the American Anthropological Association's 1973 *Principles of Professional Responsibility*:

> Anthropologists work in many parts of the world in close personal association with the peoples and situations they study. Their professional situation is, therefore, uniquely varied and complex . . . In a field of such complex involvements, misunderstandings, conflicts and the necessity to make choices among conflicting values are bound to arise and to generate ethical dilemmas. It is a prime responsibility of anthropologists to anticipate these and to plan to resolve them in such a way to do damage neither to those whom they study nor, in so far as possible, to their scholarly community.

The Society for Applied Anthropology's 1975 *Statement on Professional and Ethical Responsibilities* offers similar advice:

Recognizing that any ethical stance derives from or is intimately related to one's political convictions, we are not offering any absolute set of rules or code of ethics. Ultimately we must define and accept our own responsibilities.

Although anthropologists' ethical responsibilities span the full extent of their professional involvement with the rest of the world, their major concerns have tended to center on two problems. The fieldwork situation, which often draws anthropologists into close and long-term relationships with the people they study, has contributed to their interest in ensuring that their work does not harm the subjects of their research. The social view of anthropologists, which often commits them to a humanistic as well as scientific orientation, has contributed to their interest in the larger impact of anthropology on society.

Because anthropologists have traditionally worked with people who are outside the mainstream of modern industrial society, their concern for their research subjects has not been misplaced. In small communities, the mere presence of an anthropologist can have a profound impact on the people he or she is studying. Also, field settings have often placed anthropologists in delicate situations of trust and responsibility, particularly in cases where they find it necessary to maintain relationships with two or more groups which may be in conflict. This problem becomes especially intense if, as is often the case, one of the groups an anthropologist is involved with has power over the other. Hortense Powdermaker (1966) has described tensions of this sort during her fieldwork in Mississippi in the 1930s. Rosalie Wax (1971) has provided an eloquent testimony of her work in a Japanese American relocation center during World War II and of her later research on an American Indian reservation.

The possibility of researchers abusing and being unfair toward their subjects was a real one. In testimony before a United States Committee on Government Operations, Harold Orlans (1967) provided a number of instances of behavior on the part of fieldworkers that most anthropologists today would consider abusive and unethical. Orlans cited Reo Fortune's technique for gaining the cooperation of a recalcitrant Dobu Islander:

> The sick man and his family still would tell me nothing specific . . . I used friendliness, and found it unavailing. But one day . . . I got the family of the sick man alone, used cajolery, and I mingled with the cajolery some vague threats of Government and Mission getting them for sorcery if they would disclose nothing. My time was short in their place and I had to resort to rough and ready methods. (Fortune 1932:160)

As anthropologists (and other social scientists) began to show greater interest in field research among peoples closer to the currents of modern society, their concern with the protection of "informants" intensified. Orlans points out in his testimony that a new ethical dimension was added as social scientists undertook community studies in societies where the subjects of research and their neighbors were likely to have access to the research reports. In these cases, the question of protecting the anonymity of informants became important, particularly in instances where published reports might contain information which could be used against identifiable informants. Hence, the ethical responsibilities of anthropology came to include considerations of what happened to an anthropologist's data *after* he or she left the field.

Heightened concern for the larger social responsibility of anthropologists led to an even greater appreciation of ethical dilemmas. In the United States, as in much of the rest of the world, the 1960s and the early 1970s cast a particular mold on contemporary anthropology. Not only was there a demand that anthropology be made more relevant to the human problems associated with modern society (Hymes 1974), but a major reexamination took place of the ways in which anthropologists had sometimes worked in the past. Several events of the period stand out.

1.   Sensitivity increased toward the extent to which earlier generations of anthropologists had aided Western governments in the colonial domination of the Third World. It was pointed out that this involvement was not purely unintentional— anthropologists of the colonial period had, by and large, accepted and supported the right of colonial powers to dominate the affairs of other countries (Asad 1973).

2.   The traditional subjects and hosts of anthropological research began to question their involvement with the profession. Anthropologists (along with many other Western scientists) began to find it more difficult to receive permission to conduct research in several Third World countries.

3.   *Project Camelot* emerged as a major example of how social scientists could be duped into participating in government research which had implications far beyond those made public. Ostensibly, Project Camelot was a major effort of the United States government to study the political effects of social change in the Third World. In reality, the research was directed toward counterinsurgency efforts of the United States military and was symptomatic of the government's clandestine involvement in the internal affairs of other nations (Horowitz 1967; see also Wax 1978).

4.   Several years later came the *Thailand controversy*, which was similar in intent to Project Camelot, with the important difference that evidence emerged during its investigation to suggest that some of the anthropologists involved in the research had been fully aware of the connection between their activities and the counterinsurgency efforts of the United States military (Jorgensen and Wolf 1970).

Project Camelot and the Thailand controversy, partly because of their clear association with political events of the time, had a pronounced effect on the profession. Generations of classroom discussion about the anthropologist's respect for the integrity of non-Western peoples seemed in jeopardy. Anthropologists were also concerned that these revelations would even further erode the anthropologist's standing in countries where they typically pursued research. An immediate effect of the crisis was a favorble vote by the membership of the American Anthropological Association to condemn "clandestine and secret research" on the part of anthropologists.

Ethics and Applied Anthropology

It is unfortunate that applied anthropology has had to bear the brunt of much of the blame and repercussion following the various crises described above. Too often, the root of the problem has been identified as having to do with the mere *sponsorship* of research by government and special interests, without much attempt to identify the special conditions leading to practices which, for humanistic or professional reasons, might be judged undesirable.

The events of Project Camelot and the Thailand controversy are exceptional in the extent of deception that was apparently involved. They also raise especially difficult ideological and political questions, partly because of the academic community's widespread concern for the United States' involvement in the support of "anticommunist" Third World governments. In contrast, anthropologists' involvement in intelligence activities during World War II has not been comparably criticized, even when that involvement entailed providing the military with specific (and, at the time, one would presume classified) information about the behavior of native peoples (Thompson 1979).

It is also worth considering that basic social research, regardless of how or for what purposes it is funded, is as subject to misuse as applied research. For example, much of the anthropology that was useful to British overseas administrators during the height of colonialism was basic research related to land tenure, relationships between native peoples, indigenous leadership, and so on (Asad 1973). To urge against applied research solely on the basis of its special relationship to the clients of research is to miss the important point that, in the great majority of cases, *no* researcher has control over the use of data made publicly available. Neither is it a simple matter for any social researcher to anticipate what kinds of information might be used by someone to the detriment of the people studied.

In some respects, discounting the deception apparently involved in cases like the Camelot Project and the Thailand controversy, applied research seems to have an ethical edge on most basic research because the conditions and intentions underlying the use of data can be more readily anticipated. Where applied anthropologists have found themselves in difficult ethical positions, it has often been on the basis of their inexperience and failure to clarify the ethical implications of their work prior to becoming involved in a project.

On the other hand, a number of questions of ethical responsibility are actually intensified in applied research and continue to plague even careful and experienced practitioners. For the most part, these are problems which the profession as a whole has barely begun to consider. For example, applied anthropology assumes a greater ethical responsibility toward the *clients* of research. This is true both for advocacy and administrative models of research and service. *A basic responsibility of applied anthropology is to provide a useful product.* This requires attention to all the conditions of utility discussed in this book. It also entails an understanding of the techniques and strategies of applied research and a knowledge of the policy process. Applied anthropologists not only have an ethical obligation to avoid research which might unduly harm research subjects; they also should decline opportunities which are unlikely to result in a service which responds to a *client's* expectations. Where an anthropologist suspects that a client's expectations are misplaced or unrealistic, these misgivings should be expressed early in the relationship.

As researchers, applied anthropologists also have an obligation to realistically assess a client's actual need for research and offer appropriate guidance. The basic research model which has dominated anthropology assumes that it is virtually impossible to do too much research, since new knowledge is judged to be of value for its own sake. One essential skill of the applied anthropologist is the ability and willingness to candidly advise clients as to both the strengths and *limits* of social research. In some cases, the best and most ethical service an applied anthropologist can provide is to tell a client when social research is not likely to yield added insight into a particular problem, or when existing data is likely to serve the client's needs and save the expense of new research.

Applied anthropologists face other ethical dilemmas which are not so readily resolved. In applied research involving extended periods of field research, anthropologists often need to balance their role of neutrality vis-a-vis their research subjects against the concerns for accountability of their clients. Usually for good reason, field researchers generally want to avoid making evaluative and summative judgments about their work until it is completed. Applied research clients, who are accountable to their organizational superiors, are accustomed to checking up on people's work from time to time in order to ensure that it is being done. The length of time sometimes required for fieldwork poses special reporting problems for anthropologists and their clients (Pierce-Colfer 1981; Vivelo 1980; Chambers 1977).

In some cases, confidentiality is a special problem for applied anthropologists. The evaluation of a public program, for example, is conducted in a context in which the key actors of the activity being evaluated are well known to everyone involved or interested in the evaluation effort. The anonymity of these persons cannot be protected (Chambers and Trend 1981). In cases such as these, anthropologists may have to assume an ethical stance similar to that of journalists—by virtue of their authority over others, their involvement in the public trust, and in some cases their responsibility for public funds, some "research subjects" may not be entitled to the same rules of confidentiality as others.

Applied anthropologists engaged in field research have experienced special difficulties in regard to the disposition of their field notes. Traditionally, anthropologists have regarded field notes as personal documents in which they record raw data and keep track of their impressions, problems, and experiences while conducting research. In the hands of other persons, these notes can easily be misinterpreted. Field notes also often compromise the confidentiality of informants and pose a special threat in cases where an anthropologist's research includes investigation of illegal or quasi-legal activity, such as drug use (Agar 1980). Where applied anthropologists have most often encountered difficulty is when research clients or others seek access to a researcher's field notes, claiming that *all* the products of research should be considered the property of whoever is paying for the research. In other cases, anthropologists have been asked to surrender their field notes to law enforcement agencies or government auditors (Cassell 1978).

One line of defense against such a possibility is to clarify in writing before a research project begins who will have access to field notes. This procedure has been only partially effective, however, when outside parties such as law enforcement agencies become involved. Anthropologists should realize that conditions may arise in which they will not be able to retain sole possession of their field data, and in areas of particularly sensitive research they are well advised to assume that their notes may someday be available to others, and to record them accordingly.

Another ethical problem applied anthropologists often face concerns "secret" research. When working in areas of policy concern, it is not always advisable to make the results of applied research immediately or indiscriminately available to the public. This problem can be especially acute during the active stages of research, when the early release of results might bias the subsequent responses of research subjects or result in unfavorable publicity for a research effort. (The early, tentative results of a research project might, for example, suggest that a program is a failure, whereas further research could indicate otherwise.) As a general rule, research clients have a right to expect some control over the release of research they sponsor, particularly while that research is going on. At the same time, anthropologists recognize the need for public access to their work. Whenever possible, it is advisable that conditions governing the release of research data be clearly stated at the beginning of a research effort.

Many of the ethical problems faced by applied anthropologists are complicated by contractual obligations to clients and by other legal restrictions. The greatest potential for personal risk arises when the anthropologist's ethical commitments conflict with the law (as when a law enforcement agency attempts to enforce its access to field notes). While the professional principles of responsibility that guide anthropologists specify rather clearly the priorities governing research, they do not provide for legal or financial assistance to anthropologists who run afoul of the law as a result of their ethical obligations (Chambers and Wolfe 1978).

Federal Regulation of Research

Over the past decade, social researchers in the United States have found the government to be increasingly interested in the impact their research might have on society, and especially on the subjects of research. Federal regulation of research has taken various forms, including:

1.   The protection of the public's right to know through *freedom of information* laws and regulations that ensure the public access to work supported with public funds.

2.   The protection of an individual's *rights to privacy* through regulations and laws which restrict access to information which can be traced to individuals. These laws also specify procedures for ensuring anonymity in social research as well as in many other government and private activities.

3.   Regulations ensuring the protection of *human research subjects* from involvement in research which puts them at risk unnecessarily or without their knowledge.

Anthropologists and other social researchers have been especially affected by regulations pertaining to the protection of human subjects, regulations which have extended to nearly all the research they do. The most prominent and debatable features of these regulations have been provisions calling for *institutional review* of proposed research and requirements that researchers obtain the *written informed consent* of research subjects prior to involving them in a research activity. When the proposed regulations were first published, a number of social scientists objected to these features. They pointed out that institutional review could lead to unfair restraint on the freedom to do research, especially in cases where a researcher might be investigating a controversial or politically sensitive topic. The requirement for written informed consent was especially difficult for anthropologists to accept. Some argued that the fieldwork relationship typically favored by anthropologists requires an informal and trusting relationship between a researcher and his or her informants, and that formal consent procedures might threaten the personal nature of the relationship (Wax 1980).

A major complaint registered against the proposed regulations was that they were based on a biomedical model of research and resulted from clearly abusive cases of research where subjects were put in serious physical or emotional danger without their knowledge or consent. Early criticism resulted in significant changes in the final regulations. Most social science research (except that which clearly puts individuals at risk) is now exempt from the requirement for written informed consent. Although institutional review of proposed research is still required, in most cases the process has been simplified for social science research projects.

Federal regulations pertaining to the protection of human research subjects raise another important issue. Who has the right to determine the responsibilities anthropologists should have toward the people with whom they work? I have suggested elsewhere that, in light of the far-ranging interests and involvements of modern anthropology, the anthropologist's ethical considerations should be framed in a context which recognizes that many parties have a legitimate interest in their work:

> Our professional ethics are based to a considerable degree on conditions of research and presumptions of common aim which are no longer fully representative of the work we do. Neither are the contexts of fieldwork the same as they were even a decade ago. The subjects of research are often better informed and more sensitive to being researched. Our professional associations are struggling to adapt to the diversity of modern anthropology, with the result that their very limited resources are spread far too thin to be of great impact in any one direction. The clients and sponsors of fieldwork, and of all manner of research involving human subjects, have begun to insist on their right to influence the ethical procedures associated with work they pay for, and in some cases with work they do not pay for. The employers of fieldworkers have been given considerable authority and responsibility in guiding the processes of ethical decision making. In addition, the courts have taken a renewed interest in becoming involved in issues where the rights of free inquiry are presumably in conflict with the rights of the individual and society. (Chambers 1980:340–341)

As anthropologists become more deeply involved in work that is immediately pertinent to public policy and decision making, their presence and the style of their work will be more closely scrutinized by others. Conflicts in responsibility and ethical expectations are bound to occur. The resolution of these conflicts resides only partly in the profession; it has become equally important that anthropologists recognize the legitimate concerns of other "partners" in the exchange of information and knowledge.

The Delicate Balance of Good

Applied anthropologists have long recognized the relationship between the utility of their work and their willingness to work for special-interest groups. At the same time, their ethical considerations have often included reference to a sense of "greater good." An early statement of this dual commitment appeared in a footnote to the Society for Applied Anthropology's first ethical "code," published in 1949:

> It has been emphasized in discussions that the applied anthropologist may properly work for a partisan group within a society . . . recognizing that such groups are a significant and important part of our social life and that improvements in the functioning and social understanding of any one such group can be valuable to the whole society. However, the applied anthropologist should also scrutinize all special interest groups as to the possibility of any such group becoming destructive of the larger whole.

Judging which interest groups are beneficial to a larger social good—

and which are not—is difficult and cannot be wholly resolved on the basis of professional authority. Anthropologists are still broadly influenced by personal and ideological convictions. The way individual anthropologists decide matters of social purpose helps shape the way they do their work. In applied anthropology, these problems are particularly acute. Whereas basic researchers could (with debatable success) claim the "pursuit of truth" as their ultimate client, applied anthropologists must share their interest in truth with an obligation to be useful in clearly defined contexts of decision making.

No magic formula or pristine code can save an individual from the need to decide upon a particular involvement on the basis of his or her convictions. There are, however, a few guidelines. Applied anthropologists should take the time to know their clients' and employers' interests and goals before they agree to do a piece of work. They should also accept and, if need be, question their own convictions in light of their possible employment. In nearly every case imaginable, applied anthropologists should be sincere, with themselves and with others, about what they are doing.

TRAINING FOR APPLIED ANTHROPOLOGY

The skills and orientation required of applied anthropologists must be acquired in some way. Whereas education in anthropology has traditionally emphasized preparation for careers in basic research and teaching, applied anthropologists require a different kind of preparation. The growth of interest in applied anthropology during the 1970s saw a corresponding interest in the development of academic programs designed to prepare students for careers in applied anthropology. In many respects, these programs represent the most significant changes to occur in the training of anthropologists since the earliest days of the profession.

Skills and Curricula

What specific skills do applied anthropologists require? How are they best acquired? How can training programs expand their curricula to adapt to new skill requirements without unduly sacrificing the anthropological content of their programs? During the late 1970s, John van Willigen (1979) reviewed 22 recent articles written by anthropologists who addressed these problems. He found that the most consistent recommendations for training dealt with the anthropologist's ability to function as a generalist. The articles suggested that students in applied anthropology acquire "competence in general social science research," a "knowledge of complex society," "quantitative skills," and "training in related substantive skills."

These recommendations are consistent with the applied anthropologist's need to respond to policy problems from a variety of points of departure, and to participate in a research or decision-making activity on the basis of strategies that are responsive to specific information and knowledge needs, rather than from the biases inherent in attempting to apply a singular kind of training (for example, ethnographic research) to all problems.

An evaluation of one training program (Wolfe, Chambers, and Smith 1981) offers more detailed indications of the kinds of skills and competencies many applied anthropologists require. The evaluation includes a survey of students who completed an applied internship in a government or private agency. When asked to indicate what skills were important to the work they accomplished, the students identified three broad categories of competency. The *ability to write* (and particularly, the ability to write reports) was ranked especially high, as were competencies related to interpersonal activities (the ability to meet with the public and other specialists, conduct meetings and make oral presentations, and so on). Many of the students also indicated that research skills were important to their work. Specific applied research approaches, such as program evaluation, ranked high. Skills which might be typically associated with anthropology (such as informal interviewing) were ranked as high or higher than other social research skills (such as survey research).

One way of thinking about these observations is to consider that the employment orientation of applied anthropologists encourages them to evaluate their training and performance primarily in terms of those characteristics they *share* with other social researchers and decision makers. This view is consistent with observations offered throughout this book. It is quite different from the departmental focus of most academically employed anthropologists, where competition between university departments encourages greater consideration of the uniqueness of disciplines than of their similarities. (At the same time, academically employed anthropologists do often have occasion to consider what they have in common with other disciplines; and applied anthropologists working outside universities do need a specific orientation and preparation which makes them different from other practitioners if the idea of an applied *anthropology* is to remain viable.)

One major problem in applied training has been figuring out how to give students both the general and anthropological competencies they require. In large part, the problem results from the rapidity with which interest in applied training has grown. It has been difficult for academic programs to keep pace with the need for faculty with a suitable range of experience in applied work. As a result, departments developing applied programs often have to compromise, both by directing their students to training opportunities outside anthropology departments and by encouraging their existing faculty to refocus their interests toward applied concerns. As a result, students and faculty alike often feel a gap between the more traditional concerns of anthropology and the acquisition of applied competency, with much of the burden for the latter training being taken up by courses taught in other university departments.

This approach presents two problems. First of all, it is inefficient. While students certainly ought to be encouraged to complete "elective" courses in other disciplines, something is missing when a program must rely on other departments to provide *essential* applied skills to its students and then must offer courses to "teach the anthropology." Ideally, major applied skills should be taught from the perspective of anthropology by fully competent anthropologists who have practical experience in application.

The other problem is that "farming out" many of the competencies central to applied work leaves less of an incentive for anthropology faculty to become fully proficient in application—and, until the profession has *many* such faculty, the essential bridges between anthropology and application will remain incomplete and hazardous.

The current difficulties anthropology departments face in training future applied anthropologists lag well behind their interest in doing so. The lag is not surprising, and the willingness to forge ahead on the part of an increasing number of anthropology departments is commendable. As much as interest in applied anthropology began to take shape and solidify in the 1970s, it seems more than likely that in the future we can expect continuing innovation and significant improvement in the teaching of applied anthropology.

Internships and Practice

It is important to realize that competency in applied anthropology is not acquired solely in the classroom. For some of the more essential skills required of applied anthropologists, experience is clearly the best teacher. Recognition of the importance of practical, "hands on" experience has led most departments offering training in applied anthropology to require their students to undertake internships or practice in "real world" applied settings.

The idea of locating a major part of a student's education in a field setting is not at all foreign to anthropology, where fieldwork experience has always been regarded as a major rite of passage from student to professional status. Most anthropologists have been comfortable with the idea that much of what an anthropologist needs to know cannot be taught in the usual sense but has to be experienced at first hand.

The purpose of internship training is to place a student in an institutional setting under the supervision of an experienced practitioner. Interns are generally expected to contribute service to the institution in which they are placed, as well as conduct research or other activities leading to fulfillment of their degree requirements. The length and intensity of current internship programs in anthropology vary considerably, often in relation to the level of training being conducted. Some anthropology programs, for example, offer part-time undergraduate practica, usually equivalent to the work of one or two academic courses. Graduate degree programs often require full-time internships, with the length of the experience varying for master's and doctoral level training.

The potential variety of internship placements in anthropology is as wide and diverse as the potential for employment. At the University of South Florida, which has offered an M.A. program in applied anthropology since 1974, students have interned in government agencies, for advocacy groups, and in private research companies. Their work as interns has included applied social research, program administration and planning, and other staff activities related to institutional activities. A present limitation of applied anthropology internship programs is their tendency to reflect the same skewed distribution of opportunities as we find in the employment choices applied anthropologists have made. So far, there have been few internships in commercial or industrial settings, and most internships have emphasized research rather than administrative, policy making, planning, or implementation activities.

Applied Training at the Master's Level

More than twenty years ago, Ward H. Goodenough suggested that the master's degree might be the most appropriate level at which to train applied anthropologists to work in settings outside academia. What Goodenough was recommending was a course that has been followed by other practitioner oriented disciplines, such as business administration and social work. But in anthropology, the idea has been slow in gaining acceptance. Traditionally, the status of anthropologist has been closely equated with possession of the Ph.D. degree. It was—and in some quarters remains—difficult to imagine an "anthropologist" without all the honored regalia of long-term fieldwork and cross-cultural experience normally associated with attaining a doctoral degree in anthropology.

It took a decade for Goodenough's suggestion to find a home. The University of South Florida was the first to announce, in unambiguous terms, that it would train students for "nonacademic" careers in anthropology at the master's level. Dozens of other programs have followed.

Why should the master's degree be considered an appropriate degree level for training in applied anthropology? One reason is that it offers an excellent orientation for training *generalists*, a characteristic which we have seen to be important for many anthropologists working outside academia.

Most Ph.D. level training is, on the other hand, directed toward specialization.

Many applied anthropologists do have Ph.D. degrees, and a number of anthropology departments have begun to offer doctoral level training in applied anthropology. A need exists, both in and out of academic settings, for individuals trained to this high a degree of specialization. But the need and opportunities are much greater for applied anthropologists trained at the master's level, for a number of reasons. In a sense, applied anthropologists trained at the master's level might be the best equipped to mediate knowledge and its uses. Their graduate training should sensitize them to the anthropological approach, equip them with criteria for evaluating information and knowledge, and introduce them to the complex decision-making settings in which they will work. In their work, they will be called upon to *apply* knowledge to problems in decision making much more often than they will be called upon to *produce* knowledge.

Master's level applied anthropologists are prepared to work at the most immediate levels of the policy process—the planning and implementation of project activities. They may work as applied researchers, developing needs assessments, evaluating program activities, and so on. They may become decision makers and administrators, directly involved in the planning and supervision of project activities. In either case, as *anthropologists* they can be the important link between the knowledge and insight of the profession and its utility.

For the first time in the history of the profession, anthropology departments have begun to offer a clear professional role to people who want to involve themselves directly in the affairs of the world—individuals who are more motivated to take part in the actual processes of change than they are content to solely reflect upon the dynamics of social and cultural phenomena.

The idea is still new, and its implementation is even more recent. There are still obstacles within the profession, which has traditionally rewarded one attitude toward doing anthropology at the expense of facilitating many other interesting possibilities. Those students who have entered master's level applied training programs are as much pioneers as their faculty have been. No one can tell with certainty what will come of it, but it may well be one of the most exciting and promising events to occur in anthropology for quite some time.

Training Programs for the Future

Education is, by its very nature, oriented to the future. Today's students are tomorrow's practitioners. The way their discipline is presented to them will influence the direction of their personal careers and help shape the profession as a whole; the students' imaginations and the limits and promises of their generation will do the rest. As much as education is oriented to the future, it almost invariably lags some distance behind the potential of a profession. In a sense, education is the process by which students catch up with and surpass their teachers.

As early as 1978, approximately 50 anthropology departments were advertising special training of some sort in applied anthropology in the American Anthropological Association's *Guide to Departments of Anthropology*. The type of training offered varies considerably depending on each department's resources, faculty experience, and so on. Assuming an interest in a career in applied anthropology, how is a student to select from among the growing number of offerings? The following suggestions should be useful:

1.   At what degree level is training being offered? Programs are currently offering special training in applied anthropology at the bachelor's, master's, and doctorate levels. It is likely that master's level training will become further identified as a practitioner oriented degree, with greater emphasis on using knowledge than producing knowledge.

2.   What, if any, areas of specialization are offered? Some programs are limited to training in a single subarea, such as medical anthropology or public archeology. Others maintain several specific "tracks," and some simply offer training in "applied anthropology." It is likely that many programs will become more highly specialized in the near future.

3.   What part of an anthropology department's total effort is devoted to training in applied anthropology, and how many faculty members are involved in the applied program? As a rule, departments which have made a major commitment to applied training, with a commitment of the majority of their faculty resources to this end, are best equipped to offer the kind of preparation students should receive.

4.   What is being taught? How well are the skills of application and the perspective of anthropology integrated in specific course offerings? To what extent does a department have to rely on courses outside the department to provide *major* skills in application?

5.   What are the anthropology faculty's *actual* experiences in application?

6.   What level and type of practical experience is offered as a part of the training program? Most programs offer some type of internship or practicum experience. Much of the direction of a particular program can be discerned from the types of agencies and institutions in which students typically intern. Programs also vary in the extent to which they encourage cooperative or "team" internship experiences and independent, individual placements of interns, as well as in the amount of choice students have in selecting their own internship experience.

7.   What kinds of employment do graduates typically enter? Are they employed as researchers? Administrators? Does there seem to be a clear relationship between the training they receive and the types of work they obtain?

8.   What kind of background is expected of students? Some graduate programs assume students will enter with a background in anthropology. These programs tend to emphasize the acquisition of applied skills. Other programs deliberately seek students with experience outside anthropology and emphasize training in anthropology. The differences may be subtle, but they can often be important to students beginning their training with one or another background.

Training programs in applied anthropology involve students, faculty and, generally, the community outside the university in finding a place for anthropology in the processes of policy decision making and implementation. On the basis of my experience, I believe a sense of adventure should pervade such activities. In this respect, applied anthropology differs little from what anthropologists have done all along. The promise of the profession as a whole is invested in a willingness to face the ambiguities that inevitably arise from experiencing human societies as shifting continents of interpretation and change. Within the profession, the idea of applied anthropology currently represents a major source of such ambiguity. To the extent that we can clear it up, we should. But it is equally important to recognize the extent to which applied anthropology remains a creative endeavor, unfinished and with an uncertain future.

When I discuss with students the possibility of seeking training and careers in applied anthropology, I tend to emphasize how important it will be for them to accept the creative aspects of their choice. In the past decade or so, we have barely been able to outline the vague parameters of what is and what might be. If a student wants to begin his or her career on a rock hard foundation, other careers offer greater certainty. Some people prefer living in houses others have built. But for people who like to hold their future in their own hands, and who like to construct their own possibilities, applied anthropology offers a unique opportunity.

PERSPECTIVE

The increased attention anthropologists have begun to pay to the professional aspects of their field is in part a result of a growing interest in applied anthropology. I feel it is important to recognize that even the intellectual content of a field of inquiry is in many respects shaped by seemingly mundane professional concerns—such as the way anthropologists organize themselves, the kinds of ethical issues they consider most important, and the way they educate and train future generations of their kind. We have noted, for example, that an early emphasis on the study of relatively isolated, small-scale societies led anthropologists to an ethical stance which emphasized the protection and well-being of these peoples. In turn, these ethical commitments came to have a strong influence on the types of settings in which subsequent generations of anthropologists chose to do their work, as well as on the way in which they defined their relationship to their own society. What had once been largely a matter of scientific priority and practical necessity (anthropologists wanted to study "primitive" peoples before they disappeared) soon became so closely intertwined with a sense of ethical responsibility that it was difficult for anthropologists to broaden their priorities and respond to new challenges without an uncomfortable feeling that they were doing something wrong.

There have always been exceptions to the rule, but it is only recently that anthropologists have shown a willingness to study the institutions of their own society and, even more dramatically, have sought to play an active role in the development of those institutions. This is not to say that anthropologists have accomplished, or should even attempt, a complete about-face in their priorities. It should be recognized, however, that recent changes in the kinds of intellectual challenges anthropologists have undertaken are leading to new ways of looking at the profession's ethical stance. Many of the issues are unresolved, and different anthropologists have significantly different ideas about the ethics of their profession. My biases, as might be clear, tend toward recognizing greater responsibility to research clients and, in some respects, assuming less responsibility to research subjects. Ethical positions are, however, so dependent upon the context of particular research or action settings that it is difficult to generalize. The reader should look at some of the pertinent references cited at the end of this chapter for additional points of view.

What I have had to say about ethics applies equally to the other aspects of the profession of anthropology discussed in this chapter. The way we train students, for example, is not only reflective of the intellectual content of our discipline, but also helps shape that content. Again, we have lots of choices. There is no "best" way to train students in applied anthropology, any more than there is a "best" way to be an applied anthropologist. In the latter part of this chapter I have described some of the differences in applied programs, with the hope that students interested in the field might be able to better choose a way that is likely to be responsive to their particular interests.

RECOMMENDED READINGS

Readers interested in the general problems of ethics in anthropology can refer to Dell Hyme's *Reinventing Anthropology* (Vintage, 1974); Ralph Beal's *Politics of Social Research* (Aldine, 1968); Michael A. Rynkiewich and James Spradley's *Ethics and Anthropology* (John Wiley, 1976); and G.N. Appell's *Ethical Dilemmas in Anthropological Inquiry* (Crossroads, 1978).

Ethical problems related to fieldwork and federal regulation are discussed in Murray Wax and Joan Cassell's *Federal Regulations: Ethical Issues and Social Research* (Westview, 1979), as well as in a special issue of the journal *Social Problems* (27(3), 1980), also edited by Casell and Wax.

Other discussions of ethical problems related to applied work include Gideon Sjoberg's *Ethics, Politics, and Social Research* (Schenkman, 1967) and Margaret Mead's "The Evolving Ethics of Applied Anthropology," in Elizabeth Eddy and William Partridge's *Applied Anthropology in America* (Columbia, 1978).

Eddy and Partridge's volume also includes an article devoted to "Training for Applied Anthropology," written by the editors. Readers interested in this subject can also refer to Eleanor Leacock, Nancie Gonzalez, and Gilbert Kushner's *Training Programs for New Opportunities in Applied Anthropology* (American Anthropological Association, 1974) and William T. Vickers and Glen Howze's *Social Science Education for Development* (Tuskegee Institute, 1978). Many of the articles published in the Society for Applied Anthropology's publication *Practicing Anthropology* also have a bearing on these issues.

References

ABT ASSOCIATES INC. 1976 *Experimental Housing Allowance Program.* Annual Report 1976. Cambridge: Abt Associates Inc.

ADAMS, RICHARD NEWBOLD 1975 *Energy and Structure: A Theory of Social Power.* Austin: University of Texas Press.

AGAR, MICHAEL H. 1973A *Ripping and Running.* New York: Academic Press.

——— 1973B "Ethnography and the Addict," in *Cultural Illness and Health,* ed. L. Nader and T.W. Maretzki. Washington, D.C.: American Anthropological Association.

——— 1980 *The Professional Stranger: An Informal Introduction to Ethnography.* New York: Academic Press.

——— 1983 "Inference and Schema: An Ethnographic View." *Human Studies* 6:53–66.

ALEXANDER, CHRISTOPHER 1978 "A City is Not a Tree," in *Humanscape,* eds. S. Kaplan and R. Kaplan. North Scituate: Duxbury.

ALMY, SUSAN 1977 "Anthropologists and Development Agencies." *American Anthropologist* 79:280–292.

AMERICAN ANTHROPOLOGICAL ASSOCIATION 1978 "Profile of an Anthropologist: G. Stern." *Anthropology Newsletter* 19(9). Used with permission.

——— 1980 "Profile of an Anthropologist: Steve Barnett." *Anthropology Newsletter* 21(4):6. Used with permission.

——— 1980 "Profile of an Anthropologist: N. Gonzalez." *Anthropology Newsletter* 21(2). Used with permission.

——— 1982 "Profile of an Anthropologist: K. Buehler." *Anthropology Newsletter* 23(3). Used with permission.

—— 1982 "Profile of an Anthropologist: H. Wilson." *Anthropology Newsletter* 23(1). Used with permission.

ANDREWS, FRANK M. AND RONALD F. INGLEHART 1979 "The Structure of Subjective Well-Being in Nine Western Societies." *Social Indicators Research* 6:73–90.

ARENSBERG, CONRAD 1978 "Theoretical Contributions of Industrial and Development Studies," in *Applied Anthropology in America*, eds. E. Eddy and W. Partridge. New York: Columbia.

ARENSBERG, CONRAD AND ARTHUR NIEHOFF 1964 *Introducing Social Change: A Manual for Americans Overseas.* Chicago: Aldine.

ARON, WILLIAM S., NORMAN ALGER AND RICHARD T. GONZALES 1974 "Chicanoizing Drug Abuse Programs." *Human Organization* 33:388–390.

ASAD, TALAL, ED., 1973 *Anthropology and the Colonial Encounter.* Atlantic Highlands: Humanities Press.

BARNETT, H.G. 1956 *Anthroplogy in Administration.* Evanston: Row, Peterson.

BARTLETT, PEGGY F. 1980 *Agricultural Decision Making: Anthroplogical Contributions to Rural Development.* New York: Academic Press.

BASHAM, RICHARD 1978 *Urban Anthroplogy.* Palo Alto: Mayfield.

BASTIDE, ROGER 1974 *Applied Anthroplology.* New York: Harper & Row.

BENNETT, JOHN W. 1976 *The Ecological Transition: Cultural Anthropology and Human Adaptation.* Oxford: Pergamon Press.

—— 1980 "Management Style: A Concept and a Method for the Analysis of Family-Operated Agricultural Enterprise," in *Agricultural Decision Making*, ed. P. Bartlett.

BERREMAN, GERALD 1980 "Are Human Rights Merely a Politicized Luxury in the World Today." *Anthropology and Humanism Quarterly* 5:2–13.

BEVIS, JUDITH A. 1979 "Assisting Threatened Cultures." *Practicing Anthropology* 1:4–5.

BLAU, PETER M. 1956 *Bureaucracy in Modern Society.* New York: Random House.

BLAU, PETER M. AND MARSHALL W. MEYER 1971 *Bureaucracy in Modern Society.* New York: Random House.

BOAS, FRANZ 1910 "Changes in Bodily Form of Descendants of Immigrants." Senate Document number 208, 61st Congress, 2nd Session. Washington, D.C.: U.S. Government Printing Office.

BODLEY, JOHN H. 1975 *Victims of Progress.* Menlo Park: Cummings.

BOONE, MARGARET 1981 "Role Development of the Hospital Anthropologist." *Practicing Anthropology* 4:5–7.

BOORSTIN, DANIEL J. 1974 *The Americans: The Democratic Experience.* New York: Vintage.

BRITAN, GERALD 1981 *Bureaucracy and Innovation: An Ethnography of Policy Change.* Beverly Hills: Sage Publications, Inc.

CAMPBELL, D.T. AND J.C. STANLEY 1966 *Experimental and Quasi-Experimental Designs for Research.* Chicago: Rand McNally.

CANCIAN, FRANK 1972 *Change and Uncertainty in a Peasant Economy.* Stanford: Stanford University Press.

CAPLAN, NATHAN, ET AL. 1975 *The Use of Social Science Knowledge in Policy Decisions at the National Level.* Ann Arbor: Institute for Social Research, University of Michigan.

CASSELL, JOAN 1978 *A Fieldwork Manual for Studying Desegregated Schools.* Washington, D.C., The National Institute of Education.

—— 1980 "Ethical Principles for Conducting Fieldwork." *American Anthropologist* 82:28–40.

CENTER FOR NEW SCHOOLS 1977 "DTA Project, Overview." Chicago: Center for

New Schools.

CHAMBERS, ERVE 1975   "We Thought It Would Be the New Deal All Over Again."
Abt Associates report. Cambridge: Abt Associates, Inc.

———— 1977   "Working for the Man: The Anthropologist in Policy Relevant
Research." *Human Organization* 36:258–267.

———— 1980   "Fieldwork and the Law: New Contexts for Ethical Decision Making." *Social Problems* 27:330–341.

———— 1982   "Values and Circumstances: The Cultures of Science and Policy."
Manuscript.

CHAMBERS, ERVE, ET AL. 1978   "Cultural Compatibility in the DeSoto Elementary
School Service Area." Report, University of South Florida, Department of
Anthropology, Tampa.

CHAMBERS, ERVE AND M.G. TREND 1981   "Fieldwork Ethics and Client-Oriented
Research." *American Anthropologist* 83:626–628.

CHAMBERS, ERVE AND ALVIN W. WOLFE 1978   "Legal and Ethical Problems in
Client-Oriented Field Research." Paper presented at the 1978 Annual Meeting of the American Anthropological Association.

CHAPPLE, ELIOT D. AND CONRAD ARENSBERG 1940   "Measuring Human Relations:
An Introduction to the Study of the Interaction of Individuals." *Genetic Psychology Monographs* 22:3–147.

CHAPPLE, ELIOT D. AND LEONARD R. SAYLES 1961   *The Measure of Management:
Designing Organizations for Human Effectiveness.* New York: Macmillan.

CLARK, MARGARET 1959   *Health in the Mexican-American Culture: A Community Study.*
Berkeley: University of California Press.

CLEMENT, DOROTHY C. 1978   "Ethnographic Perspectives on Desegregated
Schools." *Anthropology & Education Quarterly* 9:245–248.

CLINTON, CHARLES 1975   "The Anthropologist as Hired Hand." *Human Organization* 34:197–204.

———— 1979   *Local Success and Federal Failure: A Study of Community Development and
Educational Change in the Rural South.* Cambridge: Abt Books.

COCHRANE, GLYN 1971   *Development Anthropology.* New York: Oxford University
Press.

———— 1979   *The Cultural Appraisal of Development Projects.* New York: Praeger.

COHEN, LUCY M. 1976   "Conflict and Planned Change in the Development of
Community Health Services," in *Do Applied Anthropologists Apply Anthropology?*,
ed. M. Angrosino. Athens, Georgia: University of Georgia Press.

COOK, THOMAS D. AND DONALD T. CAMPBELL 1979   *Quasi-Experimentation: Design
& Analysis Issues for Field Settings.* Chicago: Rand McNally.

COWAN, J. MILTON 1979   "Linguistics at War," in *the Uses of Anthropology,* ed. W.
Goldschmidt. Washington, D.C.: American Anthropological Association.

D'ANS, ANDRE-MARCEL 1979   Public lecture. University of South Florida, Tampa.
November.

DELORIA, VINE JR. 1970   *We Talk, You Listen.* New York: Macmillan.

DENZIN, NORMAN K. 1970   *The Research Act.* Chicago: Aldine.

DEWALT, BILLIE R. 1979   *Modernization in a Mexican Ejido.* New York: Cambridge
University Press.

DILLON, WILTON S. 1980   "Margaret Mead and Government." *American Anthropologist* 82:319–339.

DIXON, MIM 1982   "Socioeconomic Policy for Energy Development." *Practicing
Anthropology* 5:10–11.

EAMES, EDWIN AND JUDITH GRANICH GOODE 1977   *Anthropology of the City: An
Introduction to Urban Anthropology.* Englewood Cliffs: Prentice-Hall.

EASTMAN, CAROL 1983 *Language Planning: An Introduction.* San Francisco: Chandler & Sharp.

ERASMUS, CHARLES 1961 *Man Takes Control: Cultural Development and American Aid.* Minneapolis: University of Minnesota Press.

FISHER, J.L. 1979 "Government Anthropologists in the Trust Territory of Micronesia," in *The Uses of Anthropology,* ed. W. Goldschmidt. Washington, D.C.: American Anthropological Association.

FOREST SERVICE, U.S. DEPARTMENT OF AGRICULTURE 1977 *Social Impact Assessment: An Overview.* Washington, D.C.: U.S. Department of Agriculture.

FORTUNE, R.F. 1963 *Sorcerers of Dobu.* New York: Dutton. [Original 1932.]

FOSTER, GEORGE M. 1967 *Tzintzuntzan: Mexican Peasants in a Changing World.* Boston: Little, Brown.

———— 1969 *Applied Anthropology.* Boston: Little, Brown.

FOSTER, GEORGE M. AND BARBARA GALLATIN ANDERSON 1978 *Medical Anthropology.* New York: John Wiley.

FRANKE, RICHARD HERBERT 1979 "The Hawthorne Experiments: Re-View." *American Sociological Review* 44:861–865.

FRANKE, RICHARD HERBERT AND JAMES D. KAUL 1978 "The Hawthorne Experiments: First Statistical Interpretation." *American Sociological Review* 43:623–643.

GARCIA, MARIA-PILAR AND RAE LESSING BLUMBERG 1978 "The Unplanned Ecology of a Planned Industrial City: The Case of Ciudad Guiyana, Venezuela," in *Urbanization in the Americas from its Beginning to the Present,* eds. R. Schaedel, J. Hardoy, and N. Kinger. The Hague, Netherlands: Mouton.

GEARING, FREDERICK O. 1970 *The Face of the Fox.* Chicago: Aldine.

GEERTZ, CLIFFORD 1971 *Agricultural Involution: The Processes of Ecological Change in Indonesia.* Berkeley: University of California Press.

GOLDE, PEGGY 1981 "The Practice of Clinical Anthropology: An Illustration of Cultural Consultation." *Practicing Anthropology* 4:12–13.

GOODENOUGH, WARD H. 1963 *Cooperation and Change.* New York: Russell Sage Foundation.

———— 1970 *Description and Comparison in Cultural Anthropology.* Chicago: Aldine.

GOODWIN, LAWRENCE 1979 "Applied Anthropology in the Public School System." M.A. Thesis in Anthropology, University of South Florida, Tampa.

GRAHAM, OTIS L. JR. 1976 *Toward a Planned Society: From Roosevelt to Nixon.* New York: Oxford University Press.

GREEN, JAMES W. 1982 *Cultural Awareness in the Human Services.* Englewood Cliffs: Prentice-Hall.

HARDING, JOE R. 1979 "Anthropology and Architectural Planning." *Practicing Anthropology* 1:3–5.

HARRINGTON, MICHAEL 1963 *The Other America: Poverty in the United States.* Baltimore: Penguin.

HAYS, SAMUEL P. 1975 *Conservation and the Gospel of Efficiency: The Progressive Conservation Movement 1890–1920.* New York: Atheneum.

HICKS, GEORGE AND MARK HANDLER 1978 "Ethnicity, Public Policy, and Anthropologists," in *Applied Anthropology in America,* eds. E. Eddy and W. Partridge. New York: Columbia University Press.

HILL-BURNETT, JACQUETTA 1978 "Developing Anthropological Knowledge Through Application," in *Applied Anthropology in America,* eds. E. Eddy and W. Partridge. New York: Columbia University Press. Used by permission of Columbia University Press.

HINKLEY, ALDEN D. 1976　*Applied Ecology: A Nontechnical Approach.* New York: Macmillan.

HINSLEY, CURTIS M. JR., 1979　"Anthropology as Science and Politics: The Dilemma of the Bureau of American Ethnology, 1879 to 1904," in *The Uses of Anthropology,* ed. W. Goldschmidt. Washington, D.C.,: American Anthropological Association.

HOFSTADTER, RICHARD 1963　*The Progressive Movement: 1900–1915.* Englewood Cliffs: New Jersey.

HOLLINGSHEAD, A. AND F.C. REDLICH 1958　*Social Class and Mental Illness.* New York: John Wiley.

HOLMES, LOWELL D. 1980　"Antropology and Age: An Assessment," in *Aging in Culture and Society,* ed. Christine L. Fry. New York: J.F. Bergin.

HOLMBERG, ALLAN R. 1958　"The Research and Development Approach to the Study of Change." *Human Organization* 17:12–16.

———　1962　"Community and Regional Development: The Joint Cornell-Peru Experiment." *Human Organization* 21:107–124.

———　1965　"The Changing Values and Institutions of Vicos in the Context of National Development." *American Behavioral Scientist* 8:3–8.

HOLZBERG, CAROL S. AND MAUREEN J. GIOVANNINI 1981　"Anthropology and Industry: Reappraisal and New Directions," in *Annual Review of Anthropology,* ed. Bernard J. Siegel. Volume 10, Palo Alto: Annual Reviews Inc.

HOROWITZ, IRVING LOUIS, ED. 1967　*The Rise and Fall of Project Camelot: Studies in the Relationship Between Social Science and Practical Politics.* Cambridge: The M.I.T. Press.

HOWELL, JOSEPH 1973　*Hard Living on Clay Street: Portraits of Blue Collar Families.* Garden City: Anchor.

HYMES, DELL, ED. 1974　*Reinventing Anthropology* New York: Vintage.

JACOBS, JERRY 1974　*Fun City: An Ethnographic Study of a Retirement Community.* New York: Holt, Rinehart and Winston.

JACOBS, SUE-ELLEN 1979　"Putting Us to Work on Their Terms." *Practicing Anthropology* 1:4–5.

JANSEN, WILLIAM H, III, ED. 1980　"Anthropology in the United States Agency for International Development." Special section of *Practicing Anthropology* 3 (1).

JEROME, N.W., R.F. KANDEL AND G.H. PELTO, EDS. 1980　*Nutritional Anthropology: Contemporary Approaches to Diet and Culture.* Pleasantville: Redgrave.

JONES, DELMOS J. 1979　"Not in My Community: The Neighborhood Movement and Institutionalized Racism." *Social Policy* 10:44–46.

JORGENSEN, JOSEPH, ET AL. 1978　*Native Americans and Energy Development.* Cambridge: Anthropology Resource Center.

JORGENSEN, JOSEPH AND ERIC WOLF 1970　"Anthropology on the Warpath in Thailand." *New York Review of Books:* 26–35.

JOYCE, WILLIAM W. 1971　"MACOS: A Report from the Inner-City." *Social Education* 35:305–308.

KANE, MICHAEL 1976　*Educational Change in Rural America.* Cambridge: Abt Associates Inc.

KELLEY, JOHN C. 1977　"A Social Anthropology of Education: The Case of Chiapas." *Anthropology & Education Quarterly* 8:210–220.

KIMBALL, SOLON T. 1978　"Anthropology as a Policy Science," in *Applied Anthropology in America,* eds. E. Eddy and W. Partridge. New York: Columbia University Press.

KLEINMAN, ARTHUR 1980　*Patients and Healers in the Context of Culture: An Exploration of the Borderland Between Anthropology, Medicine and Psychiatry.* Berkeley: University of California Press.

KURTZ, DONALD V. 1973 *The Politics of a Poverty Habitat.* Cambridge: Ballinger.

KUSHNER, GILBERT 1973 *Immigrants from India in Israel: Planned Change in an Administered Community.* Tuscon: University of Arizona Press.

LANDES, RUTH 1965 *Culture in American Education.* New York: John Wiley.

LANDSBERGER, HENRY A. AND CYNTHIA N. HEWITT 1970 "Ten Sources of Weakness and Cleavage in Latin American Peasant Movements," in *Agrarian Problems & Peasant Movements in Latin America,* ed. R. Stavenhagen. Garden City: Doubleday.

LERNER, RICHARD N. 1980 "Federal Cultural Heritage Responsibilities." *Practicing Anthropology* 2:11–14.

LEWIS, JOHN VAN D. 1981 "The Growth of an Anthropological Presence in an AID Washington Functional Bureau." *Practicing Anthropology* 3:23–25.

LEWIS, OSCAR 1952 "Urbanization Without Breakdown: A Case Study." *Scientific Monthly* 75:31–41.

———— 1968 *La Vida: A Puerto Rican Family in the Culture of Poverty.* New York: Vintage.

LINDBLOM, CHARLES E. 1959 "The Science of Muddling Through." *Public Administration Review* 19:79–88.

LUBOVE, ROY 1975 *The Professional Altruist: The Emergence of Social Work as a Career.* New York: Atheneum.

LURIE, NANCY OESTREICH 1966 "Women in Early American Anthropology," in *Pioneers of American Anthropology,* ed. J. Helm. Seattle: University of Washington Press.

MAKIELSKI, SALLY KIMBALL 1978 "Population Policy for the United States: The Role of Applied Anthropology," in *Applied Anthropology in America,* eds. E. Eddy and W. Partridge. New York: Columbia University Press.

MANGIN, WILLIAM 1979 "Thoughts on Twenty-four Years of Work in Peru: The Vicos Project and Me," in *Long-term Field Research in Social Anthropology,* eds. G. Foster, et al. New York: Academic Press.

MANNERS, ROBERT A. 1974 "Introducing Changes." *Science* 184:699–702.

MARCHIONE, THOMAS J. 1977 "Food and Nutrition in Self-Reliant National Development: The Impact on Child Nutrition of Jamaican Government Policy." *Medical Anthropology* 1:57–79.

MAYER, ENRIQUE 1979 *Land Use in the Andes.* Lima, Peru: Centro Internacional de la Papa.

McELROY, ANN AND PATRICIA TOWNSEND 1979 *Medical Anthropology in Ecological Perspective.* North Scituate: Duxbury.

MEDICINE, BEATRICE 1978 "Learning to be an Anthropologist and Remaining 'Native'," in *Applied Anthropology in America,* eds. E. Eddy and W. Partridge. New York: Columbia University Press.

MENCHER, JOAN 1977 "Change Agents and the Villager," in *Anthropology in the Development Process,* ed. H.M. Mathur. Atlantic Highlands, N.J.: Humanities Press.

MENCHER, SAMUEL 1967 *Poor Law to Poverty Program.* Pittsburgh: University of Pittsburgh.

MITCHELL, EDNA 1973 "The New Education Plan in Nepal: Balancing Conflicting Values for National Survival," in *The Anthropological Study of Education,* eds. C. Calhoun and F. Ianni. Chicago: Mouton.

MODIANO, NANCY 1973 *Indian Education in the Chiapas Highlands.* New York: Holt, Rinehart and Winston.

MONTGOMERY, EDWARD AND JOHN W. BENNETT 1979 "Anthropological Studies of Food and Nutrition: The 1940s and the 1970s," in *The Uses of Anthropology,* ed. W. Goldschmidt. Washington, D.C.: American Anthropological Association.

NADER, LAURA 1974   "Up the Anthropologist—Perspectives Gained from Study-ing Up," in *Reinventing Anthropology*, ed. D. Hymes. New York: Random House.

——— 1982   "Barriers to Thinking about Energy." *Physics Today* 34:9.

NAGEL, STUART AND MARION NEEF 1979   "What's New about Policy Analysis Research?" *Society* 16:24–31.

NAKAJIMA, WESLEY N. 1979   "From Census Tracts to Neighborhood Plans." *Practicing Anthropology* 1:5–6.

NUNEZ DEL PRADO, OSCAR 1973   *Kuyo Chico: Applied Anthropology in an Indian Community*. Chicago: University of Chicago Press.

OGBU, JOHN U. 1974   *The Next Generation: An Ethnography of Education in a Urban Neighborhood*. New York: Academic Press.

ORLANS, HAROLD 1967   "Ethical Problems and Values in Anthropological Research," in *The Use of Social Research in Federal Domestic Programs*. Washington, D.C.: U.S. Government Printing Office.

PADFIELD, HARLAND AND WILLIAM E. MARTIN 1965   *Farmers, Workers and Machines: Technological and Social Change in Farm Industries of Arizona*. Tucson: University of Arizona Press.

PARDEE, MICHAEL 1981   "Anthropology in Community Development." M.A. Thesis in Anthropology, University of South Florida, Tampa.

PARTRIDGE, WILLIAM 1979   "Anthropology and Development Planning." *Practicing Anthropology* 1:6–7.

PEATTIE, LISA 1968   "Reflections on Advocacy Planning." *Journal of the American Institute of Planners* 36:405–410.

——— 1970   "Drama and Advocacy Planning." *Journal of the American Institute of Planners* 36:405–410.

——— 1970B   *The View from the Barrio*. Ann Arbor: University of Michigan Press.

PETERSON, JOHN H. JR., CHARLES A. CLINTON AND ERVE CHAMBERS 1979   "A Field Test of Environmental Impact Assessment in the Tensas Basin," in *Proceedings*, 14th Annual Mississippi Water Resources Conference. Mississippi State: Water Resources Research Institute.

PIERCE-COLFER, CAROL J. 1981   "Rights, Responsibilities, and Reports: An Ethical Dilemma in Contract Research," in *Ethics and Anthropology*, eds. M. Rynkiewich and J. Spradley. Malabar: Krieger.

POWDERMAKER, HORTENSE 1966   *Stranger and Friend: The Way of an Anthropologist*. New York: W.W. Norton & Co., Inc.

QUIMBY, GEORGE I. 1979   "A Brief History of WPA Archaeology," in *The Uses of Anthropology*, ed. W. Goldschmidt. Washington, D.C.: American Anthropological Association.

RAPOPART, AMOS 1977   *Human Aspects of Urban Form: Towards a Man-Environment Approach to Urban Form and Design*. New York: Pergamon.

REICHARDT, CHARLES AND THOMAS COOK 1979   *Qualitative and Quantitative Methods in Evaluation Research*. Beverly Hills: Sage Publications, Inc.

RHOADES, ROBERT AND VERA RHOADES 1980   "Agricultural Anthropology: A Call for the Establishment of a New Professional Speciality." *Practicing Anthropology* 2:10–11.

ROUNDS, J. 1981   "Organizational Diagnosis: An Underdeveloped Role for Anthropologists." *Practicing Anthropology* 3:13–16.

RULE, JAMES B. 1978   *Insight and Social Betterment: A Preface to Applied Social Science*. New York: Oxford University Press.

SAMOVAR, LARRY A. AND RICHARD E. PORTER, EDS. 1982   *Intercultural Communication: A Reader*. Belmont: Wadsworth.

SCHENSUL, JEAN J., ED. 1981 "Applied Anthropology in the Connecticut Region." Special section of *Practicing Anthropology* 3 (3).

SCHENSUL, STEPHEN L. 1974 "Skills Needed in Action Anthropology: Lessons Learned from El Centro de la Causa." *Human Organization* 33:203–209.

SCHENSUL, STEPHEN L. AND JEAN J. SCHENSUL 1978 "Advocacy and Applied Anthropology," in *Social Scientists as Advocates*, eds. G. Weber and G. McCall. Beverly Hills: Sage Publications, Inc.

SCHLESINGER, ARTHUR M. 1968 *The American as Reformer*. New York: Atheneum.

SCHUMACHER, E.F. 1973 *Small is Beautiful: Economics as if People Mattered*. New York: Harper & Row.

SCOTT, CLARISSA S. 1978 "Health and Health Practices Among Five Ethnic Groups in Miami, Florida," in *The Anthropology of Health*. ed. E. Bauwens. St. Louis: C.V. Mosby.

SCUDDER, THAYER AND ELIZABETH COLSON 1979 "Long-term Research in Gwembe Valley, Zambia," in *Long-term Field Research in Social Anthropology*, eds. G. Foster, et al. New York: Academic Press.

SENNETT, RICHARD 1970 *The Uses of Disorder: Personal Identity & City Life*. New York: Knopf.

SOLOMON, R. CHARLES, ET AL. 1977 *Water Resources Assessment Methodology (WRAM)*. Vicksburg: U.S. Army Engineer Waterways Experiment Station.

SOWELL, THOMAS 1980 *Knowledge and Decisions*. New York: Basic Books.

SPICER, EDWARD 1979 "Anthropologists and the War Relocation Authority," in *The Uses of Anthropology*, ed. W. Goldschmidt. Washington, D.C.: American Anthropological Association.

SPINA, SUZANNE MEYER 1980 "Kids on Kids: Anthropology Begins at Home." *Practicing Anthropology* 3:27–29.

SPRADLEY, JAMES P. 1970 *You Owe Yourself a Drunk: An Ethnography of Urban Nomads*. Boston: Little, Brown.

SPRADLEY, JAMES P. AND DAVID W. McCURDY 1975 *Anthropology: The Cultural Perspective*. New York: John Wiley.

SROLE, LEO, ET AL. 1962 *Mental Health in the Metropolis: The Midtown Manhattan Study*. New York: Harper & Row, Pub.

STACK, CAROL B. *All Our Kin: Strategies for Survival in a Black Community*. New York: Harper & Row, Pub.

ST. LAWRENCE, THEODORA AND JOHN SINGLETON 1976 "Multi-culturalism in Social Context: Conceptual Problems Raised by Educational Policy Issues." *Anthropology and Education Quarterly* 7:4–6.

SWARTZ, THEODORE 1978 "The Size and Shape of a Culture," in *Scale and Social Organization*, ed. F. Barth. Oslo, Norway: Universitetsforlaget.

TAX, SOL 1958 "The Fox Project." *Human Organization* 17:17–19.

TEXTOR, ROBERT B. 1980 "The Art of Anticipation: Ethnographic Futures Research." *Practicing Anthropology* 3:21–23.

THOMPSON, LAURA 1979 "The Challenge of Applied Anthropology." *Human Organization* 38:114–120.

TREND, M.G. 1978A "Anthropology and Contract Research: Managing and Being Managed." *Practicing Anthropology* 1:13–17.

———— 1978B *Housing Allowances for the Poor: A Social Experiment*. Boulder: Westview.

———— 1978C "Research in Progress: The Minnesota Work Equity Project Evaluation." *Human Organization* 36:200–203.

———— 1978D "On the Reconciliation of Qualitative and Quantitative Analyses: A Case Study." *Human Organization* 37:345–354.

———— 1980   "The Anthropologist as Go-fer." *Practicing Anthropology* 3:13–14.

UHLMAN, JULIE E. 1977   "The Delivery of Human Services in Wyoming Boomtowns," in *Socio-Economic Impact of Western Energy Development*, eds. B. Crawford and E. Allen. Ann Arbor: Science Publishers.

UNITED STATES BUREAU OF RECLAMATION 1975   *Social Assessment Manual*. Denver: U.S. Department of the Interior, Bureau of Reclamation.

UNITED STATES DEPARTMENT OF HEALTH, EDUCATION AND WELFARE 1977   "The Impact of the New Boomtowns: The Lessons of Gillette and the Powder River Basin," in *New Dimensions in Mental Health*. Washington, D.C.: U.S. Department of Health, Education and Welfare.

VALENTINE, CHARLES A. 1968   *Culture and Poverty: Critique and Counter-proposals*. Chicago: University of Chicago.

VAN DUSEN, ROXANN AND ROBERT PARKE 1976   "Social Indicators: A Focus for the Social Sciences," in *Anthropology and the Public Interest*, ed. P. Sanday. New York: Academic Press.

VAN WILLIGEN, JOHN 1979   "Recommendations for Training and Education for Careers in Applied Anthropology: A Literature Review." *Human Organization* 38:411–416.

———— 1980   *Anthropology in Use: A Bibliographic Chronology of the Development of Applied Anthropology*. Pleasantville: Redgrave.

VAN ZANTWIJK, R.A.M. 1967   *Servants of the Saints: The Social and Cultural Identity of a Tarascan Community in Mexico*. Atlantic Highlands: Humanities Press.

VESPERI, MARIA 1980   "The Reluctant Consumer: Nursing Home Residents in the Post-Bergman Era." *Practicing Anthropology* 3:23–24.

VIVELO, FRANK ROBERT 1980   "Anthropology, Applied Research, and Non-academic Careers." *Human Organization* 39:345–356.

WALLACE, ANTHONY 1976   "Some Reflections on the Contributions of Anthropologists to Public Policy," in *Anthropology and the Public Interest*, ed. P. Sanday. New York: Academic Press.

WARHEIT, GEORGE J., ROGER A. BELL AND JOHN J. SCHWAB 1977   *Needs Assessment Approaches: Concepts and Methods*. National Institute of Mental Health. Washington, D.C.: U.S. Government Printing Office.

WARNER, SAM B. 1973   *Streetcar Suburbs: The Process of Growth in Boston 1870–1900*. New York: Atheneum.

WAX, MURRAY L. 1978   "Once and Future Merlins: The Applied Anthropologists of Camelot." *Human Organization* 37:400–408.

———— 1980   "Paradoxes of 'Consent' to the Practice of Fieldwork." *Social Problems* 27:272–283.

WAX, ROSALIE H. 1971   *Doing Fieldwork*. Chicago: University of Chicago.

WEBB, EUGENE J., DONALD J. CAMPBELL, RICHARD D. SCHWARTZ, AND LEE SECHREST 1966   *Unobtrusive Measures: Nonreactive Research in the Social Sciences*. Chicago: Rand McNally.

WEIDMAN, HAZEL H. 1978   *Miami Health Ecology Project Report*. Volumes I & II. Miami: University of Miami School of Medicine.

WEISS, CAROL H. 1972   *Evaluation Research: Methods of Assessing Program Effectiveness*. Englewood Cliffs: Prentice-Hall.

———— 1980   *Social Science Research and Decision-Making*. New York: Columbia University Press.

WENDELL, WALTER I. 1979   "Critique of a Recent Professional 'Put-Down' of the Hawthorne Research." *American Sociological Review* 44:858–861.

WEPPNER, RICHARD 1973   "An Anthropological View of the Street Addict's World." *Human Organization* 32:111–112.

WEST, STANLEY A. 1979 "A Framework for Multiobjective Environmental Planning." *Practicing Anthropology* 2:4–5.

WHYTE, WILLIAM FOOTE 1978 "Organizational Behavior Research—Where Do We Go From Here?" in *Applied Anthropology in America,* ed. E. Eddy and W. Partridge. New York: Columbia University Press.

WIEBE, ROBERT 1967 *The Search for Order: 1877–1920.* New York: Hill and Wang.

WILDAVSKY, AARON 1974 *The Politics of the Budgetary Process.* Boston: Little, Brown.

WOLCOTT, HARRY F. 1967 *A Kwakiutl Village and School.* New York: Holt, Rinehart and Winston.

———— 1977 *Teachers Versus Technocrats: An Educational Innovation in Anthropological Perspective.* Eugene: Center for Educational Policy and Management, University of Oregon.

———— 1980 "How to Look Like an Anthropologist Without Really Being One." *Practicing Anthropology* 3:6–8.

WOLFE, ALVIN W. 1980 "Introduction," Symposium on Applied Anthropology Internships at the Master's Level. *Florida Scientist* 43:198–201.

WOLFE, ALVIN W., ERVE CHAMBERS AND J. JEROME SMITH 1981 *Internship Training in Applied Anthropology: A Five-year Review.* Tampa: Human Resources Institute, University of South Florida.

WOLFE, ALVIN W., MARY RUST AND PATRICIA M. SORRELLS 1980 "Electronic Ethnography: Human Services Information Program." Paper presented at the 40th Annual Meeting of the Society for Applied Anthropology, Denver, Colorado. Used by permission of Alvin W. Wolfe.

YEZZI, RONALD 1980 *Medical Ethics: Thinking About Unavoidable Questions.* New York: Holt, Rinehart and Winston.

YOUNG, PHILLIP 1980 "Plan Guaymi: Perceptual Divergences." *Practicing Anthropology* 2:7–8.

Index

A

Abernathy, Virginia, 99
Aboriginal Protection Society, 21
Abt Associates Inc., 115
Acculturation studies, 27
Action research, 21–23 (*see also* Applied anthropology)
Adams, Richard N., 40, 179
Ademuwagun, Z. A., 98
Administered communities, 92
Advocacy planning, 108
Advocacy research, 21–23 (*see also* Applied anthropology)
Africa, 98, 99
Agar, Michael, 79–80, 98, 117, 175–76, 222
Agency for International Development, 29, 71, 93–94, 158, 171
Aging, 78–79, 98
  evaluation research, 179
Agriculture (*See* Development)
Agriculture, Department of, 49
Akinsanya, Sherrie K., 135
Alaska, 178
Alexander, Christopher, 106–7
Alger, Norman, 80
Almy, Susan, 30, 200
American Anthropological Association, 16, 23, 214–15, 217, 219, 232
American Education Research Journal, 136
American Ethnology, Bureau of, 15, 17
American Folklore Society, 131
American Journal of Clinical Nutrition, 98
American Journal of Public Health, 97
American Society:
  anthropological research, 9
Anderson, Barbara G., 78, 97
Andrews, Frank M., 156
Angrosino, Michael V., 35
Anthropological perspective, 3

decision making, 209
public awareness of, 188
Anthropological Study Group on Agrarian Systems, 84
Anthropology:
  professional organizations, 213–17
Anthropology and Education Quarterly, 136
Anthropology Newsletter, 23, 215
Anthropology for Teachers Program, 136
Anthropology Resource Center, 22, 92, 213
Appalachia, 98, 126
Appell, G.N., 232
Applied anthropology:
  administration model, 19
  advocacy-action model, 21, 25–28, 34, 90–91, 113, 117–18, 133–34, 190, 213
  definition of, 8, 14, 37
  overview, 34
  research in United States, 35
  specialization in, 69, 95, 102
  training, 102, 216, 225–33
Applied research, 140–47, 177–79
  definition of, 17
  institutionalization of, 207–8
  utility of, 204–7
  varieties of, 154–74
Appropriate technology, 93–94, 100 (*see also* Development)
Archeology, 130–31, 205–6
Architects, 109–10
Architecture, 107, 133
Arensberg, Conrad, 31, 35, 89, 129, 136, 190
Army Corps of Engineers, 46, 130, 170
Aron, William S., 80
Asad, Talal, 219–20
Asia, 98
Association of Anthropology and Gerontology, 79
Ayala, Felipe, 136